# How Picturebooks Work

# Children's Literature and Culture

Jack Zipes, *Series Editor*

# How
# Picturebooks
# Work

Maria Nikolajeva
Carole Scott

Garland Publishing
New York and London

Published in 2001 by
Garland Publishing
29 West 35th Street
New York, NY 10001

Published in Great Britain by
Garland Publishing
11 New Fetter Lane
London EC4P 4EE

Garland is an imprint of the Taylor & Francis Group

Copyright © 2001 by Maria Nikolajeva and Carole Scott

10   9   8   7   6   5   4   3   2   1

Library of Congress Cataloging-in-Publication Data

Nikolajeva, Maria.
    How picturebooks work/Maria Nikolajeva, Carole Scott.
        p. cm.—(Garland reference library of the humanities vol. 2171. Children's
    literature and culture ; v. 14)
    Includes bibliographical references and index.
    ISBN 0-8153-3486-9 (hardcover)
    1. Picture books for children.   I. Scott, Carole.   II. Title.   III. Garland
    reference library of the humanities ; vol. 2171.   IV. Garland reference library
    of the humanities. Children's literature and culture ; v. 14.

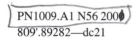
PN1009.A1 N56 2000
809'.89282—dc21

                                                                          00-062275

*Cover:* Tord Nygren, *The Red Thread* (detail)

Printed on acid-free, 250-year-life paper.
Manufactured in the United States of America.

# Contents

# Series Editor's Foreword

Dedicated to furthering original research in children's literature and culture, the Children's Literature and Culture series includes monographs on individual authors and illustrators, historical examinations of different periods, literary analyses of genres, and comparative studies on literature and the mass media. The series is international in scope and is intended to encourage innovative research in children's literature with a focus on interdisciplinary methodology.

Children's literature and culture are understood in the broadest sense of the term *children* to encompass the period of childhood up through late adolescence. Owing to the fact that the notion of childhood has changed so much since the origination of children's literature, this Garland series is particularly concerned with transformations in children's culture and how they have affected the representation and socialization of children. While the emphasis of the series is on children's literature, all types of studies that deal with children's radio, film, television, and art are included in an endeavor to grasp the aesthetics and values of children's culture. Not only have there been momentous changes in children's culture in the last fifty years, but also radical shifts in the scholarship that deals with these changes. In this regard, the goal of the Children's Literature and Culture series is to enhance research in this field and, at the same time, point to new directions that bring together the best scholarly work throughout the world.

Jack Zipes

# Acknowledgments

We wish to express our thanks to the following persons and organizations without whom this book would not have been written.

We are indebted first to our colleagues who stimulated our ideas about picturebooks with their presentations at lectures and conferences. In particular we would like acknowledge Sandra Beckett, Clare Bradford, Jane Doonan, Kristin Hallberg, William Moebius, Isabelle Nières, John Stephens, Reinbert Tabbert, and those who gave us valuable comments at our panel discussion on picturebooks at the 25th ChLA Conference organized by Jean Perrot in Paris.

We have been given many opportunities for meetings and discussions throughout the world at conferences and other events presented by the International Research Society for Children's Literature (IRSCL) and the Children's Literature Association (ChLA). In addition, the symposium on picturebooks in Stockholm in October 1998, sponsored by the Wenner-Gren Foundation for Scientific Research, and the symposium on children's literature at Åbo Akademi, Finland, organized by the program in Children's Literature Pure and Applied (ChiLPA), gave special opportunities and support for our research.

Maria Nikolajeva's work was carried out during her year as the Donner Visiting Chair at Åbo Akademi, which provided a stimulating intellectual climate with outstanding colleagues and graduate students, the opportunity to offer a picturebook course, and time for research.

Carole Scott was assisted by a grant from the Swedish-American Foundation, which sponsored research at the Swedish Children's Book Institute in Stockholm. She owes special thanks to Sonja Svensson, director of the Institute, and to John Norton, the San Diego Swedish consul, for their interest and encouragement.

Kristina Rollfelt of the Stockholm Municipal Library was an unfailing source of enthusiastic help and advice.

We want to offer our warm thanks to Jack Zipes for his confidence in us and his interest in our project.

The wonderful support and endless patience of our husbands, Staffan Skott and Christopher Scott, have been invaluable and greatly appreciated.

# Illustration Acknowledgments

We are grateful to the following for permission to reproduce illustrations: Lena Anderson for *Majas alfabet* (© 1984); Kaj Beckman for *Tummelisa* (© 1967); Anthony Browne for *Gorilla* (© 1983) and *The Tunnel* (© 1989); Patrick Couratin for *Chute!* (© 1974); Inger Edelfeldt for *Genom den röda dörren* (© 1992), *Nattbarn* (© 1994), and *Stackars lilla Bubben* (© 1996); Eva Eriksson for *The Wild Baby* (© 1980), *Sam's Cookie* (© 1981), *The Wild Baby Goes to Sea* (© 1982), *Little Sister Rabbit* (© 1983), *The Wild Baby Gets a Dog* (© 1985), and *Titta Max grav* (© 1991); Ann-Madeleine Gelotte for *Tyra i 10: an Odengatan* (© 1981); Fibben Hald for *Ägget* (© 1978); Anna Höglund for *Jaguaren* (© 1987) and *Mina och Kåge* (© 1995); Tove Jansson for *Moomin, Mymble and Little My* (© 1952), *Who Will Comfort Toffle?* (© 1960), *The Dangerous Journey* (© 1977), and *Finn Family Moomintroll* (© 1952); Mati Lepp for *Röda hund* (© 1988); Pija Lindenbaum for *Else-Marie and Her Seven Daddies* (© 1990), *Boodil My Dog* (© 1991), and *Britten och prins Benny* (© 1996); Linda Lysell for *Tummelisa* (© 1982); Sven Nordqvist for *Willie in the Big World* (© 1985), *Pancake Pie* (© 1985), *Fox Hunt* (© 1986), *Hat Hunt* (© 1987), and *Mamma Mu gungar* (© 1993); Tord Nygren for *I'll Take Care of the Crocodiles* (© 1977), *Come Into My Night, Come Into My Dream* (© 1978), *The Red Thread* (© 1987), and *Fanny och fåglarna* (© 1995); Elisabet Nyman for *Tummelisa* (© 1991); Piret Raud for *Keeruline lugu* (© 1994); Lasse Sandberg for *Little Anna and the Magic Hat* (© 1965), *Little Ghost Godfrey* (© 1965), *Titta där, sa Pulvret* (© 1983), *ABCD* (© 1986), and *Jaa, det får du, sa Pulvret* (© 1993); Colin Thompson for *Looking for Atlantis* (© 1993); Anna-Clara Tidholm for *Resan till Ugri-La-Brek* (© 1987); Cecilia Torudd for *A Worm's Tale* (© 1985); Ilon Wikland for *I Don't Want to Go to Bed* (© 1988); Andersen Press, London, for *Not Now, Bernard* (© 1980 by David McKee), *I Hate My Teddy Bear* (© 1982 by David McKee), and *Charlotte's Piggy Bank* (© 1996 by David McKee); Penguin Books, U.K., for *Princess Smartypants* (© 1986 by Babette Cole); Random House, London, for *Come Away from the Water, Shirley* (© 1977 by John Burningham), *Granpa* (© 1984 by John Burningham); and Frederick Warne & Co. for Beatrix Potter's *The Tale of Peter Rabbit* (© 1902, 1987).

If I catch a fish we can cook it for supper.

*What if you catch a whale, Granpa?*

From *Granpa*, by John Burningham.

# HOW PICTUREBOOKS WORK

From *Princess Smartypants,* by Babette Cole.

# Introduction

The unique character of picturebooks as an art form is based on the combination of two levels of communication, the visual and the verbal. Making use of semiotic terminology we can say that picturebooks communicate by means of two separate sets of signs, the iconic and the conventional.

Iconic, or representational, signs are those in which the signifier and the signified are related by common qualities; that is, where the sign is a direct representation of its signified. A picture of a printer on a computer's command menu is an icon, a direct representation of the printer. In most cases, we do not need special knowledge to understand a simple icon.

Conventional signs have no direct relationship with the object signified. The word *print* in a menu only conveys a meaning if we possess the code; that is, we must know what letters stand for, put letters together to produce words, and understand what the words stand for. Conventional signs are based on an agreement among the bearers of a particular language, both the spoken language and communications, such as gestures, dress code, or emblems. For anyone outside the given community, conventional signs do not carry any meaning, or, at best, the meaning is ambivalent.[1]

Both conventional and iconic signs have existed in human culture from its beginning, and have given rise to two parallel types of communication, the visual and the verbal. However, a growing number of art forms and media make use of different combinations of the verbal and the visual signs: from Chinese scrolls and Egyptian mural paintings to theater, cinema, video, comics—and picturebooks.

Pictures in picturebooks are complex iconic signs, and words in picturebooks are complex conventional signs; however, the basic relationship between the two levels is the same. The function of pictures, iconic signs, is to describe or represent. The function of words, conventional signs, is primarily to narrate. Conventional signs are often linear, while iconic signs are nonlinear and do not give us direct instruction about how to read them. The tension between the two functions creates unlimited possibilities for interaction between word and image in a picturebook.

Hermeneutic analysis starts with the whole, proceeds to look at details, goes back to the whole with a better understanding, and so on, in an eternal circle known as the hermeneutic circle. The process of "reading" a picturebook may be represented by a hermeneutic circle as well. Whichever we start with, the verbal or the visual, it creates expectations for the other, which in turn provides new experiences and new expectations. The reader turns from verbal to visual and back again, in an ever-expanding concatenation of understanding. Each new rereading of either words or pictures creates better prerequisites for an adequate interpretation of the whole. Presumably, children know this by intuition when they demand that the same book be read aloud to them over and over again. Actually, they do not read the same book; they go more and more deeply into its meaning. Too often adults have lost the ability to read picture books in this way, because they ignore the whole and regard the illustrations as merely decorative. This most probably has to do with the dominant position of verbal, especially written, communication in our society, although this is on the wane in generations raised on television and now computers.

Reader-response theory, with its central notion of textual gaps[2] is also valuable in approaching picturebook dynamics. Both words and images leave room for the readers/viewers to fill with their previous knowledge, experience, and expectations, and we may find infinite possibilities for word–image interaction. The verbal text has its gaps, and the visual text has its own gaps. Words and images can fill each other's gaps, wholly or partially. But they can also leave gaps for the reader/viewer to fill; both words and images can be evocative in their own ways and independent of each other.

## Current Approaches to Picturebooks

Most general studies of children's literature include a chapter on picturebooks, and a number of studies concentrate on picturebooks alone. Few if any of these books have focused upon the dynamics of the picturebook, how the text and image, two different forms of communication, work together to create a form unlike any other.

We find a number of approaches to picturebooks among the existing studies. A predominant focus is the consideration of picturebooks as educational vehicles, including aspects such as socialization and language acquisition. The examples are too numerous to mention, and include chapters in general handbooks on children's literature as well as separate handbooks on picturebooks. One of the most recent contributions is the bilingual volume *Siest du das? Die Wahrnehmung von Bildern in Kinderbücher—Visual Liter-*

*acy* (1997).[3] Ellen Handler Spitz's *Inside Picture Books* (1999)[4] is an example of a similar, yet more profound, study in which picturebooks are examined in connection with developmental psychology and their therapeutic effect on the child reader. Though Spitz is an art critic, this work concentrates on the messages that picturebooks send, and the chapters are organized by the relevance of the lessons they address: "It's Time for Bed," "Please Don't Cry," and "Behave Yourself."

Another line of inquiry examines picturebooks as objects for art history and discusses topics such as design and technique. Some early books in the field were Diana Klemin's *The Art of Art for Children's Books* (1966), introducing sixty-four illustrators, and Patricia Cianciolo's *Illustrations in Children's Books* (1970),[5] the latter also containing pedagogical applications. In Lyn Ellen Lacy's *Art and Design in Children's Picture Books* (1986), with the self explanatory subtitle "An Analysis of Caldecott-Winning Illustrations," the author states in her preface that her object of study is the "book as a work of graphic art."[6] This is pure art criticism, focusing on aspects such as line, color, contrast, shape, and space. Only the visual level of the book is taken into consideration. Often such studies take the form of a catalogue, and indeed some of them are produced in connection with illustration exhibitions.[7]

A number of historical and international surveys focus on thematic and stylistic diversity; for instance, Bettina Hürlimann's *Picture-Book World* (1968), Barbara Bader's *American Picturebooks: From Noah's Ark to the Beast Within* (1976), or William Feaver's *When We Were Young. Two Centuries of Children's Book Illustrations* (1977).[8] In most of these studies, as in catalogues, each illustrator is represented by a single picture. The specific sequential nature of picturebooks is ignored, as individual pictures are taken out of context and considered without their relationship to the narrative text. However, Barbara Bader's six hundred-page volume on the history of American picturebooks has certainly contributed to theoretical thinking, for instance by discussing openings (also called doublespreads) rather than single pages in picturebooks.

Sometimes picturebooks are treated as an integral part of children's fiction, with critics employing a literary approach, discussing themes, issues, ideology, or gender structures. Occasionally some aesthetic/narrative aspects are touched upon, for instance by Stephen Roxburgh.[9] However, literary studies often neglect the visual aspect or treat pictures as secondary. Although many of the texts discussed by John Stephens in his well-known study *Language and Ideology in Children's Fiction*[10] are picturebooks, he focuses on the topics, the depiction of society, ideological values, adult control, and so on, rather than upon the dynamics of the picturebook form. This is in fact the way picturebooks are often treated in general surveys of children's literature, in reviews, academic papers, and conference presentations.

Concentrating on pictures are Joseph Schwarcz's pioneer book *Ways of the Illustrator* (1982), with the subtitle "Visual Communication in Children's Literature,"[11] and Jane Doonan's *Looking at Pictures in Picture Books* (1993).[12] These works offer an important counterbalance to many studies of picturebooks where pictures are ignored or treated as mere decorations. Both Doonan and Schwarcz discuss thoroughly the *pictures* in picturebooks, each picture by itself and its specific way of conveying such elements as space and movement.

Schwarcz's second, posthumously published, book, *The Picture Book Comes of Age* (1991),[13] offers a panorama of themes and issues in picturebooks (for instance, the family, the representation of grandparents, the quest for identity, the portrayal of the socially disadvantaged, war and peace, and so on), but it does not develop any of the semiotic approaches to picturebooks presented in his first study. It pays little attention to the word–image interaction. Instead, it concentrates on educational and social functions of picturebooks, as well as the psychological aspects of visual perception. In fact, in neither book does Schwarcz make any distinction between picturebooks proper and illustrated books, and both books include illustrated children's novels that are primarily text. However, the second book is distinctly more focused on picturebooks as a specific art form.[14]

Perry Nodelman's comprehensive work *Words about Pictures* (1988)[15] repeatedly states that the meaning in a picturebook is revealed only through the interaction of words and pictures, but on the whole, the focus is primarily on the visual aspects. Also, despite the subtitle of the book, "The Narrative Art of Children's Picture Books," most of his discussion does not explore the purely narrative aspects, but rather examines individual communicative elements of the visual text, such as color, shape, the position of objects in relation to each other, or the depiction of movement. Thus the book emphasizes extracting information from particular pictures rather than extracting a meaning out of the interaction of picture and words. The title "Words *about* pictures" is therefore a correct description of the book's primary thrust, though the concluding chapters clearly make a significant contribution to the study of text–picture interaction. Nodelman's book provides an excellent grammar for reading and understanding pictures in picturebooks, which, because of their sequential nature, need a very different approach from that which views pictures as individual works of art. A similar comprehensive grammar is to be found in William Moebius's classic essay "Introduction to Picturebook Codes" (1986).[16]

Together, Schwarcz, Moebius, Nodelman and Doonan introduce enough tools to decode pictures in picturebooks. But we still lack tools for decoding the specific "text" of picturebooks, the text created by the interaction of verbal and visual information.

In English-language criticism, two scholars have identified the importance of the counterpoint of text and image in picturebooks, Peter Hunt (of England) and Clare Bradford (of Australia), although neither has as yet produced a whole book on the topic. In his thirteen-page chapter in *Criticism, Theory and Children's Literature,* Hunt draws our attention to the obvious lack of metalanguage for discussing the complexity of modern picturebooks,[17] while Bradford regards the complex text/image interaction as a part of the general "postmodern" trend in contemporary literature for young readers.[18]

One of the most recent English-language contributions to the theoretical discussion, also offering a useful survey of terminology, is Lawrence R. Sipe's attempt at a Peircian analysis of Maurice Sendak's *Where the Wild Things Are.*[19] However, after a prolonged introduction on the importance of text/image interaction in picturebooks, Sipe starts his analysis by saying: "Let us first consider the text alone, without reference to the illustrations."[20] As in most Peirce-inspired models, Sipe's interpretation favors the schematic and abstract.

Germany is a country where much research is devoted to picturebooks, and several excellent collections have recently appeared. One of the earliest endeavors in the field, *Aspekte der gemalten Welt,* published in 1968 and edited by Alfred Clemens Baumgärtner, was a pioneer work in the field.[21] The essays discuss mostly visual aspects, for example, the influence of contemporary art on picturebooks, with some focus on picturebooks and children's own drawings, as well as psychological and educational aspects. Baumgärtner raises the question of the relationship between words and pictures, but he gives the verbal text priority in the creative and interactive process, considering primarily how textual structures are transformed into images. In a much later essay,[22] Baumgärtner touches upon the unique nature of picturebooks in their combination of spatial (image) and temporal (word) means of expression. He is therefore moving from his earlier standpoint, toward accentuating the complete parity of word and image in this form. This evaluation of the balance between text and image is congruent with the basic premise of our book.

Each chapter in the essay collection *Neue Erzählformen im Bilderbuch*[23] is an analysis of a concrete picturebook, but few of them address text/picture interaction. In the introductory chapter, Jens Thiele calls for a syntax of picturebook language, for working tools and concepts necessary to read and understand what he calls "new" picturebooks, that is, picturebooks based on complex interrelations between word and image. Several scholars in the volume emphasize this interrelationship and make some comments regarding specific traits of picturebook narrative, such as movement from left to right, linear development, framing, simultaneous succession and the use of point of view.

In Sweden, a considerable amount of research is done on picturebooks, and some useful tools and concepts have been brought forward. One is the notion of iconotext, coined by Kristin Hallberg in 1982,[24] originating from hermeneutics and widely established among Scandinavian scholars. Ulla Rhedin's 1993 study, provocatively titled *Picturebook: Toward a Theory,* proposes the categorizing of picturebooks as epic, expanded, and genuine.[25]

In summary, a number of scholars, notably Baumgärtner, Thiele, Hunt, Bradford, Hallberg, and Rhedin, problematize the relationship between word and image and investigate the ironic counterpoint of the verbal and visual text that has become prominent in contemporary picturebooks. But what we still lack and need is a consistent and flexible terminology, a comprehensive international metalanguage, and a system of categories describing the variety of text/image interactions.

## Attempts at Picturebook Typology

Some helpful steps in defining a picturebook typology have been made. Torben Gregersen (of Denmark) makes the following distinctions:

(a)  the exhibit book: picture dictionary (no narrative)

(b)  the picture narrative: wordless or with very few words

(c)  the picturebook, or picture storybook: text and picture equally important

(d)  the illustrated book: the text can exist independently[26]

Kristin Hallberg distinguishes between the illustrated book and the picturebook, the latter based on the notion of iconotext, an inseparable entity of word and image, which cooperate to convey a message.[27]

Joseph Schwarcz does not, as already pointed out, identify any principal difference between illustrated book and picturebook; however, he does pay attention to the quantitative ratio of text and pictures in different types of illustrated books, using the expression "verbal-visual narration."[28] For what he calls the picture storybook, the concept of "a composite text" is proposed,[29] similar to Hallberg's iconotext. Further, discussing the function of illustrations, Schwarcz outlines several ways in which words and pictures cooperate:

(a)  congruency

(b)  elaboration

(c)  specification

(d)  amplification

(e)  extension

(f) complementation

(g) alternation

(h) deviation

(i) counterpoint[30]

As discussed, Perry Nodelman in *Words about Pictures* does not problematize the notion. His material ranges across many categories from exhibit books to illustrated fairy tales; he also includes photographic books and non-fiction illustrated books.

Ulla Rhedin, partly leaning on Nodelman, suggests three picturebook concepts:

(a) The epic, illustrated text, exemplified by *Look, Mardy, It's Snowing,* the text of which is a chapter from Astrid Lindgren's novel, with pictures by Ilon Wikland.

(b) The expanded (or staged) text, exemplified by Barbro Lindgren and Eva Eriksson's *The Wild Baby Gets a Puppy.*

(c) The genuine picturebook, exemplified by Maurice Sendak's *Where the Wild Things Are.*[31]

While we can accept Rhedin's first category, the illustrated text (which also appears in the other scholars' classifications), her two other categories are somewhat artificial, for the difference is very subtle and obviously subjective, and no clear criteria are proposed by Rhedin once she has exemplified her two categories by means of two existing picturebooks. Further, though it is thought provoking, the classification is insufficient to describe the vast spectrum of interrelationship between word and picture that we find in picturebooks.

Joanne Golden, in her chapter on visual-verbal narrative, discusses several types of interaction:

(a) the text and pictures are symmetrical (creating a redundancy)

(b) the text depends on pictures for clarification

(c) illustration enhances, elaborates text

(d) the text carries primary narrative, illustration is selective

(e) the illustration carries primary narrative, the text is selective[32]

Like Rhedin's classification, Golden's is an excellent starting point, but we believe that the spectrum is wider, and that we need more categories to describe the variety of relationships between words and pictures. For instance, between categories (b) and (c), different degrees of "dependence" and "enhancement" can be observed, as well as different natures of dependence and/or enhancement.

None of the many other ways of labeling the text–image interaction seems satisfactory to us: "duet" and "polysystemy," which Lawrence Sipe refers to, as well as his own suggestion, "synergy";[33] "imagetext," used by W. J. T. Mitchell;[34] to name a few. While all these notions, like Hallberg's iconotext, capture the essence of picturebooks, they ignore the wide diversity of word–image relationship. We will, therefore, start by describing the two extremes of the spectrum and then place other varieties of picturebooks between them. We have also, in the argument above, taken a firm standpoint by adopting the spelling "picturebook" for the phenomenon we are discussing, to distinguish it from picture books, or books with pictures.

## Between Word and Image

The two extremes in the word–picture dynamic are a text without pictures and a wordless picturebook. Even these two clear-cut categories can each be further divided into narrative and nonnarrative. On the verbal side of the spectrum we will then have either a story (narrative) or a nonnarrative text (a poem, a dictionary, a nonfiction text), and on the visual side a picture narrative (Jan Ormerod's *Sunshine,* 1981, and *Moonlight,* 1982; Mitsumasa Anno's *Journey,* 1977; Tord Nygren's *The Red Thread,* 1987; Quentin Blake's *Clown,* 1995) or an exhibit book (picture dictionary).

A verbal narrative may be illustrated by one or several pictures and thus becomes an *illustrated story:* the pictures are subordinated to the words. The same story may be illustrated by different artists, who may impart different interpretations to the text (often contrary to the original intention), but the story will remain basically the same and can still be read without looking at the pictures. This relationship is, in a way, similar to that between novels and their film versions. The many illustrated editions of Bible stories, folktales, Perrault's, Grimms' or Andersen's tales fall into this category. So do short stories and chapters from novels by Astrid Lindgren, published as picturebooks with different illustrations, for instance *Christmas in Noisy Village* (1964) and *Springtime in Noisy Village* (1966; cf. Rhedin's example, *Look, Mardy, It's Snowing,* 1983). Even if we have preferences for certain illustrations, perhaps because we have grown up with them, the text is not dependent on illustrations to convey its essential message.

A nonnarrative text (for instance, a poem) may be illustrated by one or several pictures, and examples can be found in the work of C. M. Barker (England), Ernst Kreidolf (Switzerland), Ottilia Adelborg (Sweden), and in a vast number of contemporary picturebooks from Eastern Europe. The text may be also written afterward, to accompany the existing illustrations. The focus of

Barker's Flower Fairies series (beginning in 1923) is upon the meticulously correct botanical representations, and the books include childlike fairy figures dressed in costumes tailored from flower parts. The verse that accompanies each illustration often appears to be an afterthought. The same can be said about Kreidolf's several collections of flower fairy tales. Lena Anderson's *Majas alfabet* (1984) in the Swedish original takes a different approach to the relationship between children and plants (in an obvious dialogue with Ottilia Adelborg's *The Princes' Flower Alphabet,* 1892), developing Maja as character and observer both in the plates and in the verse as well as featuring the plants. Interestingly, the American version, *Anna's Summer Songs* (1988), selects some of the pictures and rewrites the verse to focus upon the child and her feelings and activities, with little attention to the plant features. The origin of *Anna's Summer Songs* has thus a relationship between words and pictures the reverse of an illustrated poem: the words are written to suit the existing pictures, as in the case of Barker. However, dealing with the completed book, not knowing about its origins, we see clearly that the poems can exist on their own, without illustrations, just as a fairy tale can exist without illustrations, even though illustrations certainly add to our experience of it.

Let us revert to the opposite extreme: pictures without words. An exhibit book (picture dictionary, *Baby's First Things* or the like), which has no narrative, presents no problems, being quite straightforward. Single words may accompany the pictures. Actually, exhibit books may be the only category of picturebooks where a total correspondence of verbal and visual text is possible: the picture of a table or chair (iconic sign) is directly connected to the word *table* or *chair* (conventional sign), unless of course there is irony: cf. René Magritte's famous picture *This is not a pipe.* Inger and Lasse Sandberg's *Little Anna and the Magic Hat* (1965), although not strictly speaking an exhibit book, is based on the same type of irony, or incongruence between verbal and visual signs: the conjuror promises in words to produce a dog, a spoon, a glove, a teddy bear, an airplane, an orange, a fish, and a radio, while the pictures show a cat, a fork, a shoe, a doll, a car, a banana, a bird, and a television set. The book presupposes that the reader has enough linguistic skills to recognize irony. For a sophisticated reader, the device interrogates the conventionality of language: Why is the image of a dog connected to the letter combination D-O-G? And indeed, in Swedish, it is not; it is instead connected to the combination H-U-N-D.

While picture dictionaries are relatively simple, a wordless picture narrative is an extremely complicated form, since it demands that the reader/viewer verbalize the story. A wordless picturebook may show different levels of sophistication, depending on the amount and nature of textual (or rather iconotextual, visual) gaps. Jan Ormerod's *Sunshine* and *Moonlight* are very simple stories where all of the individual frames—between two and ten on each spread—depict consecutive moments with almost no temporal

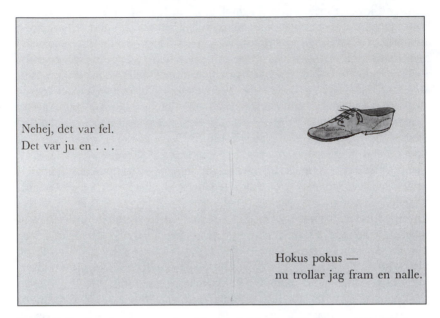

Ironic discrepancy between word and depicted object in *Little Anna and the Magic Hat,* by Inger and Lasse Sandberg.

ellipses between them. There are no substantial gaps for the reader/viewer to fill, and the story will most probably be "read" similarly by all readers. Quentin Blake's *Clown* is perhaps more demanding visually, but there is also, as in Ormerod's books, a clear sequence of events and few gaps that cannot easily be bridged by the reader.

Tord Nygren's *The Red Thread,* with its highly sophisticated self-conscious focus on the nature of the narrative itself, offers a strong contrast to Ormerod's or Blake's work for it stimulates the reader to create an infinite number of narratives to fill the gaps the pictures present. The concept of the thread itself, metaphorically used so often to represent the "thread of the story" or narrative progression, challenges the eye's tendency to dwell upon the details of the picture. This tension alerts the reader to the interplay inherent in picturebooks between the linear narrative usually presented in the text and the apparent static aspect of the pictures, and argues for a reevaluation of their interaction.

The teasing presence of the thread continually reminds the reader of the different kinds of order that exist. One doublespread provides a very specific narrative presented through a series of fifteen miniature pictures. This series tells a clear story of a man who dreams of a woman and goes on a journey to find her, the pictures revealing the events of his journey and ending with the

A picture open to many interpretations: Tord Nygren's *The Red Thread*.

happy couple standing with their arms around each other. But most of Nygren's doublespreads are far less revealing, presenting more questions than answers. What meaning lies behind the doublespread of the magician, the masks, and the mirrors, with their reflections and refractions? What is the story of the skywatchers' doublespread, where a tightrope walker traverses the sky on the red thread anchored to a crescent moon? And what is the connection between the diverse spreads, a connection posited not only by the thread itself, but by, for example, the appearance of certain characters in a number of spreads, or the inclusion of several disparate figures and scenes in the final one?

## Consonant, Symmetrical, Complementary

Having thus investigated the two ends of the spectrum, we must now try to categorize the picturebooks that lie in between. The word/image table gives a preliminary summary of the categories of picturebooks we will explore.

Most picturebooks match Kristin Hallberg's inventive notion of iconotext and her definition of a picturebook as a book with at least one picture on each spread.[35] The notion does not, however, reflect the variety of dynamics between words and picture. Let us therefore take a closer look at some books, proceeding further on from the wordless side of the spectrum.

**WORD**

narrative text                                                                    nonnarrative text

narrative text with
occasional illustrations                                                          plate book
                                                                                  (ABC book,
narrative text with at least                                                      illustrated poetry,
one picture on every spread                                                       nonfiction illustrated book)
(not dependent on image)

symmetrical picturebook
(two mutually redundant narratives)

complementary picturebook
(words and pictures filling each other's gaps)

"expanding" or "enhancing" picturebook
(visual narrative supports verbal narrative,
verbal narrative depends on visual narrative)

"counterpointing" picturebook
(two mutually dependent narratives)

"sylleptic" picturebook (with or without words)
(two or more narratives independent of each other)

picture narrative with words                                                      exhibit book with words
(sequential)                                                                      (nonnarrative, nonsequential)

picture narrative without words
(sequential)

wordless picturebook                                                              exhibit book
                                                                                  (nonnarrative, nonsequential)

**IMAGE**

One of the rare examples of a Russian picturebook,[36] titled *Picture Stories* (1958), with text by Daniil Kharms and other poets and illustrations by Nikolai Radlov, carries a separate narrative on each doublespread, divided between several frames, similar to comic strips. These picture sequences are very dynamic, constituting an accomplished and coherent plot. Some stories are accompanied by short verses, while in others the title is the only verbal support to the visual narrative. The visual plot is so clear that the pictures are not really dependent on the words, and indeed there are some Russian editions of the book without the verses.[37] While the verses of course add some-

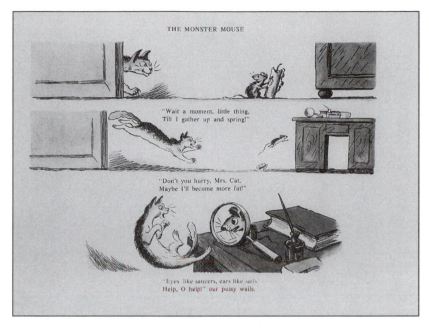

THE MONSTER MOUSE

"Wait a moment, little thing,
Till I gather up and spring!"

"Don't you hurry, Mrs. Cat,
Maybe I'll become more fat!"

"Eyes like saucers, ears like sails
Help, O help!" our pussy wails.

From *Picture Stories,* by Daniil Kharms and Nikolai Radlov.

thing to the stories, not least humor and verbal play, they are not essential to extract meaning from the book.

The Sam books by Barbro Lindgren and Eva Eriksson provide another excellent illustration for the notion of picture narrative. Although there are some very short, simple sentences to accompany the pictures, the plot can easily be understood from the pictures alone. Unlike Ormerod's wordless picture narrative, or Kharms/Radlov's word-and-picture narrative, Sam books have only one picture on each spread, so the "drama of page turning" is fully realized here. Each of the Sam books is focusing on one problem, or rather one object, featured in the title: *Sam's Teddy Bear* (1981), *Sam's Ball* (1982), *Sam's Wagon* (1986), and so on. They portray everyday situations that any child can easily recognize. There are few details that have no correspondence in the verbal text, but all details are essential. The settings are sparsely depicted. The books are addressed to a very young child whose experience of the world is quite limited. The universe consists only of the immediate surroundings and does not stretch beyond the material things the child is able to see here and now. The temporal span is extremely tight, and there are few gaps to fill.

Åke Löfgren and Egon Möller-Nielsen's *The Story About Somebody* (1951) is a good example of what Joanne Golden calls a symmetrical

Here comes Doggie.

Picture narrative supported by a few words: a nearly symmetrical picturebook. *Sam's Cookie,* by Barbro Lindgren and Eva Eriksson.

relationship. The mutually redundant nature of the interaction is especially striking as compared to the wordless *The Red Thread,* since this book also has a literal red thread running through it. However, the words tell us exactly the same story as the one we can "read" from the pictures. Naturally, the words draw our attention to some details in the pictures, but they leave very little, if anything, to the imagination.

The vast majority of picturebooks seemingly fall into this category, and can be labeled symmetrical, consonant, or complementary works. Among them are many of the so-called classics and award-winners, which are outstanding in their themes, styles, exciting designs, or educational values: Babar (1931) books, by Jean de Brunhoff, *Curious George* (1941), by H. A. Rey, *The Little House* (1942), by Virginia Lee Burton, *Bread and Jam for Frances* (1964), by Russell and Lillian Hoban, *Sylvester and the Magic Pebble* (1969), by William Steig, or *Frog and Toad Are Friends* (1970), by Arnold Lobel, to name only a few. We say "seemingly" since at closer examination most of these books have at least some interesting counterpoint details, as we will show in later chapters.

Let us, however, take a brief look at Steig's *Sylvester and the Magic Pebble,* a Caldecott Medal winner and thus appraised as a highly distinguished work. To begin with, we might observe that the verbal text does not initially mention that Sylvester is a donkey. The text merely states that Sylvester Duncan lives with his mother and father and collects pebbles as a hobby. But for the pictures, we would assume that Sylvester is a boy. Later in the story, when the parents go searching for their vanished son, they meet other animals, mainly pigs and dogs. An interesting feature of this book, which makes it in some ways different from many picturebooks involving humanized animals, is that the characters are only partly anthropomorphic. For instance, some of them wear clothes and walk on their hind legs, while others behave more like animals, like the dogs who sniff the neighborhood in search of Sylvester. Sylvester himself does not wear clothes, but otherwise seems to behave like a human child.

Apart from these elements of visual characterization, there is little in the verbal text that allows expansion by pictures. We may find the pictures charming, and we may note the richness of the characters' postures and facial expressions, corresponding to words describing their emotions, but we must admit that the pictures do not add much to the narrative. Moreover, the text is richer than the pictures: several episodes in the verbal text are not illustrated, and there are textual gaps that pictures could have filled. For instance, when Sylvester realizes that the pebble can grant wishes, the text conveys his joy at being able to have anything he wants and to give his family and friends anything they want. Here a great chance to visualize the phrase "anything they want" is lost. Another missed pictorial opportunity occurs when the didactic narrator elaborates on what Sylvester could have done when confronted with a lion: he could have made the lion disappear, or wished himself safe at home, or wished the lion to turn into a butterfly. And Sylvester's thoughts and feelings when he is transformed into a rock are not visualized.

*The Little House,* another Caldecott winner, has, as many critics have noted, charming illustrations and a simple, yet poignant plot that can be interpreted at many different levels. It is also, if not unique, quite unusual in its use of an inanimate object to represent the child. Definitely unique in this book is its fixed point of view, where the reader/viewer is placed in front of the house, as if it were a theater stage. However, while the perspective does not change, the scenery does: from day to night, spring to summer, fall to winter, and then through a rapid urbanization and technologizing. While these changes create a dynamism of the narrative, the relationship between words and images is rather unimaginative, since everything that happens around the Little House in the pictures is extensively described in the text. There is little for the reader to discover beyond the words. Moreover, the text is built around the key word "watch": "She watched the grass turn green," "She watched the harvest gathered," and so on. The text mainly describes what the Little House sees, although the pictures are better suited for this purpose. Further, the words suggest that we as readers share the Little House's literal point of view, while in the pictures we are situated in front of her. Thus while the story and the pictures must surely be enjoyed together, they inevitably create a mutual redundancy.

In *Frog and Toad Are Friends,* words carry the main load in the narrative. Most of the story is a dialogue, which by definition cannot be directly rendered by images. However, there is no attempt to render it indirectly either, for instance, Frog's vivid descriptions of the coming summer. The pictures focus on the two characters, most often showing them in close-ups (amplifying the direct speech of the verbal text) and thus contributing primarily to characterization. Most of the information conveyed by pictures is duplicated by words. Frog and Toad books have been published in the United Kingdom by Puffin and in the United States by Harper & Row, in the I Can Read series. Is the verbal dominance perhaps inherent in them, so that the pictures have merely a decorative function?

All three aforementioned books are thus quite static in visual text; the pictures are more decorative than narrative. We are not questioning artistic quality but simply offer these books as examples of a certain concept of a picturebook. Sometimes this concept is the result of the way picturebooks are produced. While some picturebooks are created by notable teams, too many double-author picturebooks in the United States are created by a writer producing a text that is then sent by the writer's literary agent to a publisher, which then finds a suitable illustrator. The writer has no say in the choice of the illustrator or in the illustrator's choice of pictorial solutions. A picturebook text must therefore necessarily include all the details the writer regards as important, such as the setting, the appearance of the characters, and so on. This means that the text can be read and apprehended independently, and the final product is, in fact, not a picturebook, but an illustrated book.

This imperfect collaboration between verbal text and picture is, of course, not a concern with a single author/illustrator. Among the best picturebooks of all times and countries we find examples by Beatrix Potter, Elsa Beskow, Wanda Gág, Maurice Sendak, John Burningham, Anthony Browne, David McKee, or Sven Nordqvist. In Potter's case, we see an extraordinary balance in complementarity between remarkable pictures and unique prose style. This provides a number of avenues of expression that rarely overlap, but rather work together to strengthen the ultimate effect.

An illustration of this is the second picture of *Peter Rabbit* (1902), which offers complementary expression of both transformation and prediction. The picture of the rabbits illustrates a metamorphosis from the first page's depiction of ordinary wild creatures on all fours to characters with human attributes; they are standing up and wearing clothes, and distinctive clothes at that. This instant humanization is reinforced by the text on the opposite page, where Mrs. Rabbit is talking to her children, addressing them with an endearment, and giving them advice and a little family history. In addition, in a combination of backshadowing and foreshadowing, while the text refers backward in time to Mr. Rabbit's "accident," the picture is alerting us to the future: the girls are clustering around and paying attention to their mother, but Peter stands apart with his back to her. The combination of text and image communicates to the reader a sense of imminent peril, the meeting of a dangerous situation (text) with the refusal to be guided by past experience (picture).

## Enhancement and Counterpoint

If words and images fill each other's gaps wholly, there is nothing left for the reader's imagination, and the reader remains somewhat passive. The same is true if the gaps are identical in words and images (or if there are no gaps at all). In the first case, we are dealing with the category we have named "complementary," in the second, "symmetrical." However, as soon as words and images provide alternative information or contradict each other in some way, we have a variety of readings and interpretations.

Many of the most exciting examples of counterpoint between text and picture are to be found in books created by a single author/illustrator who is completely free to choose either of the two aspects of the iconotext to carry the main load of the narrative. However, we also have examples of successful teamwork, such as Barbro Lindgren and Eva Eriksson (The Wild Baby books, Sam books), or Stefan Mählqvist and Tord Nygren, not to mention wife–husband cooperation, for instance Russell (text) and Lillian (picture) Hoban, Margret (text) and H. A. Rey (picture), or Inger (text) and Lasse (picture) Sandberg—note the opposite gender patterns! The apparent prerequisite is a close collaboration between author and illustrator, in which the author leaves gaps for the illustrator to fill with visual images. Indeed, in Sweden, unlike the United States, most double-author picturebooks are created with close collaboration between writer and artist.

Pat Hutchins's *Rosie's Walk* (1968) is often used to exemplify words and pictures telling two completely different stories.[38] John Burningham's *Come Away from the Water, Shirley* (1977) and *Time to Get Out of the Bath, Shirley* (1978) are two more favorites.[39] However, the nature of interaction is radically different. In *Rosie's Walk,* words and pictures contradict each other. The visual narrative is more complicated and exciting than the verbal one, which comprises a single, twenty-five-word sentence. In Shirley books, words are fully in accord with one set of pictures but totally contradictory to the parallel story told by the pictures on the right-hand pages, which thus constitute a wordless narrative. The two narratives in Shirley books are, among other things, conflicting in their genres: one is "realistic," the other a fantasy.

Jan Lööf's *The Tale of the Red Apple* (1974) is sometimes treated as a Swedish counterpart to *Rosie's Walk,* since it also has a villain figure in every picture, not mentioned by words.[40] However, unlike *Rosie's Walk,* the story told in the pictures—the stolen apple and the confusion arising from this—is doubled by words, except for some pictures portraying the bandit. The pictures do not really provide a counterpoint to the words, but rather "expand" (Rhedin) or "enhance" and "elaborate" (Golden) the words. In the case of

*Rosie's Walk,* we may use Golden's notion of the text being dependent on the pictures, but the picture definitely does not carry the primary narrative, the text being selective. Words and pictures actually tell two different stories, from two different points of view.

The same duality is the narrative principle of Satoshi Kitamura's *Lily Takes A Walk* (1987). In fact, the verbal story is almost as uninteresting and uneventful as *Rosie's Walk.* A girl takes a walk with her dog, going first through a green suburban landscape, and then down some streets, stopping to shop and to point out the stars for the dog (ironically enough, the Dog Star), waving to a neighbor, watching the ducks in a canal, and returning safely home. The text specifies that Lily "is never scared, because Nicky is there with her." Looking at the pictures, on the other hand, we see that the dog is extremely frightened, and following his gaze—that is, sharing his perspective rather than the girl's or the omniscient narrator's—we discover the sources of his fear: a huge snake winding around a tree stem, a tree formed in a monstrous grin, a mailbox gaping with sharp teeth and dropping letters from a ghastly red tongue, an arch and two streetlamps metamorphosing into a dragon, the moon and the tower clock together building a pair of huge eyes, a giant emerging from a shop window, a dinosaur stretching its long neck from a canal on the other side of the bridge, and finally a garbage bin full of dreadful creatures.

One of the final spreads shows the smiling Lily and her parents around the dinner table, accompanied by words, "Lily's mother and father always like to hear what she has seen on her walks." Apparently, her account is as unexciting as the preceding verbal story itself. The thought balloons coming from the dog reiterate, in images, what he has seen, which also is a way to alert the readers in case they have missed any of the details. Eventually, disguised behind the flap on the last spread, we see the dog's basket being invaded by an army of mice, accentuating that at least some of his fears are true. Lily, sound asleep, is oblivious of the event. If we open the flap so that it instead becomes part of the very last picture, we see the dog asleep and the mice retreating into their hole, so this episode as well may be interpreted as the dog's imagination or nightmare.

The fact that the focalizing character of the visual narrative is a dog in an otherwise realistic story—that is, the dog is not a humanized, talking animal—creates an interesting situation for the reader. Like a very young child, the dog cannot verbalize his fears, which obviously stimulates the reader's empathy. The images make a clear statement that the character does have emotions even though he cannot articulate them. As readers, we are allowed to feel superior to both the girl and the dog. We see clearly that the girl is unobservant and perhaps lacks imagination (she has the role in the story usually ascribed to the neglecting parents), but we also see the dog's overdimensioned fancies, and this irony is the main point of the book. The visual story would perhaps be understandable in itself, but it is the girl's total inattention, expressed by words, that creates the counterpoint.

David McKee's *I Hate My Teddy Bear* (1982) is still another often-discussed example of a book where pictures make the reader aware of things happening around the oblivious protagonists. The two children sent out to play with their teddy bears are preoccupied with quarrelling over whose teddy is best, and the verbal story mostly conveys their dialogue. However, the teddy-centered narrative is only a tiny part of what is going on in the book. The most prominent side narrative, which the children do not notice but the reader cannot ignore, involves all the people bearing gigantic plaster hands. This provokes intense curiosity in the reader as the story progresses, though in the end the people appear to be part of an open-air exhibition. Further, the children are completely disinterested in other things going on around them (which on the psychological level is an excellent illustration of a young child's total solipsism). Brenda's mother is obviously telling John's mother some horrible story involving many letters and a photo of a man. Other life stories are depicted, some of which stretch through several pages (the woman with a ball of yarn, the woman who loses a glove), while others are mere sketches, drawn with humor and sympathy. There are people waiting for their dates, women gossiping, strangely clad travelers, and so on. Notably, many figures are pointing at something or looking upward, as if stressing that there are activities outside our field of vision. The book is deliberately drawing our attention to the fact that the visual story is not only different, but considerably richer than the simple story the words are telling.

In Babette Cole's *Princess Smartypants* (1986; most often analyzed for its feministic implication rather than its fascinating text–picture relationship), the verbal text, clever as it is, allows considerable expansion. The verbal text begins: "Princess Smartypants did not want to get married. She enjoyed being a Ms." The accompanying picture shows the princess lying on her stomach on the floor in front of a television set, surrounded by her pets (including two little dragons). She is eating chocolates from a box; around her is a mess of dirty clothes and dishes, a banana peel and apple cores, a crushed Coke can and a Mars bar wrapper. Her horse is spread comfortably on the sofa. Apparently this is visualization of the joys of "being a Ms." and deciding for herself. On the next page, the verbal statement "she was very pretty and rich" is expanded partly by her painting her nails, partly by her sitting on a golden throne. The phrase "all the princes" is expanded by the picture of three unattractive figures in military uniforms looking at the princess with stupid smiles.

The tasks the princess gives her many suitors are described by words: "stop the slugs from eating her garden," "feed her pets," "challenged [ . . . ] to a roller-disco marathon," "invited [ . . . ] for a cross-country ride on her motorbike," "rescue her from her tower," "chop some firewood in the royal forest," "put her pony through its paces," "take her Mother, the Queen, shopping," and "retrieve her magic ring from the goldfish pond." The pictures show why the unfortunate suitors cannot accomplish the tasks: the slug is as large as a dinosaur, her pets are a horde of fierce dragons, the tower is made of glass, the forest is enchanted, the goldfish pond is inhabited by an enormous shark, and so on. In each case, the words antedate the picture; the picture is the result of what is decreed by words. When the last suitor arrives, the words state only that he accomplishes all the tasks, while the pictures show exactly how he manages it, with a great deal of humor and inventiveness in details. The verbal story ends, after the princess has got rid of her successful but still unwanted suitor, by stating that she "lived happily ever after," the pictures expanding the words by showing the princess leaning back in a beach chair, wearing a bikini, and once again surrounded by her hairy and scaly pets. Thus while the story the pictures tell is not radically different from the one told by words, much of the humor and irony of the narrative would be gone if the pictures were withdrawn. The feminist content of the book may perhaps be conveyed by the verbal narrative alone, but its aesthetic whole would be destroyed. The complete narrative is definitely dependent on the pictures to produce the desired effect.

Together with David McKee, Babette Cole is one of the contemporary picturebook creators who indeed leave the pictures to do most of the work in the storytelling. The best examples are to be found in her *The Trouble with Mum* (1983). The protagonist/narrator seems to be either totally unaware of the peculiar nature of his mother, or he deliberately avoids mentioning any revealing details. He says, for instance: "The trouble with mum is the hats she wears . . ." a statement many young readers can easily relate to. The picture, however, discloses more than the words. The mother's hat is not only strange, it is strange in a very special way, making the reader wonder about this character. Our suspicions are immediately confirmed on the next spread. The narrator merely states that other children were amazed when his mother took him to his new school. The picture shows the mother in her funny pointed hat flying a broom, with her son perched behind her. After this, we have no doubts about the mother's true self; however, the ambiguity of the verbal text is maintained throughout the story. "She didn't seem to get on . . . with other parents" corresponds to the two facing pictures. In the first, the mother passes a row of ordinary and rather cross-looking parents, while in the second we see a row of frogs sitting on the same bench, one wearing a tie, another a beret, and still another continuing her knitting as if nothing has happened. The matter-of-fact tone of the verbal story creates an ironic counterpoint to the humorous and unpredictable pictures. The essence of the story is that while the parents definitely disapprove of the deviating mother (the usual fear of "the other," which can be translated into a variety of situations), the children not only do not mind but truly enjoy the witch castle, the enchanted food, and the pets (a huge raven, a dragon, and a spider, only depicted visually).

In *The Trouble with Gran* (1987), the narrative device is slightly different. The narrator says from the beginning that his grandmother is an alien, and as readers we are encouraged to watch out for symptoms. Some are rather obvious, like her green antennae popping up through her hat. But while the text maintains: "None of the other OAP's suspected a thing . . ." we see that the grandmother has taken off her shoe, which is apparently hurting her, showing a green flipper instead of a foot. On a school outing, the bored granny starts to transform, acquiring a sucker for a nose, metallic tongs for hands, hairy green legs, and a crocodile-like tail. She disposes of a bad singer, wins a beauty contest by metamorphosing into a ravishing young lady, makes the merry-go-round horses come alive, and so on. Perhaps the funniest episode is her meeting "some friends" in the Lunar Landscape Tour and taking them to tea. The text does not describe the friends, but the picture shows an assortment of green and blue monsters, reflecting all the known stereotypes of space aliens. On the whole, this book lacks the subtlety of *The Trouble with Mum* and gets fairly symmetrical toward the end. This is still more true about *The Trouble with Grandad* (1988), which, humorous and inventive as it is, does not make much of the text–image interaction.

## Dual Audience

Many picturebooks are clearly designed for both small children and sophisticated adults, communicating to the dual audience at a variety of levels. Colin Thompson's *Looking for Atlantis* (1993) is an excellent example of a book that plays to an audience extending from nonreader to literate adult. Adults are thoroughly steeped in the conventions of the book and are practiced at decoding text in a traditional manner, following the expected temporal unfolding of events and scanning from left to right. But Thompson's intricate iconotexts, with illustrations comprising a multitude of miniscenes and tangential pictorial events, are ideally suited to the child's less practiced but perceptive eye. Thus he levels the playing field for his varied audience by requiring less tutored skills of perception and picture decoding. Clearly the best audience is a team of adult and child together, each offering special strengths.

The array of images, like the presentation, addresses a spectrum of ages and experience. The doublespread portraying Grandfather's chest offers the nonreader a chance to laugh at images such as a chamber pot sporting a mast and sail; a Swiss army knife with the usual blades interspersed with such anomalies as a paintbrush and a mushroom; and a tiny hand protruding from a clasp-closed notebook, implying that someone is trapped within. For the

"Grandfather's Chest" from Colin Thompson's *Looking for Atlantis.*

reader a further dimension is offered: the Swiss army knife is labeled Swiss
Navy Knife (consonant with the book's watery theme), and the chamber pot
carries a play on words, being noted as suitable for "sailing the china seas."
The subtle gradations of understanding are illustrated by the various levels of
sophistication of the verbal jokes: while the younger reader can enjoy the
Fabulous Jewels Beyond Price, where among the drawers labeled "pearls,"
"rubies," "emeralds," and "diamonds" is one for treacle toffees, the adult will
respond with a cynical smile to the antiaccountant pills included among those
designated for seasickness, liver problems, and other ills. Thompson thus
acknowledges a variety of levels of reading ability, sophistication, experiences of life, and the sense of humor characteristic of these levels, so that no
one is excluded from feeling a part of the audience.

The humor of *Atlantis* largely depends on the anomalies present both in
the images and in the intraiconic text. The complexity of the narrative elements presented visually appears at first to be in contrast with the rather simple textual narrative perspective of the child protagonist, who tells the story of
his Grandfather's death and the message Grandfather left him, to learn how to
look with imagination, to "shut your eyes [ . . . ] and open your heart." However, the dual audience concept in fact continues in the retelling of, for
instance, Grandfather's extraordinary yarns that the child presents in literal
fashion. The boy tells us seriously that Grandfather "sailed across every
ocean a hundred times and traveled through every country of the world [ . . . ]

had seven wives and eleven children, was a prince and a pirate." While the younger audience of the book wonders at these colorful adventures, the adult sees through the narrator to Grandfather's viewpoint, watching his grandson's eyes light up with amazement at the amazing events. And the voice of cynical adulthood also penetrates the boy's narrative in the description of the probable adult reaction to his quest: " 'It's just a silly old man's dream they would have said.' " The narrative text thus does mediate to some extent the child/adult audience, but because the text is bound by the stricter conventions and expectations of the linear narrative, this is less significant than the interplay of the multifaceted illustrations.

The counterpoint between textual and iconic narrative is an important point of tension in communicating the book's theme. The formal text states, "You have to learn how to look," and the protagonist relates his ongoing and at first fruitless search where "all I could see is all I could see." But Thompson continually reveals to the reader, through the cross-section technique of his illustrations, the hidden world below the floorboards, within the chair, or inside the plumbing that is invisible to the boy. Thus the narrative perspective presented to the reader through the iconotext is richer, more advanced, and actively involves him or her in the unfolding development of the boy's visioning skills.

Of particular interest in understanding the narrative perspective are the strangely jolting shifts in visual perspective that are a hallmark of Thompson's style. The juxtapositions that counterpoint both indoor and outdoor scenes, and close-ups with more distanced perspectives subvert the reader's approach to meaningful interpretation and disarm attempts to make sense of the whole. While the notion of the title page's miniature sea world inside a toilet tank is comprehensible, a closer look reveals that the ballcock enclosed within the tank is in fact a globe depicting the universe. In similar fashion, one illustration depicts a close-up view of a few large volumes resting on a table with a distant view of the sea. This perspective is subverted by the movement of the water depicted on the page, for the seawater behaves as though it is suspended directly above the table. It is shown leaking from the sea onto the table, running across it in rivulets, and then cascading into a miniature waterfall on the other side measuring a path from the top to the bottom of the page. In this manner Thompson breaks pictorial conventions for representing space and perspective, and disturbs readers' expectations.

The surrealism of the fluctuating perspective emphasizes the shifting ambiguity of Thompson's address. This effect is supported by the combination of objective and subjective elements involved in the textual and the visual narrative, and by the constant counterpoint between the humor of the illustrations and the serious subject and message of this book, which addresses death and presents a philosophy of life. Although the verbal and the iconic texts may not always seem harmonious, if the ultimate subject of the book is the breaking of the conventional and the support of an imaginative perspective, then they work together toward a common end.

## Varieties of Counterpoint

Clearly, the picturebooks that employ counterpoint are especially stimulating because they elicit many possible interpretations and involve the reader's imagination. They do this in a wide variety of ways.

**Counterpoint in address.** Textual and visual gaps are deliberately left to be filled differently by child and adult. In our approach, we are not concerned about pedagogical or cognitive aspects of picturebooks, that is, in questioning whether young readers understand different textual or pictorial codes, or whether certain books can be used for educational purposes. However, we are interested in the way picturebook creators handle the dilemma of the dual addressee in picturebooks, and in the possible differences between the sophisticated and unsophisticated implied reader.

**Counterpoint in style.** In a picturebook, words can be ironic while pictures are nonironic, or the other way around. Further possibilities include contradictions such as "serious"/humorous, romantic/realistic, realistic/naivistic (a very common feature in "everyday" picturebooks), historical/anachronistic (e.g. phones and TV sets in "Cinderella"), "artistic"/"popular," and so on. Many contemporary picturebooks are deliberately eclectic, both in words and images, and in the interaction word/image.

**Counterpoint in genre or modality.** Words may be "realistic" while images suggest fantasy. In most fantasy picturebooks, there is a tension between the "objective" and "subjective" narrative expressed by words and pictures (Sendak's *Where the Wild Things Are,* 1963, Tove Jansson's *The Dangerous Journey,* 1977, Lindgren and Eriksson's *The Wild Baby Goes to Sea,* 1982, and others). While the verbal story is often told from a child's point of view, presenting the events as "true," the details in pictures suggest that the story takes place only in the child's imagination.

Thus, picturebooks successfully interrogate the conventional notion of genres. John Stephens identifies the distinction between fantasy and realism as "the single most important generic distinction in children's fiction."[41] In many picturebooks, words and pictures tell different stories from the genre viewpoint, challenging Stephens's statement. Some of the most provocative contemporary picturebooks probe this ironic counterpoint, such as John Burningham's Shirley books, *John Patrick Norman McHennessy—the Boy Who Was Always Late* (1987), and *Aldo* (1991), David McKee's *Not Now,*

*Bernard* (1980), Anthony Browne's *Gorilla* (1983) and *The Tunnel* (1989), and many others. In fact, picturebooks seem to have a better immediate facility for expressing genre eclecticism than novels.

**Counterpoint by juxtaposition.** In some contemporary picturebooks, we find two or more parallel visual stories, either supported or unsupported by words, for instance in Burningham's Shirley books and *Granpa,* Mitsumasa Anno's *Journey,* Sven Nordqvist's Festus and Mercury books, and many others. Since these stories are connected by the device known in narratology as *syllepsis,* we have named such books *sylleptic,* placing them between picture narratives and counterpointing books in our spectrum.

**Counterpoint in perspective,** or point of view. In narratology a distinction is made between who is speaking (in picturebooks expressed primarily by words) and who is seeing (expressed either metaphorically, by words, or literally, by picture). This aspect is especially interesting if there is a discrepancy between a child's point of view and an adult narrative voice (and occasionally the other way around).

The notion of perspective does not only include the perceptional point of view, so we can equally speak about certain degrees of contradiction in ideology, since words and picture can express different ideological attitudes. A specific aspect is contradiction in gender construction: while words are "feminist," pictures may express conservative gender stereotypes, and the other way around.

**Counterpoint in characterization.** Words and images can present characters in different and contradictory manners, thus creating irony and/or ambiguity. The verbal text can mention characters who are not portrayed in pictures (for instance, such important characters as mothers in Sendak's *Where the Wild Things Are* or Browne's *The Tunnel*); pictures can portray characters not mentioned by words.

**Counterpoint of metafictive nature.** Words can express notions that cannot be portrayed in images: round squares, green colorless ideas, or fillyjonks. Many contemporary picturebooks challenge this, for instance P. C. Jersild and Mati Lepp's *German Measles* (1988). Some picturebooks are based on metaphors treated literally in pictures. A growing number of picturebooks also explore the possibilities of multiple framing, thus successfully implementing the most daring challenges of "postmodern" aesthetics. Further, picturebooks have unlimited possibilities for counterpoint in paratexts: titles, covers, title pages, and endpapers can introduce contradictory elements to the book itself, as well as manipulate the reader/viewer to read in a certain manner (e.g., the title *The Red Thread* encourages us to follow the thread).

**Counterpoint in space and time.** Spatiotemporal relations is the only area in which words and pictures can never coincide. The picture, the visual text, is mimetic; it communicates by showing. The verbal text is diegetic; it communicates by telling. As previously stated, conventional (verbal) signs are suitable for narration, for creation of narrative texts, while iconic (visual) signs are limited to description. Pictures, iconic signs, cannot directly convey causality and temporality, two most essential aspects of narrativity. While pictures, and especially a sequence of pictures in a picturebook, successfully confront this problem in a number of ways, it is in the interaction of words and images that new and exciting solutions can be found. Likewise, while words can only describe spatial dimensions, pictures can explore and play with them in limitless ways.

In the following chapters, we will explore the variety of text–image interactions in picturebooks, using these categories to shape our discussion. Since we are interested in the way words and pictures collaborate in telling stories, we will concentrate on narratives, leaving aside, for instance, picture dictionaries, illustrated poems, the many nonfiction books with pictures, and other kinds of illustrated books, which demand special attention. We have also decided not to include photographic books, although they provide several interesting types of text–image interaction. Finally, we are not dealing with comic books, since they have a poetics of their own, which has been the subject of several major studies.[42]

## Notes

1. Conventional signs are sometimes called symbols, for instance in Peircian semiotics, but we prefer to avoid this term because it has a different connotation in other fields.

2. See Wolfgang Iser, *The Implied Reader* (Baltimore: Johns Hopkins University Press, 1974); Wolfgang Iser, *The Act of Reading: A Theory of Aesthetic Response* (London: Routledge & Kegan Paul, 1978).

3. *Siest du das? Die Wahrnehmung von Bildern in Kinderbücher—Visual Literacy* (Zurich: Chronos, 1997).

4. Ellen Handler Spitz, *Inside Picture Books* (New Haven: Yale University Press, 1999).

5. Diana Klemin, *The Art of Art for Children's Books* (New York: Clarkson N. Potter, 1966); Patricia Cianciolo, *Illustrations in Children's Books* (Dubuque, Iowa: Wm. C. Browne, 1970).

6. Lyn Ellen Lacy, *Art and Design in Children's Picture Books: An Analysis of Caldecott Award–Winning Illustrations* (Chicago: American Library Association, 1986), vii.

7. See, e.g., Brian Alderson, *Looking at Picture Books* (London: National Book League, 1973); John Barr, *Illustrated Children's Books* (London: The British Library, 1986).

8. Bettina Hürlimann, *Picture-Book World,* trans., ed. Brian W. Alderson (London: Oxford University Press, 1968); Barbara Bader, *American Picturebooks: From Noah's Ark to the Beast Within* (New York: Macmillan, 1976); William Feaver, *When We Were Young: Two Centuries of Children's Book Illustrations* (London: Thames and Hudson, 1977).

9. Stephen Roxburgh, "A Picture Equals How Many Words? Narrative Theory and Picture Books for Children," *The Lion and the Unicorn* 7–8 (1983): 20–33.

10. John Stephens, *Language and Ideology in Children's Fiction* (London: Longman, 1992).

11. Joseph H. Schwarcz, *Ways of the Illustrator: Visual Communication in Children's Literature* (Chicago: American Library Association, 1982).

12. Jane Doonan, *Looking at Pictures in Picture Books* (Stroud: Thimble Press, 1993).

13. Joseph H. Schwarcz and Chava Schwarcz, *The Picture Book Comes of Age* (Chicago: American Library Association, 1991).

14. Ibid., 5–13.

15. Perry Nodelman, *Words about Pictures: The Narrative Art of Children's Picture Books* (Athens: University of Georgia Press, 1988).

16. William Moebius, "Introduction to Picturebook Codes," *Word and Image* 2 (1986) 2: 141–158. Also in: *Children's Literature: The Development of Criticism* ed. Peter Hunt, 131–147 (London: Routledge, 1990).

17. Peter Hunt, *Criticism, Theory, and Children's Literature* (London: Blackwell, 1991): 175–188.

18. Clare Bradford, "The Picture Book: Some Postmodern Tensions," *Papers: Explorations in Children's Literature* 4 (1993) 3: 10–14; "Along the Road to Learn: Children and Adults in the Picture Books of John Burningham," *Children's Literature in Education* 25 (1994) 4: 203–211.

19. Lawrence R. Sipe, "How Picture Books Work: A Semiotically Framed Theory of Text–Picture Relationships," *Children's Literature in Education* 29 (1998) 2: 97–108.

20. Ibid.: 104.

21. Alfred Clemens Baumgärtner, ed., *Aspekte der gemalten Welt: 12 Kapitel über das Bilderbuch von heute* (Weinheim: Verlag Julius Beltz, 1968).

22. Alfred Clemens Baumgärtner, "Das Bilderbuch. Geschichte-Formen-Rezeption." In *Bilderbücher im Blickpunkt verschiedener Wissenschaften under Fächer,* ed. Bettina Paetzold and Luis Erler, 4–22 (Bamberg: Nostheide, 1990).

23. Jens Thiele, ed., *Neue Erzählformen im Bilderbuch* (Oldenburg: Isensee, 1991).

24. Kristin Hallberg, "Litteraturvetenskapen och bilderboksforskningen," *Tidskrift för litteraturvetenskap* 3–4 (1982): 163–168.

25. Ulla Rhedin, *Bilderboken: På väg mot en teori* (Stockholm: Alfabeta, 1993).

26. Torben Gregersen, "Småbørnsbogen," In *Børne-og ungdomsbøger: Problemer og analyser,* ed. Sven Møller Kristensen and Preben Ramløv, 243–271 (Copenhagen: Gyldendal, 1974).

27. Hallberg, op. cit.

28. Schwarcz 1982: 11.

29. Ibid., 13.

30. Ibid., 14–18. Lawrence Sipe only refers to congruency and deviation as Schwarcz's categories, thus reducing the variety of interaction to two polarities; see Sipe, op. cit.: 98.

31. Rhedin, op. cit.

32. Joanne M. Golden, *The Narrative Symbol in Childhood Literature: Exploration in the Construction of Text* (Berlin: Mouton, 1990): 93–119.

33. Sipe, op. cit.: 97f.

34. W. J. T. Mitchell, *Picture Theory: Essays on Verbal and Visual Representation* (Chicago: University of Chicago Press, 1994).

35. Hallberg, op. cit.: 164; cf. Ulla Rhedin's definition in Rhedin, op. cit.: 15.

36. This statement may seem astounding to anyone even briefly acquainted with some of the excellent Russian book illustrators; however, most of the Russian books with pictures are illustrated fairy tales, stories, or poems rather than picturebooks. See Maria Nikolajeva, "Bilderboken som försvann. Några tendenser i den sovjetiska bilderbokskonsten," in *I bilderbokens värld,* ed. Kristin Hallberg and Boel Westin, 127–142 (Stockholm: Liber, 1985). Maria Nikolajeva, *Children's Literature Comes of Age: Toward a New Aesthetic* (New York: Garland, 1996): 82–90.

37. There is an extraliterary explanation to this: during a certain period, one of the contributing poets, Daniil Kharms, was considered a "nonperson" by the Soviet regime.

38. See, e.g., Nodelman, op. cit.: 224f; Stephens, op. cit., 162ff.

39. See, e.g., Schwarcz 1982: 17f.

40. Gustaf Cavallius, "Bilderbok och bildanalys," in *Bilden i barnboken,* ed. Lena Fridell, 31–60 (Gothenburg: Stegeland, 1977).

41. Stephens, op. cit.: 7.

42. See, e.g., Scott McCloud, *Understanding Comics* (Northampton, MA: Tundra, 1993).

# CHAPTER 1

# Whose Book Is It?

## Author-Illustrators and Author-Illustrator Teams

In our introduction we touched briefly on the balance between pictures and text produced by a single picturebook creator (both author and illustrator), picturebooks created by an author-illustrator team, and those where author and illustrator work separately, without collaboration.

We will begin by examining some products of these relationships, for a look at situations where ownership of the book is problematic dramatizes the complexity of the relationship between the verbal communication and the iconic communication that picturebooks embody—that dynamic interrelationship and creative tension between the two modes of communication that we are exploring. While purists may declare that the iconotext is all and supports whatever interpretations seem appropriate, the interpretation of the relationship between image and text also becomes increasingly complex as the number of people involved in its creation increases and their collaboration diminishes. Multiple ownership and multiple intentionality lead to ambiguity and uncertainty in the validity of the interpretation.

Many readers will have experienced the jolt that comes when the familiar beloved books of childhood are met with in other forms. As children we relate to our picture books in a holistic fashion, merging sensations of the eye and the ear (for first we are read to), which marries the image and the sound of the words, and later, as we learn to read, the look of the words. Thus when Beatrix Potter's stories appear with other illustrations, they are no longer Potter picturebooks. Dr. Seuss's *The Cat in the Hat* in the Russian version with Russian illustrations is certainly not Theodore Geisel's. The American version of *Den vilda bebiresan* is another surprise. Not only has the book been translated with a cavalier freedom, but illustrations have been reordered, some have been cut out of the book, and one has been partially obliterated. Whose book is this?

John Stephens has some comments about the relationship between text and image in what he calls "intelligent picture books." He believes that an important principle is

> a capacity to construct and exploit a contradiction between text and picture so that the two complement one another and together produce a story and a significance that depend on their differences from each other. Further, because individual pictures do not have grammar, syntax or linear flow, but freeze specific moments in time, rarely presenting more than one event within a single frame, this relationship between text and picture is one between differently constructed discourses giving different kinds of information, if not different messages. Hence the audience will experience a complicated process of decoding, so that a text which by itself is a series of inconsequential events structured as a language lesson, and as such might be expected to strive for clarity and precise, simple meaning, becomes only a surface beneath which other kinds of meaning can be perceived, and meaningfulness itself becomes problematic.[1]

This comment raises a point central to our discussion. How do we approach the "contradiction between text and picture" and decide whether it is a contradiction that leads to the two "complementing one another" and producing "a story and a significance that depend on their differences from each other," or whether it is a contradiction that simply creates confusion and ambiguity— the kind of contradiction that arises from a mismatch of text and image, which might be due to an author and illustrator who do not work as a team, to a series of illustrators for a single text, or a series of authors for a series of illustrations.

Beatrix Potter's *The Tale of Peter Rabbit* (1902) provides an excellent example to begin this examination. If we look at the opening doublespread (picture on the left, words on the right), there are some apparent contradictions, some devices to keep the reader alert and involved. The picture is quite simple and straightforward, and the reader is drawn directly into it since mother rabbit looks us right in the eye. But the text tells us there are four little rabbits and the picture shows only three. Knowing that there is one creator for the book encourages us to look more closely and ask whether the hind legs and tail on the left belong to a rabbit whose head is underneath the tree root rather than to the rabbit whose head appears the other side of the root. With greater discrimination, it becomes increasingly apparent that the body of the rabbit would have to be long and rather distorted to reach the head on the other side of the root. Beatrix Potter's drawings are so anatomically correct that it is safe to conclude that the tail must belong to the fourth rabbit. This little puzzle immediately sets up a tension between picture and text, because

ONCE upon a time there
were four little Rabbits,
and their names were—

Flopsy,
Mopsy,
Cotton-tail,
and Peter.
They lived with their Mother
in a sand-bank, underneath the
root of a very big fir-tree.

Complementary iconotext created by Beatrix Potter in *The Tale of Peter Rabbit.*

we want to figure out how to resolve the discrepancy. And because we know that Potter is responsible for both image and text, we know that this apparent discrepancy is intended. When we read the book next time we know that it is probably Peter who is checking out his surroundings underground instead of taking his cue from what his mother is looking at.

Another device is in the text. Unlike the usual left to right motion, the names of the rabbits are listed in a slanted line that leans, like a backslash, from right to left, bringing the eye toward the picture and the puzzle of the four names and three rabbits. The text and picture are thus interrelated in several ways: in the apparent discrepancy between the information that is imagistically (iconically) and verbally (symbolically) presented; in the impact on eye movement that plots a back-and-forth pattern between text and picture pages, reinforced by the line of names that points to the picture; and in the interpretive questions provoked by the behavior of the rabbit whose head is hidden from the reader—questions that introduce the subversive message of the book (motives for behavior may be hidden, subversive, antiauthoritarian, and exciting and adventurous).

This kind of confident interpretation becomes problematic when the book's "ownership" is shared. We will first examine what happens to a book translated from the original language to another. The question that challenges us is, what kind of transformation takes place when the text is translated? Is

Fast morgonen blir förmiddag
hon gör sej ingen brådska.
Hon lockas inte upp ens
av en stor bit mandeltosca!

"Her brilliant mind is always at work." Pija Lindenbaum's *Boodil My Dog.*

this now another work altogether? This comparison will reveal more about the tension between text and pictures, for here we have the illustrations held constant, while different texts are applied.

Our first example is Pija Lindenbaum's picturebook, *Boken om Bodil* (1991; Am. *Boodil My Dog,* 1992). One of the earliest illustrations shows the dog lying belly up in an armchair, head and two paws hanging down to the ground, totally oblivious to her surroundings. The original Swedish text in literal translation reads:

> Boodil the dog in her usual spot. She is nice, but lazy and stubborn
> —never pays attention.
> Although early morning turns into late morning
> She is not in a hurry.
> And she is not even tempted
> By a big piece of almond cake.

The American version (incidentally, the title page tells us it's not "translated" by Gabrielle Charbonnet, but "retold" by her) reads as follows:

This is Boodil, my dog.
She's sleeping in her favorite chair.
My dad used to think it was his chair,
but he knows better now.
Boodil is a bullterrier. She's
the best dog in the whole world.
Her brilliant mind is always
at work. Her guard is never down.

A second illustration shows Boodil cowering under the sofa away from the vacuum cleaner. The Swedish version in literal translation reads:

But, when the floor must be cleaned
—Boodil knows all about it—
then she becomes scared and small.
You can wonder where she has disappeared to.

The American version:

Boodil has never really gotten
used to the vacuum cleaner.
It probably looks like a dangerous enemy to her. I bet
only Boodil's amazing superdog
self-control keeps her from
ripping the vacuum to pieces.

The pictures are identical in each of these versions, as is their depiction of the animal, which is unmistakable. The Swedish text simply provides a little

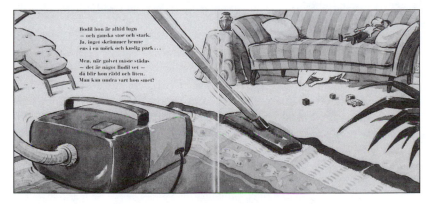

"Boodil's amazing superdog self-control."

more detail about what we already know; text and pictures are complementary or symmetrical, and the voice of the speaker is straightforward, unemotional, objective and detached. But the relationship between the Swedish text and pictures versus that between the American text and pictures is completely different. To begin with, since the American text and pictures are completely contradictory, the reader first asks whether the relationship is ironic, or whether the perception implied in the text is simply mistaken. Of course it is both: the narrator loves the dog and is unable to see its true nature; every action is misinterpreted in a rejection of reality, which is replaced by a heroic ideal—what the speaker would like the dog to be. The author of the text is being heavily ironic, creating a discrepancy so apparent that it makes the reader laugh. But because the persona is innocent and loving, although the reader's laughter provoked by the dog is loud, the laughter at the person's misapprehension is softer and somewhat poignant. One could say that the Swedish original is ironically humorous too, in an understated fashion, because people feed the dog (with almond cake yet!) and allow it to take possession of the most comfortable chair. Even so, the complexity of the dual perception is in no way present. The two books are not the same even though the pictures are unchanged, and we must make different interpretations.

The Wild Baby books have made an international impact and offer a more complex situation for examination since the series is produced by the partnership of Barbro Lindgren and Eva Eriksson rather than a single individual. We will be analyzing their teamwork in detail in later chapters, so we will simply say here that they work collaboratively so that interpretation of intent is not problematic. Instead, we will examine what happens to their book, *Den vilda bebin får en hund* (1985), when it moves into two different cultures, in its British and its American versions. To make a fair comparison, we've made a literal translation of the Swedish text to compare with the rhymed text of the British and American verses, and have selected one small but significant sequence where the baby opens up his birthday present to find a toy dog in place of the real dog he had hoped for.

While the verbal translation would seem the most important, the change in layout also demands our attention. The Swedish original and the British translation both present the sequence on one double-spread, with one picture and a verse on the verso, and two more pictures on the recto, although the Swedish version has a three-line verse, picture, five-line verse, four-line verse, picture, while the second page of the British version differs in that it has picture, ten-line verse, picture. The American version changes this, expanding the sequence to two doublespreads (four pages). On the first page comes the verse, with the picture on the facing page. Turning over we find the verse, picture, verse sequence similar to the top half of the Swedish version, but then a two-line verse and the final picture on a page of their own.

The layout of *The Wild Baby Gets a Dog,* by Barbro Lindgren and Eva Eriksson, is changed in the American edition.

Let us now concentrate on the unfolding of events and emotions of just one page (two in the American version). In the original Swedish text, the baby's descent into disappointment is the first emotion featured, because for a moment he is convinced that the dog is real: "The baby becomes almost shy," says the text, and then he is hit with the realization that "THE BODY IS MADE OF CLOTH!" (The impact of the realization is expressed through capital letters.)

The picture of the baby holding up the cloth dog by its back accompanies this verse, for the baby's head is level with the top line and the left of the picture underneath its words, although the picture extends to the right and below the verse. The emotion of the baby is hard to tell from the drawing. Surprise? Dismay? We must rely on the words here for the specifics.

The next emotion is disappointment giving way to anger: "I WANTED A DOG THAT COULD BARK! I WANTED A DOG THAT WAS ALIVE, NOT ONE LIKE THIS! I AM GOING TO SHOOT IT WITH MY GUN!"

In the next stanza the dog is forgotten. Mama gets the cake, the baby devotes his attention to it, eats it, and then opens his other presents.

> Then Mama gets the cake
> the baby is very fond of it
> He eats it up in half a second
> and then opens parcel after parcel.

The picture provides the illustration for just two of the events cited in the verse, juxtaposing what in the text are two separate rather than concurrent events: "I am going to shoot it with my gun," and "Then Mama gets the cake." The baby stands on one leg pointing a gun as big as he is toward the already lifeless dog, while Mama holds the cake above the toy toward the child. While the baby is presented as a focus of energy, the facial expression not clearly communicating specific emotion, the mother's posture and expression openly express her aim to please.

The U.S. version makes an interesting comparison. First, the drama of the initial misrecognition is gone. This baby is savvy and more sophisticated; he isn't taken in for a moment, and his disappointment is expressed in an objective analysis of the toy.

> There's a puppy in here,
> but the puppy's not real.

Admittedly this statement is "exclaimed with a squeal," but the diction is controlled. The picture intervenes, placed centrally in the middle of the page, with no overlapping text.

The text continues in the same sedate manner. "It's made out of rags, it can't run, it can't bark." And then a momentary "I" statement, "I can't ever take it for walks in the park." There is no mention of the gun, no mention of violence, but an analysis of the situation in rather gentle terms: "Mama, I think that you've made a mistake."

The picture seems to us to be very much in contrast with the tone of the words. Wild Baby pictures are notable for their sense of action, but they are not pretty or polished. They tend toward caricature rather than naturalistic description, with exaggerated stance and gesture that appeals more to a tactile involvement than a visual seductiveness. The Wild Baby in the American text has lost his wildness and become quite civilized, and the pictures' function has changed.

The final page of the sequence is thus quite surprising.

> "Don't be angry," said Mama,
> have some of your cake."

Tied to Mama's mistake by rhyme, the cake as pacifier is made explicit, though the child's anger is so controlled and muted as to be really unexpressed, and Mama strongly advises against whatever impulses to anger lie hidden. Since the mature voice of the baby is not heard on this page, the importance of the picture becomes more pronounced. As noted, it is the mother who verbalizes the child's anger for him, an anger that the picture, with its image of the child with the gun, does express. But the mother has become the primary focus here, taking charge of the child's feelings and emphasizing her need to manipulate his emotions with the cake. To support this, the picture, which was over to the right-hand side of the page in the Swedish version with the baby thus closest to the center of the page, has been shifted over to the left, moving mother closer to the center. Although the picture is in the same place on the page, the text is not, so that the visual positional relationship between picture and text has changed. While in the original version the text downplays the mother's urgency in intervening while the picture tends to stress it, in this American version, mother's statement at the top of the page puts her in control, reinforcing the picture's intensity depicted in her stance, her pleading face, and the upward swing of her tasseled belt suggesting speedy movement.

The American version is very different from the British, where the anger and violence are magnified. In this British version, the baby is initially excited, which provides a contrast with his instant realization that "oh no" the dog is not alive. The child's feelings are not at first expressed directly; instead the description focuses upon the toy's shabbiness, as though it is the quality of the toy that is in question.

> A saggy, baggy, home-made pup,
> With wobbly legs that won't stand up,
> A long limp tail, and button eyes.

The child's disappointment and anger are thus expressed in the rejection of the toy he's been given, culminating in:

> I don't want this old thing," he cries
> And in a tantrum gets his gun,
> He feels like shooting everyone.

Thus while the Swedish baby is ready to shoot the toy with his toy gun and says so, and the American child suppresses his anger and doesn't mention violence, the British child has murder in his heart and wants to kill everyone in sight. Interestingly, the author doesn't trust him to tell us this himself, but has the narrative voice provide this information for us. The cake is not mentioned until later. The emphasis is thus placed entirely on the baby's anger, focusing the reader on his perspective and making the mother somewhat irrelevant and part of the scenery. Interestingly, though the position of the picture is not shifted, the text is, so that it is the figure of the dog that draws our attention. The energy of the text is very much more in accord with the pictures. The description of the dog captures the essence of the images and develops them in greater detail, and the text's exaggeration of feeling and the caricaturish name of Bodger given to the baby emphasize the wild, uncivilized nature of the baby.

Turning our attention from this particular incident to the book in general, we see that another significant change made to the Swedish original by the translations involves the dog itself. In the original, the dog feels unhappy: "The dog lies quiet on the floor and wishes it were alive at least someday." The coming alive is thus initiated by the dog's wish as much as by the baby's. This motif of toys transformed into living beings is well known in children's literature (*Pinocchio, The Velveteen Rabbit*[2]), and the Swedish text may be alluding to it. But nothing similar is ever mentioned in the British or American translations. Instead, the dog is given several rather strange lines that characterize it in a peculiar manner: "Zip nodded his head and modestly said, 'Did I mention that one of the things I can do if I try is quite easily fly if I spread out my fold-away wings.' " As the picture clearly shows, the dog's wings are made from the baby's umbrella, so the dog has neither had them before nor known about his ability to fly. On the contrary, it is part of the magic, and just as much a surprise to the dog as it is to the baby.

The narrative presence is also significantly altered in ways that strongly affect the mood and tenor of the book. The omniscient narrator of the original makes few didactic comments and they concern Mama: "She answers, just as mothers always do," and "She waits for them as she always does; mothers cannot help being anxious all the time." Otherwise, the narrator keeps in the background, focalizing the baby (and occasionally other characters). This means that the narrator is primarily introspective, and the adult narrative voice does not interfere with the child's point of view. Since the visual, perceptional point of view is apparently that of a child (among other things we are always positioned on the same level as the baby or lower), the narrative voice is respectful and supportive. As narrative theory suggests, a good test of possible focalization is to transpose third-person narrative into first person. Most of the original can easily be told in the first person, from the baby's point of view. For example, "Everyone wants to have a little dog, and the baby most of all," can equally be an omniscient narrator's comments and the baby's opinion, an internal focalization of him. The same is true about "to wait is the worst thing in the world for the baby, five minutes is an eternity."

While the narrator of the American translation is quite similar to that of the original, the narrator of the British version states at once: "Alas, this *wild* child's *crazy pranks* go on *from bad to worse*" (emphasis added), immediately positioning the narrative perspective at the adult, condemning and didactic level. That the baby throws "a tantrum" when he is angry is a similar didactic comment. Further, we read that the baby's urging that they jump from the window "wasn't very good advice," and that eating too much ice cream "was, (I think) a great mistake." Most intrusive of all is the sugary, Victorian-style invocation, "But, dear children, don't despair." Here, the child perspective is totally abandoned, and instead the authoritative, intrusive adult narrator addresses the implied audience in a patronizing tone.

If we return once again to the dominant question "whose book is it," it is clear that we have, in a sense, three different books. Even though the pictures are basically the same, the dynamic between the illustrations and text is dramatically different. Certainly the sensitive translator must adapt the idiom creatively to the new language and culture, and the two English translations have responded to what they perceive as cultural imperatives and cultural context.

We cannot leave the Lindgren-Eriksson partnership without referring to one more incident where the American translation significantly reinterprets the original intention, this time in *Den vilda bebiresan* (1982; Am. *The Wild Baby Goes to Sea,* 1983). The relationship between mother and baby and that between text and picture are especially revelatory in the storm scenes.

In a prior incident, the mother's voice has penetrated the baby's fantasies, calling him to dinner, but the baby has rejected her intrusion into his imaginary journey. This is expressed in both text and illustration in the Swedish edition. As the danger of the imaginary world increases, the illustration goes far beyond the text in expressing the baby's fears and incorporating Mama into the fantasy. The text reads simply:

> Then comes the storm
> terrible and big.
> Then Mr. Rabbit
> And Mr. Giraffe
> Call Mama.
> And the cock crows
> As loudly as he can.
> It is certainly only the baby
> Who is happy.

The illustration subtly and dramatically expands the text's hints at the child's insecurity, suggested by his toys, and comments on the nature of the child's imagination and his mother's place in supporting it. While the baby is away on his fantasy adventure, the mother's presence is always in the background. Although the baby resists her call to come home for dinner when real fear threatens, rather than abandon his journey, he weaves her into it. While his toy giraffe and rabbit express the fear that he represses, Mama suddenly appears as part of the sea scene, sitting in her armchair, which floats on the waves, and holding her umbrella to keep herself dry. She is always patient and loving, and her characterization is consistent in her appearance in the journey. She brings with her aspects of ordinary life, the armchair, the umbrella, her smile and her wave, as well as a sense of humor: her slippers have metamorphosed into little boats and float in the water in front of the chair. A duck in a teacup, doll floating in a bed, and dog floating in a bowl and wearing a saucepan hat accompany her presence.

Mama participates in the imaginary journey in *The Wild Baby Goes to Sea.*

This special moment in the original book is omitted in the American translation. The sequence where Mama interrupts is absent, and the image of her floating in the armchair is excised from the page, leaving the baby alone. This decision is extremely significant, and while it might simply be taken as an expression of cultural difference, it might also be considered censorship or tampering with the artists' intent. In this case the ownership of the work is clearly put in question, for the relationship of mother and baby is dramatically redefined.

Seeing the effect of these changes in verbal and iconic translation helps us see even more clearly the nature and the success of the Lindgren-Eriksson partnership and heightens our appreciation of it. This partnership appears to

A storm came up, the ocean swelled,
"Oh, save us, please!" the rooster yelled.
But baby Ben was undismayed,
he chuckled as they pitched and swayed.

In the American version, Mama is deleted.

be an excellent example of a team effort that produces a work whose ownership is not in question.

## One Text and Several Illustrators: *Thumbelina*

Apart from translations, few books have two sets of verbal text accompanying the same illustrations, although such examples do exist, and there are several studies of these rare cases.[3] The range of interpretation when the same text is illustrated by different artists has been thoroughly discussed in criticism, especially regarding some popular fairy tales by Charles Perrault and the Grimm brothers, such as *Little Red Riding Hood, Cinderella, Hansel and*

*Gretel,* and *Snow White,*[4] and by Hans Christian Andersen.[5] The pictures do not only reflect the individual style of the artist and his or her response to the story, but also the general style in illustration at a particular period, ideology, pedagogical intentions, the society's views on certain things, such as naked-ness (for instance in *The Emperor's New Clothes*), and so on.

We have chosen a number of illustrated versions of Andersen's *Thumbe-lina,* one of the most popular of his fairy tales and also one of the dozen most often included in children's editions, to explore the impact of the variety of illustration. There are many picturebooks made out of the text, and a compar-ison between them reveals once again many of the dilemmas in picturebook creation. Our books are illustrated by Swedish, Danish, German, Austrian, and American artists, the year of publication ranges from 1907 to 1996, and we have included mass-market as well as "artistic" books.

Like all Andersen's fairy tales, *Thumbelina* was not meant to be illus-trated, since at the time of publication, in 1835, the printing technique made illustrated books too expensive to be mass-produced. The collection *Fairy Tales Told for Children,* in which *Thumbelina* first appeared, although expressly addressed to children, had no illustrations. The first illustrations to Andersen's fairy tales were made by Vilhelm Pedersen in 1849; Andersen chose the illustrator himself and was very pleased with his work. Pedersen made three woodcuts to *Thumbelina:* an initial vignette portraying Thumbe-lina and the elf-king[6] worshipped by their subjects, a full-page picture of Thumbelina floating on a water-lily leaf tugged by a butterfly, and a final vignette depicting Thumbelina emerging from a flower (we admit that the logic of this order is somewhat strange).

The text of the fairy tale, like most of Andersen's texts, is extremely visual in itself, that is, abounding in vivid descriptions. Andersen elaborates on what the flower looked like, what kind of objects surrounded the tiny Thumbelina and how she used them, describes the nature around her, the rat's home, and so on. Descriptions are also widely used in characterization. Thumbelina is "graceful and delicate," the toad is "loathsome [ . . . ] ugly, big and wet," the swallow's "beautiful wings pressed close against its sides, its legs and head huddled into its feathers," and the flower elf is "as fine and del-icate as if he were made of glass" with "the prettiest beautiful golden crown upon his head, and bright and shining wings."

The text leaves very little to expand in pictures, for there are practically no gaps that would allow the artist a free interpretation. Still, we will see how different the artists' approaches to the text are. The illustrators' decisions about their pictorial solutions depend highly on their background, artistic and pedagogical context, and so on. Some of the versions are child-adapted, accentuating the plot and the adventurous aspect of the text, as well as the helplessness and exposure of the tiny child in the big world, while others bring forward the enigmatic and mythical elements, emphasize the natural

Bladet ned ad Aaen, bort med Tommelise, langt bort, hvor Skrubtudsen ikke kunde komme.

Tommelise seilede forbi saa mange Steder,

71

Original illustration by Vilhelm Pedersen to *Thumbelina.*

setting, and focus on the character, and will probably appeal more to a sophisticated reader. Some pictures are artistically refined, while others are playful and ironic; some are romantic, some are comic. The style manipulates the reader's apprehension of the story.

There are some significant initial questions regarding the number of illustrations and the episodes selected by the illustrator. In the books we have studied, the number of pictures the artist has chosen to illustrate the text varies between eleven and thirty-two. The visual density reflects radically opposed approaches to illustration. The larger number of illustrations tends to make them more decorative. Some artists strive to evoke the sense of the text with minimal means, for instance by making pictures dynamic and prefiguring the action, while those with the larger number of illustrations tend to be more decorative.[7] Very dynamic effects can be conveyed by using the whole doublespread and especially with wordless spreads, as can be found, for instance, in Susan Jeffers's version. Surprisingly, most of the versions use a traditional layout with text and picture on facing pages, and the pictures are framed to create a sense of distance and detachment. We assume that because they are illustrating a 19th-century text, the artists feel compelled to use a traditional layout.

The artist's selection of episodes for illustration suggests that these are the ones apprehended as key events in the story. But it is also possible that key episodes have not been selected for various reasons. Additional questions are more subtle and concern settings, characterization, and point of view, and it is interesting to see whether there are there any details, characters, or other features that appear in the illustration, but are not featured in the text. Finally, there is the question of whether the artist has imposed any additional meaning upon the text. (An excellent and much-discussed example of the latter is Sendak's illustration to *Dear Mili* with holocaust images implanted in the fairy-tale setting, which is a way a contemporary artist can make an older text "up-to-date.") All these questions lead to the most crucial one: Are the illustrations merely decorative, or do they enhance—and if so, in what way—our experience of the text?

In *Thumbelina,* her emergence from the flower at the beginning of the story and her wedding with the elf-king at the end seem especially appropriate for illustration. In between, the text encourages a recurrent change between "positive" (peaceful, harmonious) and "negative" (dramatic, disturbing) images. For instance, pictures of Thumbelina rowing around in a boat made of a tulip petal or sleeping in her hammock of grass convey a sense of peace, while the scenes of her desperate crying on the water-lily leaf or freezing in winter have a strong disturbing effect. Another example of a harmonious picture is Thumbelina drinking "the dew which lay on the leaves every morning," foregrounding some gorgeous thistle flowers and a snail, whose quiet gaze contemplating Thumbelina we almost feel compelled to share. This picture from Elisabet Nyman's Swedish version counterbalances the dramatic events preceding and following it.

It is illuminating to see how some artists seem to deliberately emphasize Thumbelina's hardships, while others, more overtly addressing a young audience, subdue or omit them. For instance, the picture of the swallow flying away is seldom included, perhaps because of its emotional charge. The swallow has offered to take Thumbelina away from the rat, but the girl is loyal to her benefactor and decides to stay. The picture in Nyman's version conveys Thumbelina's point of view as she watches the swallow flying against the setting sun, with wide fields and two rabbits in the foreground. The picture expresses a longing for freedom, which Thumbelina so far has rejected. It also can be said to combine two episodes: the swallow flying away (spring) and Thumbelina going out in the fields to watch the sun (late summer); the picture conveys a temporal duration of several months.

There is in Andersen's text an obvious alternation of static and dynamic episodes, the latter including the toad and the cockchafer kidnapping Thumbelina. These dramatic episodes are accentuated in some versions and toned down in others. The accents are slightly different, as most artists choose the very event of Thumbelina being carried away, others focus on the confrontation on the water-lily leaf, and still others show the toads on the bottom of the lake. While some artists emphasize the cockchafer carrying away Thumbelina, others omit this action and instead portray either Thumbelina alone with the cockchafer or the other cockchafers inspecting her. Interestingly enough, none of the artists depict the scene in which the cockchafer rejects Thumbelina under his friends' pressure. The text says: "She sat and wept because she was so ugly"—an emotionally disturbing scene that the artists definitely prefer to exclude.

The overall atmosphere of the story, as well as its rhythmical pattern, thus becomes totally different according to the illustrator's strategy. The static episodes often convey a long span of time, while the dynamic pictures are by definition swift and passing. The dominance of either type creates a specific sense of narrative duration. By omitting "disturbing" episodes, for instance the dead swallow in the tunnel, some artists make a clear adaptation to the young audience. By contrast, one of the artists visualizes the swallow's story about how he injured his wing on a thorn. The picture is a visual flashback and also a sharp contrast to the preceding picture of Thumbelina in the dark and narrow passage mourning the swallow, whom she believes dead. The picture of the injured swallow may be disturbing with its bloodstained thorn and drops of blood (the allusion to Christ's crown of thorns is obvious), matched by the red berries. However, the brightness of the scenery conveys a reminder of summer, in contrast to the words, which describe the cold, snowy winter. This is a good example of an artist going far beyond a simple illustration of the story.

There is, as we see it, a difference between dynamic pictures that actively contribute to a picturebook and static "illustrations" of a text. A dynamic picture of Thumbelina floating on a leaf can also portray the cockchafer flying toward her, about to snatch her and carry her away. Dynamic pictures convey a sense of motion, as when the toad stretches out its front leg, about to seize the walnut cradle with the sleeping Thumbelina.

Of the more profound differences in the artists' visual interpretations, characterization is perhaps the most essential. In some books Thumbelina is a sugar-sweet child with blond curly hair. In fact, the text makes no mention of

Elsa Beskow's Thumbelina is an innocent child.

Thumbelina's coloring, but, most illustrators choose the blond stereotype associated with the Nordic type of female beauty. Sometimes she emerges from the flower as a baby, naked and plump, sometimes wearing a dress. She can remain unchanged to the end of the story, grow up a little to the age of four or five, or evolve into a more mature feminine form. Some artists use a wide range of visual means to convey the feelings of the heroine, showing fear or despair through facial expression and body position. Others depict her as lacking any emotions whatsoever, a cupidlike, sexless child.[8]

Another way of depicting Thumbelina is perhaps the most "traditional" and true to the text: a slender, almost ephemeral feminine creature, a fairy. However, quite a few artists have chosen to depict Thumbelina as a young woman. In Lisbeth Zwerger's version she is red-haired, with her hair in two neat plaits, healthily red-cheeked, and dressed in a sort of peasant costume with a white blouse, red flowery skirt, and vest. She does not change much, and her grown-up shape makes her encounter with the elf a more natural and a clearly erotic event. In fact, the pose of the couple in the last picture suggests two peasant youths petting, rather than a romantic wedding.

Still another version most obviously exposes the Otherness in Thumbelina. The fact that the tiny girl comes out of a magic seed provided by a witch is seldom noticed by critics, perhaps because of the literary convention that compels us to identify with main characters and apprehend them as good and their adversaries as evil. The Swedish artist Linda Lysell not only interrogates the changing notion of female beauty (what exactly do the words "sweet and fine" signify?), but also accentuates that Thumbelina is an "alien child," not a human being. Her Thumbelina is a grown-up woman, with long, wavy, reddish hair, reminiscent of Pre-Rafaelite paintings, with a sensual mouth and pronounced dark eyes. There is definitely something of a witch about her.

Linda Lysell's Thumbelina is an enticing woman, perhaps a witch. Note the "green chair" she is sitting on.

Still another surprising interpretation of the protagonist is to be found in Arlene Graston's version. Her Thumbelina bears an unmistakable resemblance to the woman in the beginning of the story. Is the artist suggesting that Thumbelina's story is the imaginary projection of a childless woman longing for a child? Incidentally, the appearance of the woman and the witch in the pictures is revealing in itself. These characters are so marginal in the story and disappear so quickly that one would expect them to be too insignificant to be featured in a picture at all. In fact, Andersen disposes too easily of the woman who has longed so much to have a child and loses it so soon. Nevertheless, several artists devote a whole page to the woman, depicting her sometimes as an old, worn-out peasant, sometimes as a typical 19th-century, middle-class woman, sometimes as young and pretty. However, none of the artists has chosen to depict the woman planting the seed or kissing the flower just before it opens, an emotionally charged scene that would probably draw too much attention to the woman.[9]

The animal characters are much more central to the story than the woman. The general style of the books naturally determines the way the animals are represented. Some are realistic, almost naturalistic, even though they may wear clothes. Other are traditional fairy-tale anthropomorphic animals, and in the mass-market books they are reminiscent of comic-strip figures. Characterization is the area where the text provides the artists the most freedom. Some of them choose to depict the toad decorating the room with rushes and water lilies "to make it look nice and bright for her new daughter-in-law." Even though we, identifying with Thumbelina, apprehend her enemy as evil, this picture intensifies the fact that the toad does not mean any harm and is on the contrary nice and well-wishing, from her own viewpoint. The same is true about the cockchafer who gives Thumbelina food, corresponding to the text: "[ . . . ] gave her honeydew from the flowers to eat, and told her that she was very pretty [ . . . ]." The cockchafer is nice to Thumbelina in the text, but apparently few artists want to draw our attention to it.

The depiction of the elf, as already hinted, in many ways manipulates our apprehension of the message of the story. In the Danish original, the elf is called "the angel of the flower." The text also says that "in each flower there lived a tiny man or woman." Some translations say "a boy or girl." However, even when the translation mentions "men and women," the child-adapted versions depict the elves as children. These books' closures, even though the text mentions marriage, are reestablishments of the happy and innocent paradise of childhood. Other versions show the elf as a young boy, somewhat reminiscent of Peter Pan, his gaze revealing his overtly erotic interest in Thumbelina.

In all the versions, the omniscient perspective is used, which is natural in a fairy tale and corresponds well to the omniscient narrator of the verbal text. The composition of most pictures is a general, theatrical view with Thumbelina in the center. No close-ups or unusual angles are used. No attempts are

Kaj Beckman's final illustration suggests the paradise of fairy-tale childhood.

made to convey a subjective point of view. As already mentioned, frames create a further sense of detachment. The metafictive comment in the end, mentioning "the man who can tell stories," is indirectly reflected in one book, in a little vignette of the swallow by the open window; however, in Arlene Graston's version, the last picture explicitly shows the aging Andersen with the swallow perched on his finger.

Finally, setting is another textual element that allows the illustrator considerable freedom. One passage in the text that allows great imagination is the description of the warm countries: "[ . . . ] along the roadside hedges grew the most delicious green and purple grapes; lemons and oranges hung from trees; the air was fragrant with myrtle and many sweet herbs; and about the paths ran many lovely children playing among the brightly coloured butterflies." Andersen most probably had in mind Italy, where he had been the year before he wrote *Thumbelina;* the text mentions "a palace, built long ago of dazzling white marble," with a "great, white column lay fallen on the ground [ . . . ] broken into three pieces."

The artists' responses to this description are widely diverse. Some books have Roman temples or ruins in the background, others depict medieval towers or even Disney-like fairy-tale castles with pointed roofs. In Elisabet Nyman's book, in contrast to the words, the scenery is unmistakably Scandinavian. The picture of Thumbelina flying on the swallow's back imitates the

style of Swedish neo-romanticism at the turn of the 20th century, with its specific yellowish "Northern light." These different settings naturally contribute
to our interpretation of the closure. For instance, the castle suggests that
Thumbelina has come to some fairyland, where she apparently belongs, while
the text is quite ambivalent on this point; the swallow returns to Denmark, to
reality. The place where Thumbelina finds her destiny may also be interpreted
as the realm of death, especially in light of the images of angellike, winged
creatures inhabiting it. However, none of the artists imply this interpretation.

Generally, none of the books can be characterized as counterpointing or
even expanding, apparently because there are so few gaps in the text to be
filled by illustrations. Some versions have occasional figures not mentioned
in the text, mostly animals and insects, but they have merely decorative functions. Occasionally they may accentuate Thumbelina's tiny size by comparison. One interesting and somewhat anomalous feature that has given artists
some leeway is "the green chair," mentioned in the Danish original, on which
Thumbelina is sitting when the flower opens. Some of the artists actually
depict this strange green chair. In some books, Thumbelina sits on the stamen, while in most others whatever she sits on is obscured by the petals of the
flower. In some cases, the illustration derives from translations of the original,

Elisabet Nyman's landscapes allude to Scandinavian neo-romantic painting.

and emphasizes the "whose book" question even more strongly. Most Swedish translations have "a green chair," Naomi Lewis's English translation says "green center," and Erik Haugaard's, "green stigma." Some of the books omit the chair altogether.[10]

It is also interesting to observe which picture has been chosen for the cover. The covers of picturebooks signal the theme, tone, and nature of the narrative, as well as implying an addressee. Few artists create a unique cover picture not repeated inside the book. The choice of cover evidently reflects the importance attached to the particular episode. Several covers show Thumbelina's emergence from the flower, thus not signaling the plot. Some versions emphasize adventure by choosing Thumbelina floating on a leaf or the two toads carrying away Thumbelina's bed while she is standing on the leaf, surrounded by sympathetic fish. Linda Lysell's version has the idyllic scene in the hammock, which, however, reveals Thumbelina's tiny size against the background of plants, flowers, and mushrooms. Elisabet Nyman's has the picture of the rat knitting by the cozy fireplace and Thumbelina carding wool, a peaceful scene not in any way suggesting the dramatic events of the book. Susan Jeffers's cover shows Thumbelina in her wedding dress bidding farewell to the sun, with the impatient rat and mole in the background, thus anticipating the most dramatic turning point in the plot. Naturally, the artists may expect their readers, especially the adult coreaders, to know the story of Thumbelina. However, if each book is the readers' first acquaintance with the story, their anticipation of what will happen will vary dramatically depending on the cover.

The discussion of the many versions of *Thumbelina* brings us back to the question of "ownership." Every illustrator has made a very different book from the text of Andersen's original tale. Many of these books have their merits, and it has not been our intention to discuss which is "best," only to show how differently the artists interpret the text and the wide variety of pictorial possibilities the text allows, even, as we have shown, a very "tight" text like this one. Few if any of the versions take the text beyond its original intentions; however, they certainly amplify different aspects of the text, which considerably affects our perception of the story and our reaction to it.

## *I Don't Want to Go to Bed* in Two Versions

One of the few examples, besides folktales or Andersen's stories, of a text illustrated by different artists is *I Don't Want to Go to Bed*, written by Astrid Lindgren. The first picturebook with this text was produced in 1947 by Birgitta Nordenskjöld. In 1988, a new picturebook was issued, with pictures by Astrid Lindgren's frequent illustrator, Ilon Wikland. A comparison between the two books does not only reveal a divergence in style that, besides the individual artist's manner, reflects the change in picturebook design in the forty years between the two books. It also reveals the two artists' different approaches to the text.

The design of Nordenskjöld's book is traditional, with full-color framed pictures on the right page and text on the left accompanied by small vignettes. All in all, there are seven spreads in the book. The first is the establishing scene, presenting the character and the situation: the five-year-old Lasse does not want to go to bed, and the old lady neighbor offers him her magical eyeglasses. The last spread depicts the resolution, when Lasse returns to his room and goes to bed. The spreads in the middle depict the five scenes Lasse sees through the magical glasses, each portraying nice small animals going to bed: a little bear, rabbits, birds, squirrels, and mice. The pictures are static and indeed "illustrate," that is, freeze, one of the moments in the series of events described by words. The left-page vignettes supplement some of the episodes.

Ilon Wikland works with doublespreads, using the whole area of the spread and often letting the picture "bleed" beyond the frame. Instead of one establishing scene, she chooses to have three. In the first, the boy is depicted five times, in a half-circular movement around the spread, which corresponds to the words describing his actions: building with blocks, drawing, jumping down from the kitchen table, examining a hole in his sock, and hiding behind a rocking chair (it is worth pointing out that the order of pictures does not match the order of words). Some details of the continuous picture imply other games not mentioned by words: a rope tied to three chairs, a windup mouse, a troll in a wagon, a half-eaten apple lying on the floor, and a jigsaw puzzle. The picture "expands" the words, suggesting that Lasse's going to bed has been delayed by more games than those described in the verbal text. In Nordenskjöld's left-page vignettes, we see the boy building with blocks and pulling at his sock, that is, the pictures merely duplicate the text.

In the next spread in Wikland's book, the mother is putting the screaming and protesting boy to bed, and we are invited to have a glimpse of his room, untidy and overcrowded with toys. The picture is unsettling and emphasizes the conflict between mother and child. In the third spread, Wikland introduces the neighbor, who bears an unmistakable resemblance to Astrid Lindgren. The composition of the two pictures is strikingly similar, with the lady sitting in an armchair offering the glasses to the boy, who stands in front of her. Nordenskjöld characterizes the lady by the many family portraits on the wall, a ball of yarn and a half-knitted sock on the coffee table, a rose in a vase, and a cat on a cushion. There is also a little mouse by the mouse hole in the corner. In contrast Wikland has a big potted flower on a high stand, an open book, and a cup of coffee.

Most of the subsequent episodes in Wikland's book are divided between several spreads. First she shows the little bear sitting nicely in his bed eating his porridge. In the next spread, she illustrates the verbal flashback, describing the little bear's pranks during the day. The little rabbits going to bed is also divided into two episodes: a pillow fight and a rather turbulent bathroom scene, which in the verbal text is described only by the sentence: "They race to the bathroom, pushing each other to come first." The richness of detail in both pictures makes them dynamic and suggests a considerable flow of time. Nordenskjöld's picture is static and, pillow fight notwithstanding, restful. Her Bear family is, on the contrary, full of movement. While Mrs. Bear is feeding the little bear, six agile mice are cooking the porridge, sweeping the floor, putting firewood in the stove, and one of them is hanging up little bear's wet socks and shoes. The last action is the only one mentioned in words. Remarkably, the two lines about the tiny maids are deleted from the text in Wikland's book. Apparently, it was not considered politically correct in 1988 in Sweden to portray maids; however, a gratifying pictorial possibility has been lost.

The birds in Wikland's book are perhaps the less imaginative, almost naturalistic, in no way making use of the many funny details the words elicit—for instance the young fledgling's memories of his desperate attempts to fly during daytime, which Nordenskjöld depicts in the left-page vignette. She also has some minor characters in her picture, not mentioned in the text: two ladybugs in front of their mushroom house and two ants busy at work.

The squirrel family in Wikland's version is again depicted in two spreads, allowing a certain development within the sequence. Nordenskjöld's single picture is static, but it has a witty detail, Father Squirrel reading a newspaper titled "Evening Bark." The left-page vignette represents one of the baby squirrels' dream of building many toy trains. Also, the interior of the mouse home has some additional details, such as shelves marked, "Cheese,"

Expanding, dynamic picture in *I Don't Want to Go to Bed,* by Ilon Wikland.

"Jam," "Breadcrumbs," and "Empty Jars." As all intraiconic texts, these details slow down our "reading" of the visual text and add to the text–image tension.

The final picture of Wikland's book is the traditional "homecoming" in children's fiction, the safe return to the security of the bedroom. Since the setting repeats an earlier spread, albeit from another viewpoint, the viewer is not encouraged to investigate the picture any further. The chaos of the earlier spread is gone, the toys are tidily put away in a box, the drawers nicely pushed back into the chest, the clothes neatly folded on the chair. The picture reflects a sense of peace. So does Nordenskjöld's final picture, of course. However, since there is no "return" in the sense that there is no picture in the beginning of the book showing the boy's room, there is an urge to contemplate the picture and register the details: the many toys, drawings on the wall, a mobile hanging from the ceiling, a hobbyhorse in the corner, and the two *Babar* picturebooks in the bookshelf. It is only now that we are truly introduced to the protagonist of the story. Both Nordenskjöld and Wikland use characterization by setting, but Nordenskjöld does so after the closure, as a final touch.

The endpapers in Wikland's book suggest that all the animals portrayed in the "magical" scenes are Lasse's toys. Another interesting feature of the book is that many details from the boy's room appear in the animals' rooms: furniture, toys, drawings, clothes; the small rabbits have a long rope similar to the one in the first spread. Wikland thus manipulates the viewer to apprehend the "magical" scenes as products of the boy's imagination, while Nordenskjöld's version accentuates the magic of the glasses, really allowing the boy to see far into the forest and into the animals' homes.

Both artists "expand" the words they are illustrating, adding details in the pictures and contributing to the plot, setting, and characterization. However, they do this in different ways, which, among other things, result in slightly different interpretations. Neither of the two sets of pictures directly contradicts the words, but Wikland's version is apparently more sophisticated in its treatment of "objective" versus "subjective" interpretation, since in her book, the line between fantasy and reality is more flexible and fluctuating. If anything, this approach reflects the general trend we notice in contemporary picturebooks.

This trend is also confirmed by two other examples involving the same authors, *I Want to Go to School Too* and *I Want a Brother or Sister*. The first was illustrated by Birgitta Nordenskjöld in 1951 and by Ilon Wikland in 1979; the second by Nordenskjöld in 1954 and Wikland in 1978. All the changes and differences observed in the two versions of *I Don't Want to Go to Bed* are also relevant for these books. The American translations, appearing in the late '80s, use Wikland's pictures.

While we can wonder why the new illustrations were necessary for the three Astrid Lindgren books, it is quite obvious what caused a revised version of *I Can Drive All Cars,* written by Karin Nyman. It first appeared in 1965, illustrated by Ylva Källström. In 1997 it was reissued with illustrations by Tord Nygren that introduced new car models, since the ones in the original book would not be familiar to today's children.

## Picturebook Authors Illustrating Others' Texts

Our final examples are drawn from instances where authors/illustrators are asked to illustrate not their own texts, but the texts of other writers. Here the sense of ownership given full rein in one's own creation must be mitigated to form a collaborative partnership with another writer.

In *Mr. Rabbit and the Lovely Present* (1962), written by Charlotte Zolotow, Maurice Sendak is much more restricted by the words he is illustrating than he is in any of his own picturebooks. In fact, he obviously rejects some excellent opportunities to create visual images merely because they would have replicated the words.

The text is built on repetitions. The little girl wants to give her mother a birthday present, something her mother likes, and as she likes red, yellow, green, and blue, several options are suggested by Mr. Rabbit and either declined or accepted by the girl. Among the options, only a few are selected by Sendak to be visualized in illustrations. Thus, of the red, the abstract "red" is not portrayed, which corresponds to the verbally expressed doubts of Mr. Rabbit: "You can't give her red" (the same is repeated about the other three colors). Red underwear, red cardinal birds, and red fire engines in the text are not featured in the pictures, while red roofs and red apples are, the latter becoming the little girl's choice. Of the yellow suggestions, taxicabs, sun, and butter are only mentioned in the text, while canary birds, rejected, and bananas, chosen as a suitable present, are depicted in the illustration. Emeralds, green parrots, caterpillars, peas, and spinach are further suggested by Mr. Rabbit, but only his final proposal, green pears, appears in the picture. Finally, an unlikely present, a blue lake, is depicted, as are stars, and blue grapes, the girl's choice; but sapphires and bluebirds remain in the verbal text only.

The artist's decision is quite plain. Everything that can be easily found in the setting of the book (which is "realistic," disregarding Mr. Rabbit being a talking animal) goes into the picture, that is, everything that can be immediately perceived externally. However, Sendak chooses not to portray the girl's or the rabbit's (the point of view is not clear in the book) internal vision of taxicabs or fire engines, emeralds or sapphires. Of the four bird types, only one, a yellow canary, is actually placed in a picture. And the abstractions of red, yellow, green, and blue are rejected as impossible to perceive. Sendak is thus extremely careful to avoid the duplication of verbal message in his pictures. No other objects in the pictures could be associated with the particular color (this becomes more apparent if we compare the book to *Come Into My*

*Night, Come Into My Dream* (1978), by Stefan Mählqvist and Tord Nygren, where the verbal mention of the green color initiates a string of visual associations). Neither does the tone of any picture change as a new color is discussed in words.

In general, few pictorial details go beyond the verbal text. The landscape, the little girl's house, and the two characters are the only textual gaps filled by the visual images. One exception is the picture suggesting that the little girl and Mr. Rabbit may have had a picnic while discussing the mother's present. It can naturally be argued whether the positions of the characters in a page, their gestures and facial expressions are merely illustrating the words or present a slightly different story, but this is true of any picturebook, including Sendak's own.

Another artist who is most famous for his own picturebooks but also illustrates others' texts is Sven Nordqvist, author of the internationally praised Festus and Mercury series. Less known outside Scandinavia are his illustrations to a series about Mamma Moo and the Crow, written by Jujja and Thomas Wieslander. We have chosen one book from this series for a close reading, referring to others occasionally.

In illustrating *Mamma Moo on a Swing* (1993), Nordqvist, just like Sendak illustrating Zolotow, is more restrained than in his own picturebooks. The Mamma Moo stories were originally written for the radio, that is, they were deliberately nonvisual and explicit in their descriptions. Further, they are primarily based on dialogue, which is apparently nonvisual, and in the book is emphasized by close-ups, generally not characteristic of Nordqvist's work. The text often uses onomatopoeia: "KNOCK-KNOCK-KNOCK" on the door, "FLAP FLAP BUMP" (the crow flying and landing with a bump), or "BUZZ!" for the sound of a tractor. Since these are part of the preexisting verbal text, the illustrator refrains from inserting them into pictures, for instance as comic-strip sound effects. There is, however, a speech balloon in one picture, where Mamma Moo is swinging violently, shouting: "Wow, wow, here comes the swinging cow!" These words are not featured in the verbal text, but they could have been part of the radio script, and it is impossible to say whether they are the illustrator's own addition.

The settings in *Mamma Moo on a Swing* are reminiscent of those in the Festus and Mercury books in style and color, which is especially evident in comparison with the two doublespreads portraying cows in *Ruckus in the Garden* (1990). However, they lack most of the specific features of Nordqvist's usual scenery, notably the disproportional plants and vegetables, strange objects (such as oversize boots, tin cans, or musical instruments), and the small creatures living their own lives in the foreground ("running stories," or syllepses). Just one little jubilant green creature appears in the spread where Mamma Moo starts swinging, but it is almost hidden by the green grass. There is also a bird in its nest, looking out anxiously at Crow's manipulation with the swing, but it is not as fanciful and out of place as Nordqvist's own creatures. In the other Mamma Moo books, these creatures appear occasionally (*Mamma Moo Rides the Bob,* 1994) but are never as prominent as in Festus and Mercury books.

The landscape of Mamma Moo is practically "realistic." There are a few modest distortions in size, as well as several trees and bushes with "wrong" leaves, but these are neatly disguised among other vegetation and certainly not as conspicuous as in *Festus and Mercury.* The only nonrealistic element (except for Mamma Moo riding a bicycle) is a glimpse of the interior of Crow's house, portrayed in just one doublespread and quite similar to the rustic interior of Festus's house. We are given a full view of this space in *Mamma Moo Cleans Up* (1997), where the spread, abounding in detail, bears perhaps the closest resemblance to the delightful chaos of Festus and Mercury.

Among the pictorial details comparable to those of the Festus and Mercury books are the three singing birds up a tree and a fly, its trajectory marked by a dotted line, in the first doublespread. However, these details merely illustrate the verbal statement "the birds twittered, and the flies buzzed" (symmetrical interaction).

The verbal text goes on: "All the cows were grazing in the pasture. All except Mamma Moo." The last sentence is redundant, since Mamma Moo is depicted sneaking deeper into the picture and toward the edge of it, in a typical pageturner. Since all other cows are brown and white, we have no doubts about the runaway's identity. Here, a good opportunity for a verbal gap, filled by the picture, is lost.

Some other favorite devices used by Nordqvist in Festus and Mercury, such as simultaneous succession, intensified by trajectory lines, become less effective when they merely repeat the verbal statements: "He flew around Mamma Moo's head as fast as he could," or "Crow sneaked behind the bushes. He sneaked over the stones. He ran from tree to tree and hid among the branches." Very little is left for the reader/viewer to fill in these spreads. The same in true about the sledding scenes in *Mamma Moo Rides the Bob.* The only really expanding picture in the Mamma Moo series is the spread from *Mamma Moo Builds a Hut* (1995), in which Crow is depicted twenty times, corresponding to the words: "It took little time for him to build. He used all his tools almost at once."

The swinging sequences, utilizing the so-called simultaneous succession, are somewhat metaphysical in the spatial solutions. In one spread, the swing with Mamma Moo is portrayed twice, on verso and recto as if mirroring each other. The two "mirrored" branches are slightly different. In the next spread, there are four images, in the same mirror composition, but the two swings on the verso and recto, respectively, are tied at different places on the same branch, an ironic detail that easily escapes the viewer's attention. Characteristically, in the first two unsuccessful attempts, Mamma Moo is turned left, back into the story, while as she starts swinging she is turned right, toward the next spread and the continuation of the plot. The motion lines in each static picture (waving of the tail, swinging of the legs) may be a commonplace, but there is another ironic detail, doubled by the words: "Then she waved her horns."

In the third spread depicting the swinging, Nordqvist reverses the pictures, so that verso and recto are still mirroring each other, but instead of growing from the same stem in the "gutter" of the doublespread, the branches grow from the page edges. It is impossible to say whether this is the artist's deliberate decision, for instance for the sake of variety; however, the constant change of perspective, real or illusory, contributes to the dynamic character of the visual level, since the verbal level is relatively static. Applying film terminology, the artist uses "rotating camera," shooting the scene from different angles. This is again one of Nordqvist's favorite devices (see, e.g., the first spread of *Wishing to Go Fishing,* 1987). However, in *Mamma Moo on a Swing* there are no aerial views, which are quite common in Festus and Mercury books. Several other daring spatial devices are absent as well, such as the blending of two different spaces by means of a common detail (chair in *Wishing to Go Fishing*), or the merging of one object into another (curtain turning into road into tablecloth in *Pancake Pie,* 1985). The absence of all these features makes *Mamma Moo* a much more conventional book in its spatial representation.

Most of *Mamma Moo on a Swing* is symmetrical, as the actions of the

Unusual picture sequence in *Mamma Moo on a Swing*, illustrated by Sven Nordqvist. Observe the motion lines and the little creature in the bottom right corner.

characters are described both verbally and visually, while the dialogue corresponds to their positions and facial expressions. Nordqvist does, however, use some purely visual means as he portrays Mamma Moo's change of moods through several spreads: hope, disappointment, cautiousness, fear, satisfaction with the first small results, joy, and final triumph. More prominent verbal gaps in these pages are Crow's reaction, successfully filled by the pictures.

The verbal text normally only uses external focalization to show Mamma Moo's actions, so that the pictures instead describe her inner reaction to the failures and eventual success. However, on one page, both external and internal focalization is used: "The wind blew around Mamma Moo's ears. Her fringe flapped. It took her breath away." While the first two sentences are doubled by the picture, the last one cannot be directly expressed visually.

A direct remnant of the radio manuscript appears on the penultimate spread when Crow says, "Look! The farmer has lost his cap!" This detail could have remained in the picture only, especially in view of the next spread, where Mamma Moo sneaks into the cowshed wearing the cap while the farmer is milking the other cows—a Mary Poppins–type proof that the adventure has really taken place.

If Nordqvist were illustrating his own text, he would have had an option to delete some verbal statements that are doubled by the visual signs. In most cases, he avoids verbal redundancies in his own books, but far from everywhere. One example is *Wishing to Go Fishing,* when Mercury's vivacious movement across the page, expressed by simultaneous succession, is at least partly doubled by words: "He jumped on the chair, bit his own tail, jumped up on the table, took a sip of coffee, dropped a lump of sugar, chased it to the floor, up into the sofa, back to the table . . ." The picture is however so dynamic that it almost looks as if Mercury is chasing himself, and he literally bites the tail of his own image in front of him!

In illustrating others' texts, Nordqvist uses fewer expressive means, and when using some of his favorite devices, does so in a much more subdued manner. His illustrations are often symmetrical, while his own books are considerably more expanding and contradictory. In Mamma Moo we find no pictorial details/objects/images that are not featured in the text and that have no direct connection with the plot. All this contributes to the general impression of Mamma Moo books as being visually meager and definitely inferior to Festus and Mercury books.

## Notes

1. John Stephens, *Language and Ideology in Children's Fiction* (London: Longman, 1992): 164.

2. See, e.g., the treatment of this motif in Lois Kuznets, *When Toys Come Alive: Narratives of Animation, Metamorphosis and Development* (New Haven: Yale University Press, 1994).

3. See, e.g., Hugo McCann and Claire Hiller, "Narrative and Editing Choices in the Picture Book: A Comparison of Two Versions of Roberto Innocenti's Rose Blanche," *Papers* 5 (1994) 2-3: 53–57.

4. See, e.g., Joseph H. Schwarcz, *Ways of the Illustrator: Visual Communication in Children's Literature* (Chicago: American Library Association, 1982):107–117; Ulla Bergstrand, "Det var en gång - om mötet mellan sagan och bilderboken," in *I bilderbokens värld,* ed. Kristin Hallberg and Boel Westin (Stockholm: Liber, 1985): 143–163; Perry Nodelman, *Words About Pictures. The Narrative Art of Children's Picture Books* (Athens: The Univerity of Georgia Press, 1988): 264–276; Russ Mac-Math, "Recasting Cinderella: How Pictures Tell the Tale," *Bookbird* 32 (1994) 4: 29–34.

5. See Lena Fridell, "Text och bild. Några exempel," in *Bilden i barnboken,* ed. Lena Fridell (Gothenburg: Stegeland, 1977): 61–83; Schwarcz, op. cit., 101–104.

6. In the Danish original, the creature is called "the angel of the flower." The different translations, for instance into Swedish, English, German, and Russian, present him as "elf," "guardian-spirit," "angel," etc.

7. Cf. Perry Nodelman's discussion of Maurice Sendak's single illustration to Grimms' "Snow White," encompassing the whole story, in Nodelman, op. cit., 266.

8. Swede Einar Nerman's Thumbelina is a sexless baby, with short haircut, wearing a frilly vest, her bottom bare. Nerman used his infant son as a model. The picture of Thumbelina running through the dark tunnel with a torch may for today's Swedish readers seem an ironic self-quotation, alluding to Nerman's most famous image, a logo on a box of matches ("Solstickan"). But in fact, the illustrations to *Thumbelina* predate Solstickan, so Nerman borrowed his Thumbelina for the matchbox.

9. Actually, some mass-market retellings circumvent the ambiguous wish of the unmarried woman to have a child by exchanging her with a childless couple!

10. When we discovered this mysterious green chair, our first thought was that the Danish "den grønne stol" must have an additional meaning of "stamen," and that the Swedish translators had missed it. However, standard Danish dictionaries do not have this meaning, and our Danish informants categorically denied such a possibility, maintaining that the green chair was as enigmatic to Danish natives as to anyone else.

CHAPTER 2

# Setting

## Some General Remarks on Setting

The setting of a picturebook establishes the situation and the nature of the world in which the events of the story take place. At the simplest level, it communicates a sense of time and place for the actions depicted, but it can go far beyond this in establishing the genre expectations of the work (fairy tale, fantasy), in providing a pervasive affective climate that sets the reader's emotional response in a particular register (grotesque, nostalgic, everyday), in instigating plot development through contrasting or dramatic change in settings (home/away, city/pastoral, war or other disaster), and in commenting upon character. Picturebooks incorporate these functions of setting without limitation, and one book, especially a complex one, may exemplify all of them. Our use of complex books to illustrate particular functions in no way suggests that their setting is limited to this one type of communication. Setting is also an important way of assisting the creation of character, which will be more appropriately considered in the next chapter.

While these general functions of setting do not differ radically between novels and picturebooks, the text–image interaction in picturebooks creates a variety of possibilities. In a picturebook, setting can be conveyed by words, pictures, or both. The visual text of a picturebook is naturally well suited to the description of spatial dimensions, including both indoor scenes and landscape, the mutual spatial relations of figures and objects, their relative size, position, and so on. Similar to characterization, setting demonstrates very well the difference between diegesis (telling) and mimesis (showing). While words can only *describe* space, pictures can actually *show* it, doing so more effectively and often more efficiently. In narrative theory, a description is one of the signs of the narrator's presence in the text. The verbal narrator forces the reader to "see" certain details of the setting, while ignoring others. Visual representation of setting is "nonnarrated," and therefore nonmanipulative, allowing the reader considerable freedom of interpretation.

Let us first consider the dynamics of the verbal–visual interaction in the picturebook form. It is commonly believed that young readers dislike descriptions and even skip them altogether while reading, therefore in novels for children verbal descriptions of setting are often kept to a minimum. In a picturebook, with its limited scope of verbal text, verbal descriptions of setting are either totally absent or negligible. The visual description has on the contrary unlimited possibilities. However, even in the visual setting we can observe a wide spectrum of pictorial solutions ranging from no setting at all, either verbal or visual (characteristic of exhibit and ABC books but also in books where just the characters and occasional objects necessary for the plot development are present), to a fully depicted setting that may be predominantly visual, predominantly verbal, or a variety of combinations and permutations.

While even the most setting-poor books may imply some environmental connection, for example characters in certain kinds of dress, or objects that belong indoors, or outdoors, the options for text–picture interaction are multiple and sophisticated. In the simplest, most redundant case, pictures and words replicate each other, but this occurs only in very reduced settings, where words indeed describe all of the objects in the picture, including shape, color and mutual position. More frequently the pictures will expand on what the text describes, but they may go far beyond this, so that the entire setting is conveyed visually rather than verbally. At the furthest extreme, the words and pictures may not be in harmony: this may be positive and intended, for instance, to offer a dream sequence or an ironic counterpoint, or it may, unfortunately, be the result of a mismatch between author and illustrator, as we discussed in a previous chapter.

We can perhaps say that visual settings in picturebooks are similar to the scenery in theater, which can be realistic or symbolic, elaborate or simple. Often, especially in modern performances, the actors operate with a limited number of props. In this, picturebook conventions are different from film, whose screen image does not have blank areas. Indeed, it is quite common for picturebooks to have so-called negative space, that is, empty areas around characters and objects. However, unlike theater, but similar to film, picturebooks can make use of a variety of pictorial solutions in the depiction of setting, for instance panoramic views (especially on the so-called establishing pages), long shots, middle-distance shots, close-ups or multiple scenes (that is, two or more different settings on the same spread or page). Picturebooks can even have contrasting settings on verso and recto.

Framing is an extremely powerful visual element of setting. Frames normally create a sense of detachment between the picture and the reader, while the absence of frames (that is, a picture that covers the whole area of a page or a doublespread) invites the reader into the picture. The successively diminished and finally disappearing frames in Maurice Sendak's *Where the Wild Things Are* (1963) reflect the change in the character's state of mind.[1] Frames in Beatrix Potter's *The Tailor of Gloucester* (1903) provide a sense of historical distance not usually found in her unframed illustrations. The round frames on the first and last page of Tove Jansson's *The Dangerous Journey* (1977) serve to open and close the plot, while the full-page pictures inside create an effect of presence and involvement. In Barbro Lindgren and Eva Eriksson's *Wild Baby* books (1980–85), fully developed settings contrast with action vignettes focusing upon object and character without any definitive setting.

For many stories with a historical dimension, the correct and careful delineation of setting is both necessary and educational. The details of the setting can offer information about places and historical epochs that go far beyond the young reader's experience, and do so in a subtle, nonintrusive way that provides an understanding of unfamilar manners and morals and the cultural environment in which the action takes place. Examples of this may be found in Barbara Cooney's *Island Boy* (1988) and *Only Opal* (1994). In other cases, the setting may take the action literally out of this world, or at least into an unknown realm, as for instance in Sendak's *We're All in the Dumps with Jack and Guy* (1993), which moves the characters onto the moon, or Olga Pastuchiv's *Minas and the Fish* (1997), which takes us into an underwater world. Similarly, the setting of a work like Jeanie Adams's *Pigs and Honey* (1989), which moves us into the cultural realities of Aboriginal Australia, suggests a familiar landscape and time seen through an alternative perspective.

## Minimal or Reduced Setting

The tradition of reduced or minimal setting in picturebooks is closely connected with the post–World War II "hyperrealism" in children's literature, focusing on the familiar and the everyday, on the young child's immediate surroundings. A full depiction of pictorial space is assumed to be superfluous, since the reader's attentions must be fully occupied by the character and just a few details: a piece of furniture, a toy, or a tool. This is a reflection of a specific concept of the picturebook and its educational and aesthetic purposes. A number of Swedish picturebook creators who emerged in the 1950s and '60s gained worldwide reputations with this type of picturebook: Inger and Lasse Sandberg, Gunilla Bergström with her Alfie Atkins books, and Gunilla Wolde with her Thomas and Betsy books.

Whether the characters of the Sandbergs' books are children or imaginary beings, like spooks, the settings are familiar and ordinary. They are also considerably reduced, reflecting the child's limited experience of the world. Most often, only the objects essential for the plot are depicted, surrounded by negative space. However, there is wide diversity in the Sandberg series. The Anna, Daniel, and Dusty series address very young children (*What Anna Saw,*

1964, *Daniel and the Coconut Cakes,* 1968, *Dusty Wants to Help,* 1983) and are wholly concentrated on the characters and the objects. The objects are isolated, almost like those in an exhibit book. No backgrounds or other objects suggest the social status of the characters, the historical epoch, and so on. The stories are deliberately lifted out of place and time. One of the assets of this is that they do not become outdated, as books with more distinct realistic settings often do. *Dusty Wants to Help* takes place in the kitchen, so the stove and the sink are the natural elements of setting. *Look There, Dusty Said* (1983) describes a walk in the country, and some details of rural landscape are depicted: a road, road signs, fences, some flowers, a butterfly, an ant—things that a very young child observes in his immediate surroundings. In the Little Ghost Godfrey series, we find more details of setting, mainly interiors, not mentioned in words. There is a fascinating contrast between the fairy-tale (the castle) and the everyday setting: stove, butter churn, and the like.

Thomas, Betsy, and Alfie Atkins books reflect the same trend as most of the Sandberg creations. In addressing very young children, they depict limited settings focusing on the essential details and omitting anything that does not immediately concern the plot and the character. The settings are of the backdrop type. They do not stimulate long pauses at each spread, instead encouraging quick turning of pages to follow the plot. Sam books by Barbro Lindgren and Eva Eriksson do not use negative space, but the settings are just as minimal as in all the above-mentioned series.

Domestic setting in a fantastic story: Inger and Lasse Sandberg's *Little Ghost Godfrey.*

Historically authentic setting in Ann-Madeleine Gelotte's *Tyra from Odengatan no. 10.*

## Symmetrical and Duplicative Settings

In books set in the past, the setting is always integral since it provides additional information about the epoch described. In Ann-Madeleine Gelotte's three picturebooks, depicting three generations in Sweden, *Ida-Maria from Arfliden* (1977), *Tyra in Odengatan no. 10* (1981), and *We Lived in Helenelund* (1983), the author offers detailed and historically accurate visual descriptions of exterior and interior scenes, focusing on jobs, assignments, games, and recurrent events of everyday life. In the first book, the setting is rural, Northern Sweden in the 1890s. Outdoor pictures show the work and leisure time of a woodcutter's family. Interior scenes depict chores such as spinning, weaving, and sewing clothes, and events such as a peddler's visit, bathing in a tub, a lesson with a village teacher, or a parish meeting. The second book is set in Stockholm in the 1910s, and describes the family's one-room apartment crammed with furniture, the yard, the street, washing and cleaning scenes, the interior of a grocery store, a schoolroom, an amateur theater performance, a movie theater, a picnic, a fun fair, and so on. The third book takes place in suburban Stockholm in the 1930s, and presents the everyday and festive events in the life of an ordinary family. The many details in the setting are necessary to convey the atmosphere of the time as well as concrete historical knowledge.

The verbal–visual interaction is almost symmetrical. The verbal text describes practically everything presented in the pictures. Naturally, there are visual details that clarify the verbal message, but the words could almost stand on their own, while the pictures have more of a decorative function. Many details are apparently supposed to evoke nostalgic feelings in adult readers, since they describe artifacts no longer in use, as well as landscapes and cityscapes long gone. For young readers, the settings have a clear educational purpose.

Barbara Cooney's historical picturebooks *Only Opal* and *Island Boy* are likewise dependent on the setting. *Only Opal* is based on an authentic diary. The events take place in the beginning of the 20th century, and the artist is obliged to present a correct description of clothes, interiors, buildings, and so on. The pictures are idyllic, with panoramic views of the New England landscape, conveying a sense of nostalgia for times gone by. The setting is thus counterpointing the verbal narrative, which is supposed to express a child's immediate perspective, since the visual description carries adult overtones. At the same time, the child's closeness to nature is stressed in the recurrent pictures of the little girl in the fields or woods. By contrast, the indoor settings depicting the girl doing her household chores or in the schoolroom represent "civilization" and the adult world. All the settings are expanding, since the words only say, "Near the road grow many flowers," or "I talk things over with my tree," while the pictures are detailed and reflect perfectly the observant eye and contemplative mood of the young protagonist. One very emotionally charged picture shows Opal's favorite tree cut down, and conveys what the narrator cannot express with words: "Some day I will write about [ . . . ] the great tree I love." In this picture, as in most other exterior scenes, the girl's figure on the doublespread is small, stressing her oppressed and insecure position in the big world.

*Island Boy* is a different kind of story, a sort of family chronicle describing life on a little island in New England over several generations. The setting is integral and important, and the changes in landscape as the island is successively built up are an essential part of the narrative. Once again, the correct visual descriptions of settings are vital: the landscape, the buildings, and the detailed indoor scenes involving furniture, utensils, and clothes. Although one purpose of the book is certainly educational, Cooney, unlike Ann-Madeleine Gelotte, allows pictures rather than words to describe settings and explain the way things were done in the past. The many outdoor scenes are dynamic, showing people at work. In this book nostalgia is also strong, and as the protagonist grows up and becomes an old man, his love for the island is emphasized by the poetic pictures.

## Redundancy

It is not always easy to decide whether the verbal description is indeed redundant. In Anna-Clara and Thomas Tidholm's *The Journey to Ugri-La-Brek* (1987), we find the following passage:

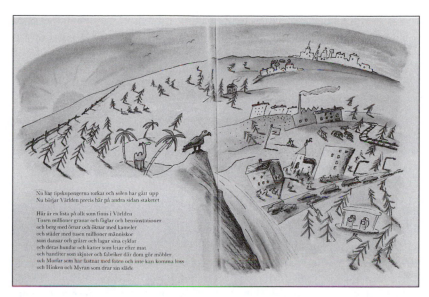

"Everything that exists in the World"—imaginary setting in *Journey to Ugri-La-Brek.*

> Here is a list of everything that exists in the World:
> A thousand million fir-trees and birds and gas stations
> and mountains with eagles and deserts with camels
> and cities with a thousand million people
> who dance and laugh and mend their bicycles
> and their dogs and cats who search for food
> and gangsters who shoot and factories where they make furniture

At first sight, the enumeration may seem redundant, since everything that the words describe is duplicated by the picture. However, the verbal setting has several additional functions. First, it is a poetic description, creating a special atmosphere in the book. It conveys the subjective experience of a young child confronted with the big and frightening world, especially in the hyperbole "a thousand million," which naturally is only verbal. In fact, the picture shows one mountain with a lonely eagle on top, one camel, one gas station, and one factory. For once, it is the words that expand the picture, making it more universal. Finally, the picture may have an educational purpose, encouraging the young reader to find all the things mentioned by words, which is not always an easy task. In any case, the verbal description demands a lengthy pause in the narrative while all the visual details are taken in.

## Enhanced and Expanded Setting: Creation of Mood

Setting can create a special mood in a story. For instance, the feeling of nostalgia inspired by the description of idyllic countryside and the contrast between rural and urban setting within a book can have ideological implications. Setting can be apprehended as a symbol, like a dollhouse representing a happy childhood, or a forest representing danger and fear.[2]

Beatrix Potter's nostalgic setting of her own home village of Sawrey not only depicts a simplicity of life, such as the village shop in *Ginger and Pickles* (1909), or cottages in *The Pie and the Patty-Pan* (1905), but finds expression also in the conventional manners of her human and animal characters, their mode of address, and their clothes, which are at least a generation out-of-date. The setting, then, is idyllic in the way nostalgic representations usually are, and in Potter's case is very much in the pastoral tradition. Though a few tales are set in large towns or cities (for example, *The Tailor of Gloucester*), most have the countryside, farmlands, and the small village as background to the action.

*The Tale of Johnny Town-Mouse* (1918) is an excellent example of words and images working together to promote the idealization of the pastoral. When Timmy Willie is accidentally transported to the small town, he finds "there was no quiet; there seemed to be hundreds of carts passing. Dogs barked; boys whistled in the street; the cook laughed, the parlour maid ran up and down-stairs; and a canary sang like a steam engine." Ironically, the one outdoor picture of the town shows a single cart standing in an old-fashioned cobbled street, a couple of dogs, the cart driver, and the housemaid, so that the sense of bustle described in Timmy Willie's analysis portrays his own very personal experience. The change is a major one for him, however, and the street shows no vestige of vegetation, supporting the sense of contrast from the countryside. Timmy Willie also finds that the food is not nourishing, derived from the scraps left by the people. The indoor pictures detail a plush interior and a formal mouse dinner party, supporting Timmy Willie's mood of unease by showing mouse figures crowded together in formal, unrelaxed postures, and very small mice set against a very large hall and stairway, with no sense of cover. Where the text points out that "the sofa smelled of cat," the picture shows the animal itself peering into the corner where the pillow lies.

When questioned by his cousin Johnny Town-Mouse about the dullness and raininess of the countryside, Timmy Willie's responds with a glowing description of his pastoral existence: "When it rains, I sit in my little sandy burrow and shell corn and seeds from my Autumn store. I peep out at the throstles and blackbirds on the lawn and my friend Cock robin. And when the sun comes out again, you should see my garden and the flowers—roses and pinks and pansies—no noise except the birds and bees, and the lambs in the meadows." The illustrations support but do not duplicate this lush description. The countryside is green, luxuriant, and teeming with edible plants: plump strawberries, delectable carrots, crunchy lettuces, a veritable cornucopia of nature's bounty.

Throughout Potter's tales, nature's profusion is detailed with joy. Wild blackberry bushes are heavy with berries, Mr. McGregor's garden is crammed with vegetables, and the houses, like Ribby's and Duchess's in *The Pie and the Patty-Pan,* have gardens filled with flowers: lilies, poppies, snapdragons, and clematis climbing over the front door. Superimposed on these succulent and eye-delighting pastoral scenes are the indoor, domestic pleasures where natural goods are transformed into civilized treats: thistledown, honeydew wine, and rabbit tobacco.

The countryside is not all innocence, however. Jemima Puddle-Duck's eggs are eaten by the hounds that chase off the fox; Mr. Rabbit is put in a pie by Mrs. McGregor, and the Flopsy Bunnies almost follow him. The latter are almost eaten by Mr. Tod, too, and certainly the veal-and-ham pie that Ribby makes involves sacrifice of animals. But the whole is presented with the cozy veneer of domesticity that makes it acceptable, and in keeping with the country life. The emotional tone of the setting is presented through complementary and enhancing interplay of words and pictures in harmony. The intention of the detail is not to instruct, but to give the color, texture, and a sensuous immediacy that involve the reader in Potter's world.

Elsa Beskow's picturebook art presents another natural environment in her fairy-tale idylls, perhaps best known from her *Children of the Forest* (1910).[3] The setting is Swedish nature, which Beskow presents accurately and lovingly, in the best traditions of Scandinavian neo-romantic painting. The scarce verbal place descriptions, like "deep under the pine roots," "in the silent and peaceful forest," "down by the lake," are expanded into detailed and colorful plates. Long shots as well as occasional middle shots are used. The tiny gnomes allow a splendid play with dimensions as they appear among plants and small forest animals: squirrels, bats, frogs, rabbits, and birds. The pictures of trees, plants, flowers, and mushrooms have a didactic purpose: readers are supposed to recognize the snowdrops and anemones, linnea and lady's mantle, sorrel and fern, blueberries and lingonberries, although most of the names are never mentioned in words. The names that do appear are those of the edible mushrooms, which the readers are supposed to learn together with the forest children.

## More Complex Settings: Contributing to Plot Development

In the examination of setting, a distinction is usually made between integral and backdrop setting. Integral setting is an indispensable component of the narrative; the story cannot take place anywhere else. For instance, historical books naturally demand a somewhat "realistic" setting in the past. A story involving Australian Aborigines demands an authentic Australian setting, and so on.[4] *Eloise* (1955), by Kay Thompson and Hilary Knight, takes place in the Plaza Hotel, and this setting is the prerequisite for the events of the story.

Backdrop settings, on the other hand, are not essential for the plot, although they may have some of the other above-mentioned purposes in the narrative.

Setting can strongly contribute to and clarify the conflict in a story, especially in plots that take the characters away from their familiar surroundings, a situation that can occur in both fantasy and everyday stories. By moving the character into an "extreme" setting, which can vary from war or natural catastrophe to a slightly unusual situation in a relative's home, a writer can initiate and amplify a maturation process that would be less plausible in a normal setting. Setting thus becomes a catalyst in the plot. A change in setting, for instance from everyday to fantasy, also contributes to plot development. William Moebius has investigated the bedroom as an important initial and final setting in picturebooks, creating a sense of security as the character is taken away from and then brought back to familiar surroundings after stirring adventures.[5]

Jean de Brunhoff's Babar books beginning in 1931 present interesting material from the point of view of setting. The narrative starts in the African jungle, an exotic-realistic setting, but in the context of children's literature, equally a fairy-tale setting. The minimal verbal description "In the great forest . . ." is expanded in the first picture and the subsequent doublespreads with palm trees, vast open plains, pink mountains in the background, shrubs and flowers.

The little orphan elephant's travels move the action, as the fairy-tale pattern prescribes, out of his ordinary surroundings to meet an alien world. While for a human being this would mean leaving civilization and entering the Otherness of the forest (alternatively cave, desert, or some other transformation of the unfamiliar space), for an animal character it implies leaving the jungle and entering a big city. The reversal of the actual setting does not affect its functional role in the narrative. However, the traditional pattern would bring the hero back to his normal surroundings (restoring order) rather than allow him to import the Other and thereby destroy the familiar. The use of exotic setting is therefore a pretext to maintain the superiority of civilization over "nature."

Something quite remarkable about the visual setting of the story is the depiction of the city. The verbal story does not specify that the action takes place in Africa, rather we extrapolate this fact from the landscape and the animals. However, several days' travel bring Babar into a typical European city with a towered church, an opera house with columns, and quite different kind of vegetation. The landscape around the city when Babar takes his daily car rides is also European, including a river with a tugboat, rushes, fields, apple trees, and a variety of European fauna. This discrepancy in setting emphasizes the fairy-tale nature of the story as well as its main underlying conflict: between nature ("Africa") and civilization ("Europe").

Babar's acquisition of human manners and behavior involves wearing clothes, living indoors, sleeping in a bed, eating at a table, using tools and machines, and so on, all carefully described in words and in pictures. Upon returning to the jungle (which luckily coincides with the old elephant king's death), Babar brings tokens of civilization with him. In *Babar the King* (1933), we witness how in order to build a city for his subjects, Babar must cut down the jungle (some of the editions omit the actual illustrations depicting this act), the result being a boring, regular settlement with identical huts and two monstrous public buildings: a Bureau of Industry and an Amusement Hall.

The changing setting of Babar books has as its main function supporting the development of character from "savage" to "civilized," which, especially in light of contemporary postcolonial theory, can be perceived as offensive. However, if we instead view Babar's evolution as a depiction of a little child's socialization, the change in setting will reflect a metaphorical rather than realistic transformation. Further, this transformation also reflects the general trend in children's fiction toward urban rather than rural settings. In the late Babar books, as well as the sequels produced by Laurent de Brunhoff, the civilization theme is muted or nonexistent; the books are mere variations on the character and his domestic and outdoor adventures, and do not add anything in terms of setting.

The contrast between rural and urban settings is a common feature in children's fiction. Rural settings reflect the adult writers' idealization of the child, which goes back to the Romantic view of childhood as innocent, happy and natural. By introducing threatening urban settings, children's writers often question this view.[6] Picturebooks allow unlimited possibilities of imagery involving the transition from a "natural" to a "civilized" state, as well as temporary escape from civilization and oppression.

*The Little Train* (1973), by Grahame Greene and Edward Ardizzone, is a symbolic representation of the child's longing for the big world, as the animated engine runs away from its idyllic branch line to explore. The visual setting in the beginning of the story matches the words: "What beautiful peaceful country and what a lovely sleepy village." The little train finally comes to a big city, called Smokeoverall, only to discover its "smell of soot and oil and glue," the noise, the "blinding lights," and crowds of people "pushing, yelling . . ." The train thinks that it has come "to a terrible cave of demons," and the pictures visualize this feeling. The authors' nostalgia forces the train to hurry back to where it belongs. The contrast of settings juxtaposes childhood and adulthood, stressing the values of the former and the horrors of the latter. This is just one of dozens of similar picturebooks.

By contrast, in many "dream" books the child leaves civilization and enters the uncorrupted natural world, real or imaginary, as in *Journey to Ugri-*

*La-Brek*. However, a growing number of picturebook authors deliberately choose an urban setting as an expression of dystopian fears. In *The Jaguar* (1987), by Ulf Stark and Anna Höglund, the imaginary journey does not take the protagonist away from the city into the idyllic freedom of nature; the dream or nightmare takes place in the city itself, with its asphalt streets, tall and impersonal tenement houses, dirty backyards and dumps, shops, and heavy traffic. The authors' view of civilization is especially stressed by the picture of a fur store. Since the character is transformed into a jaguar, showing a jaguar fur coat in the shop window is unequivocal criticism.

## Complex Setting as Actor

The setting for Nadia Wheatley and Donna Rawlins's *My Place* (1988) is especially interesting because it is continually in transition and, through its evolution, becomes an actor in the drama. The book's historical perspective, which peels back layers of time to search for the earliest time and setting, also presents an ongoing natural world–human world dynamic that places people and nature in disharmony and reveals the process of industrial pollution that has spoiled the land and poisoned the rivers. Yet this movement back in time, which reveals an early idyllic state and its metamorphosis into the current city life where "the color of the earth, back home" is represented only by a flag, simultaneously parallels the development of a multicultural society where people feel happy and at home.

The idyllic early time, paradoxically presented at the end of the book, negates space and time boundaries in the doublespread image of the great tree in which Barangaroo sits looking to the ends of the earth and of time.

> Sometimes, at the end of the day, I climb to the top of the big tree and play
> that I'm the only person in the world. If I look one way, the sea runs out till
> it meets the sky. But the other way, the land goes on till the sun sets.
> My grandmother says, "We've always belonged to this place."
> "But how long?" I ask. "And how far?"
> My grandmother says, "For ever and ever."

The waves of immigrants change the face of the land, and the idyllic past is replaced by a realistic series of events. The quality of the natural setting is eroded by the tannery, the woolen mill, and the brick pits, and the land is parceled up and fenced. As the pollution of the water traces the depredation of the natural environment, so the great tree remains as a symbol of nature's persistence. Each generation modifies the setting, which moves from the hunting and gathering culture of the aboriginal peoples through the farming economy of an agrarian setting, industrialization and township, and finally to the modern city that is the initial setting of the book.

The setting is presented through three media: a hand-drawn map, which combines text and image in a spatial-temporal account of the immediate environment, including the big tree and other landmarks as well as personal remarks; the illustrations, which picture each child narrator in a scene from his or her life, often surrounded by friends, family, and animals; and the narrative text, which tells of events and relationships and comments on the pictures and the maps. The setting is thus personalized by each of the child narrators and given historical and geographical dimension in a variety of ways. The combined personal and historical perspectives create a setting that expresses both permanence and change, short- and long-term focus, and a spectrum of modes encompassing a variety of presentation from the romantic to the realistic.

## Complex Setting: Intraiconic Text

The uncertain division between text and image in some of Sendak's picturebooks insists upon the reader's attention to the dynamics of the iconotext. *In the Night Kitchen* (1970) provides an imaginative setting of buildings formed from kitchen utensils, implements, and boxes, bottles, and tins of food. While in some cases these are purely imagistic, for example the lemon squeezer, beater, bottle opener, and whisk-shaped towers, and salt cellar buildings, in many cases the objects carry their words with them, creating a subtext within the pictures that competes with the standard text. For example, the text for two pages, placed within frames at the top of the picture, reads "till it looked okay," and "Then Mickey in dough was just on his way." Within the picture, as part of the setting, are the labels of the various boxes and containers: one reads "Patented June 10th 1928, registered, Cocoanut," and "Mill 2000 Barrels Daily Capacity, Niagara Falls NY"; another, "Safe Yeast, up with the moon." This technique is even more intense in *We Are All in the Dumps with Jack and Guy* (1993), where numerous newspaper headlines, names on boxes, and dialogue all compete with the brief identified text of the nursery rhymes.

Colin Thompson's work also uses intraiconic text to a high degree. The library shelves of *How to Live Forever* (1995) are filled with books whose titles demand attention for their word play and their jokes. *Looking for Atlantis* (1993) provides more variety, for not only do we find the amusing book titles, modified to the watery theme ("The Merry Whelks of Windsor"; "The Brine of Miss Jane Brody"), but all kinds of objects with their wordy, jokey labels ("Horse Fly Pate"), which vie with the "real" text. Inger and Lasse Sandberg's *Yes, You May, Dusty Said* (1993) provides another example of the ironic use of book titles on shelves, which are also clearly metafictional and address the adult coreader, and are backdrop, being unrelated to the plot. Besides including existing albums by contemporary Swedish illustrators and world-famous painters, and collected works of some Swedish authors, the titles include humorous books such as "Criticism of Criticism" in four volumes and "The History of Children's Literature After 2000." The final page of the book shows some advertisements and newsbills in the window of a rural grocery store: "Buy one—pay for two," "Tie in Eurovision Song Contest," and—obviously without intentional reference to Sendak's *Dumps*— "8-year-old New Prime Minister."

In these books, the words' migration into the visual pictorial setting redefines the experience of the environment, reflecting characteristics of the modern world by including the verbal cacophony (oral and visual) of today's life,

Intraiconic texts in Inger and Lasse Sandberg's *Yes, You May, Dusty Said.*

the constant intrusion of advertising into our senses, and the clutter and distraction of our experiential relationship with the world around us.

## Complex Settings: Establishing Genre Expectations

Setting readily signals a particular genre. The fairy-tale world of Babette Cole's *Princess Smartypants* (1986) or of the many versions of *Thumbelina* alert us to the nature of the story to come, be it pretty or burlesque. The domestic setting of Hoban's *A Baby Sister for Frances* (1964) sets an expectation of events with a particular significance, while an adventure setting like Tove Jansson's *The Dangerous Journey* (1977) prepares us for a broader spectrum of experience.

### Fairy Tales

It is illuminating to see how visual setting can affect our perception and even manipulate our interpretation of classic fairy tales. Comparing a number of picturebook versions of "Snow White," "Beauty and the Beast," or "Hansel and Gretel," we can easily discover that the nature of setting varies from romantic to gothic, from realistic to grotesque, from medieval to modern, and so on.[7] By choosing a particular type of setting, the illustrator not only prompts our reading the story on a certain level, but also places the story in a certain historical, social, and literary context. For instance, by introducing tokens of contemporary technology (such as a television set) in his version of *Hansel and Gretel* (1982), Anthony Browne immediately suggests a "postmodern," ironic reading, which makes us keep our eyes open for more counterpointing details. The Oriental style of Jane Ray's version of the same tale (1997) takes it out of its customary Western context and draws our attention to its universality. In Paul O. Zelinsky's *Hansel and Gretel* (1984), only the first two pictures of the witch's house show it from the children's perspective: "[ . . . ] built out of bread. Its roof was made of pancakes and its windows of sugar candy." After the children have been captured, the house in the pictures becomes quite ordinary, suggesting that the vision of pancakes and candy has been a mirage caused by hunger and desire. This change in visual setting naturally adds still another dimension to this highly ambiguous tale.

*Princess Smartypants* provides a humorous dimension to the fairy tale and a wonderful example of words and images in ironic, even sarcastic counterpoint. Like *Cinder Edna* (1994), Ellen Jackson and Kevin O'Malley's humorous send-up of the Cinderella fairy tale, *Princess Smartypants* combines aspects of the traditional with the modern and presents a feminist twist so that the Princess and Cinder Edna take charge of their lives and the unfolding of the plot to a significant extent. While Princess Smartypants's grotesquely comic suitors are sent on quests that sound appropriate to the genre, the depiction of each challenge reveals its true nature. Yet the setting clearly shows the trappings of the fairy tale with the appropriate castles and clothes, though these, like the royal pets, are comically distorted and played with. *Cinder Edna* divides the main character into two personas, Cinder Edna and Cinder Ella, and provides them with settings and clothes that reflect the two different worlds in which they live: the modern one where one puts a dress on layaway in case of future need, and the one where a fairy godmother is needed to provide one by magic (although she wonders at Cinder Ella's ineptitude and dependency). The final scenes show Cinder Edna married to the Prince's brother and taking care of stray cats and a recycling business, while Cinder Ella, married to the Prince in the castle and, engaged in stultifying royal duties, lives a life of repetitive boredom.

### *Realism/Surrealism:* **The Tunnel**

Anthony Browne's *The Tunnel* (1989) offers contrasts in setting that communicate a metamorphosis in genre expectation. The rather tame family squabbling between brother and sister, which takes place in a realistic domestic setting featuring indoor and outdoor scenes and wallpaper that expresses the relationship between the characters, suggests a simple sibling conflict and resolution. As the background of the story changes—first to the chaotic junkyard identified as waste ground, then to the transitional "dark, and damp, and slimy, and scary" tunnel, and finally to the "quiet wood," which transforms into a witchy, surrealistic setting appropriate for a nightmare—the plot is driven forward and the relationship between the characters develops.

As the settings change, so do the readers' expectations. It is not until the entrance to the tunnel that the words suggest anything out of the ordinary: "There might be witches . . . or goblins . . . or *anything* down there" (author's emphasis). The metamorphosis from the ordinary world to a surrealistic one begins in words with the sister's fears, but is taken entirely into the visual realm as words fail. In the transitional picture, what had been ordinary trees become progressively twisted, writhing into animal shapes with fearful eyes. The setting begins to take on allusory aspects: a fallen basket and a woodcutter's ax bring the girl's red hooded coat into another fairy-tale dimension. A barred hole in one tree, a rope hanging from another, and a fire burning feverishly near another (echoing Browne's version of *Hansel and Gretel*) provide hints of hidden life, while tendrilous roots spread out to trip and tangle. The wordless doublespread that features the girl blurred from her speed, the trees turned into bears, boars, wolves, and dryads, and a lone tombstone (or is it a door in the ground?) completes the fearful transformation that prepares the reader for the horror of the brother turned to stone in a field where all the trees have been chopped down.

The move back into the human, family dimension begins with the stone figure's metamorphosis into living flesh and the reinstatement of the felled trees to create a natural landscape. The journey home to domestic comfort follows the restoration of the natural world and the recapture of the familiar setting with which the book began.

### The Absurd: Nordqvist

In Sven Nordqvist's books, the settings are overtly "postmodern," eclectic, often absurd. *Willie in the Big World* (1985) starts with an indoor scene. The setting is exclusively visual, but words are introduced when Willie goes to say goodbye to his friend the Old Man before he sets on his journey. The man advises him not to collect too many possessions; he himself has only one of each thing.

This statement is in a wonderfully ironic contradiction with the picture, which shows the Old Man's abode overcrowded with things. There is indeed only one of everything (the book is in fact a counting book, with numbers one to ten introduced on every spread), but the number of objects is overwhelming. A verbal description of the setting would fill many pages and still be inadequate. There are tools, kitchen utensils, electric appliances, musical instruments, toys, decorations, and so on. Whether we indeed stop and identify every object, ordinary and exotic, or whether we take in the whole scene, we become aware of the multitude, which, besides its educational purpose, also contributes to characterization. The Old Man, who, as we learn from the verbal text, once sailed around the world, has many souvenirs, but he also must be skillful with the many tools he has. The setting is backdrop in the sense that it does not add anything substantial to the plot. It is, however, an essential part of the text–image narrative.

In the next spread, the character has moved to an outdoor setting with the limited verbal indicator "outside on the road . . ." It is, however, in this spread that the artist's hilarious play with dimensions starts. In the background landscape we find oversize spools of thread, leek plants larger than the largest trees, two gigantic stones with two elk standing on them, and many absurd details like two phone booths connected to each other, but not to anything else. The purpose of the setting is to create a comic effect. Naturally, the prerequisite is that the reader is familiar with the right size and proportions of the depicted objects and therefore is able to appreciate the nonsensical distortion.[8] Therefore, in this and the subsequent spreads, the artist uses only the objects that a young reader will easily recognize: the most common flowers and plants, animals, birds, cars, boats, and so on. However, the images grow more sophisticated as the story progresses. In the fourth spread, there are, for instance, three oversize apples and a pear, which the reader is supposed to identify as *four* pieces of fruit. The buildings are to be recognized as four churches, although they are not totally identical, and a monocycle with a quadrangle wheel demands a keen eye and some imagination. The four-headed creature is reminiscent of many of Dr. Seuss's characters. Each head is crowned, but with a different item: a pointed hat, a tin can, a teapot, and a baseball cap, all of which nevertheless function as headgear. In the fifth spread, there are five different airborne vehicles, the five cars are of different make, the five statues are scattered all over the page area, and so on. Most readers will recognize the five flags in the cake as the flags of the five Scandinavian countries. By the sixth spread, the reader is trained in the device and starts looking for the sixfold objects, which become more and more disguised.

The setting of Willie's journey changes radically and rapidly between spreads, from green meadows to deep forests, from regular gardens to hilly wilderness, and the artist has no aspiration to create a sense of logic or continuity. It is possible that the whole journey is imaginary, and the absurd details of the setting support such an interpretation. Since the setting is exclusively visual, it must be apprehended as "subjective," the boy's inner vision. In the last spread, when Willie has come home, we see him looking through the window at a much more realistic landscape outside.

Many of the devices from this early book become Nordqvist's distinctive features in his famous Festus and Mercury series. Unlike traditional settings, Nordqvist's settings are playful and humorous, allowing a practically unlimited expansion of the verbal story. In a way, the settings are stories in their own right.

Imaginative landscape in *Willie in the Big World,* by Sven Nordqvist.

### Multiple Genres: Sendak

The various settings of *We Are All in the Dumps* extend a number of different genre expectations. The initial setting pictures a shantytown of cardboard boxes, empty buckets, and cloth tented over ropes that provides the dwelling place for the homeless children. In the background stand the towers and skyscrapers of New York, identifiable by the Brooklyn Bridge and the Trump Tower, while the foreground is framed by tenements. This dystopian environment of social ills, inhumanity, greed and corruption, poverty, hunger, and lovelessness enhances and is enhanced by the words in the meager nursery rhyme text, the dialogue balloons, and the ongoing commentary provided in the newspapers whose headlines draw attention to the broader environment: "Leaner times, meaner times," "Famine in the world," "Layoff," "AIDS," "War," and "Babies starve." The interplay, both blatant and subtle, between word and image reinforces the mood of cynicism. In some cases the words are few and the images highly detailed. In others the balance of word and image is reversed—the newspapers in which the children are wrapped introduce an affluent social setting expressed in numerous advertisements for real estate and mortgages.

When the children follow the rats and the stolen boy to the bakery and orphanage, they pass through a field of grain, but the stalks are prickly, the ground beneath them is dry and lumpy, and the field stands next to a building that resembles a concentration camp with black smoke billowing from its high chimney. Mediating between the two sites is a barren terrain and a skyscape scene where winged, barefoot figures in russet robes read newspapers, and images of a gigantic cat and the moon metamorphose into one another.

Unlike the intraiconic text settings of *In the Night Kitchen* and the Colin Thompson books discussed earlier, where the text functions as a diversion distracting from the action, the interplay between text and image in *Dumps* actually contributes to the central theme and mediates among a number of genre forms. The nursery rhyme form brings with it the scent of political commentary; the dialog is often choral or operatic (for example the multiple rhythmic voices in "Look what they did! Look what they did!—The rats— stole the kittens—and the poor little kid!"); and the journalistic and advertising modes of the newspapers meld to create a crescendo of commentary on the situation. Similarly, the figures imply a variety of very different settings. The malicious rats' playing-card gowns are reminiscent of *Alice in Wonderland,* though the rats' faces and claws are fairy-tale grotesque. Jack and Guy are dressed in clothes reminiscent of Dickens. The recognizable aspects of New York City (Brooklyn Bridge and Trump Tower) are juxtaposed with a stage set of gigantic playing cards. The skyscape with the giant moon is fantastic. The field of grain stands beside a visual reference to concentration camp smokestacks. But the cartoon parent cat with the forty or so kittens is humorous and exudes warmth. Sendak draws upon many traditions to present this multiple-genre setting with its continuous surprises, which evade the ordinary and break expectations.

## Notes

1. Cf. Jane Doonan, *Looking at Pictures in Picture Books* (Stroud: Thimble Press, 1993): 17.

2. See further discussion of pictorial setting in Joseph H . Schwarcz, *Ways of the Illustrator: Visual Communication in Children's Literature* (Chicago: American Library Association, 1982): 55–64; Joseph H. Schwarcz and Chava Schwarcz, *The Picture Book Comes of Age* (Chicago: American Library Association, 1991): 112–134.

3. The versified Swedish story is rendered in English in prose, and the translator has taken great liberties in adding details not present in the original, among others some descriptions of setting. We use the Swedish original text in our own prose translation.

4. On setting conveying national character in picturebooks see John Stephens, "Representation of Place in Australian Children's Picture Books," in *Voices From Far Away: Current Trends in International Children's Literature Research,* ed. Maria Nikolajeva, 97–118 (Stockholm: Centre for the Study of Childhood Culture, 1995).

5. William Moebius, "Room with a View: Bedroom Scenes in Picture Books," *Children's Literature* 19 (1991): 53–74.

6. Cf. Schwarcz (1991: 135–145).

7. Cf. Meyer Schapiro's study of the illustrations to the Bible, *Words and Pictures: On the Literal and the Symbolic in the Illustration of a Text* (The Hague: Mouton, 1973).

8. Kornei Chukovsky argues in his famous study *From Two to Five* that the purpose of nonsense is to give young children a sense of self-assurance as they feel able to distinguish between sense and nonsense. See Chukovsky, *From Two to Five* (Berkeley: University of California Press, 1963).

# CHAPTER 3

# Characterization

## Some General Remarks on Characterization

In a verbal narrative, a number of techniques are employed to portray character. Narrative description is the most basic, involving both external, visual detail (what do the characters look like, how do they move, what are they wearing) and emotional, psychological, and philosophical characteristics. The description can involve a temporal dimension, tracing changes in appearance, situation, and internal or emotional growth or alteration. The narrative may be colored in a number of ways, depending on the choice of the narrator and the perspective from which the narrator interprets.

Events in which the character is involved provide information through the action of the character, and a testing ground for the narrative description. The behavior of the character expressed in action and by direct and indirect speech reveals dimensions of character in very immediate ways that the more static description with its inherent analytical stance cannot hope to present. This information about the character in action is presented much more directly to the reader, without the sense of narrative interpolation that sets character analysis at one remove. This technique involves the reader more intensely in the estimation of character than does simple narration.

Dialogue between the protagonist and other figures reveals another dimension of character, adding another layer of information to the reader's store. Further, the protagonist's inner monologues offer another mode of understanding of the character dynamics. Readers construct a somewhat complete picture of a character by extracting relevant information about the character from the text, by making inferences from the character's behavior, by synthesizing snippets of information included in the text, and by amplifying these from their own imagination.

Finally, a character's features may be conveyed to the reader through repetition, through comparison to other, well-known literary characters or real figures, through contrast between different features (most often good and evil), or implicitly, when the readers must make conclusions themselves. Names, especially "telling" names (Princess Smartypants, Prince Rushforth, Prince Boneshaker, or Prince Swimbladder), may add to our understanding of characters.

In picturebooks the inventory of techniques is expanded. Many picturebook critics dwell upon the interrelationship of text and image as though there is something radically different involved. As we have noted in the introduction, Lawrence Sipe for example offers a number of terms used by critics to describe the relationship: duet, counterpoint, interference, polysystemy, congruency, synergy.[1] John Stephens prefers contradiction.[2] While all of these are useful metaphors for understanding the relationship between two kinds of communicative technique, in fact the degree of friction or harmony involved can simply be considered an extension of the narrative techniques involved in telling any story. A storyteller adds visual and aural dimensions to a narrative through voice and gesture and can offer harmonic or ironic cues to aid the understanding of the audience. The techniques employed in verbal narrative can also work with or in contradiction to each other. Words spoken, words describing action, and characters' emotions expressed in inner monologues can all support a single interpretation or can produce a complex interrelationship of meaning that simulates the complexity of life. Film similarly offers a complex simulation of life that is shaped to offer a meaningful experience. Within this context, the iconic–verbal communication that the picturebook conveys is different in degree rather than in essence. While the interplay between the text and the image may, in reading, be less simultaneous than for example film and storytelling, it is less linear than purely verbal works.

However, it is clear that picturebooks allow little room for thorough characterization in the conventional sense. We may generally observe that picturebooks tend to be plot-oriented rather than character-oriented. Further, the plot itself is often too limited to allow much development, which means that most characters are static rather than dynamic, and flat rather than round.[3]

Nonetheless, the specific form of picturebooks provides a wide scope of artistic devices for characterization, and some picturebooks show a remarkable level of sophistication in this respect. Pictures allow a variety of external characterizations, while words can be used both for external description and internal "representation." Some of the most common characterization devices acquire a specific dimension in picturebooks. For instance, external description can be both verbal and visual, and these two aspects can either confirm or contradict each other. Most often, verbal external description is omitted in picturebooks, and the visual description only is used, being more efficient. Although some permanent human qualities (such as brave, clever, innocent) are difficult to communicate visually, the characters' poses, gestures, and facial expressions can disclose emotions and attitudes, such as happiness, fear, and anger. Duplicating the description in words may create redundancy and diminish the impact of the characterization.

If we consider what images and words each do best, it is clear that physical description belongs in the realm of the illustrator, who can, in an instant, communicate information about appearance that would take many words and much reading time. But psychological description, though it can be suggested in pictures, needs the subtleties of words to capture complex emotion and motivation. External and internal speech as a means of characterization is by definition verbal (although some interesting visual devices can be used to convey speech, as we often see in comic strips), as are other people's statements, while narrators' comments can be both verbal and visual. And, unlike film, picturebooks cannot provide the movement in time that the symbolism of words can offer. In addition, words provide the medium by which the narrator explains to the reader most precisely the perspective and the analytic stance, and enable the author to exert greater control over the reader's perception than do images. Conversely, though words can express emotions both obviously and subtly, their impact is challenged by the speed and efficacy of illustrations' potential to communicate emotion. Besides the simple line, images have a complex repertoire of techniques including color, design, and placement to shape responses.

Pictures naturally have a superior ability to convey the spatial position of the character, and especially the mutual spatial relationship of two or more characters, which often reveals their psychological relationship and relative status. Characters' size and placing on the doublespread (high or low, to the left, to the right) may reflect their attitude toward other characters, a permanent psychological quality, or a temporary mood; changes in the position reflect changes in the characters themselves.[4] Most of these features are based on conventions and are therefore not absolute rules. We assume that a character depicted as large has more significance (and maybe more power) than the character who is small and crammed in the corner of a page. The central position in a page emphasizes the character's central role in the story. It also conveys a young child's "centralization" (Piaget) of himself.

The character's actions can be described verbally or visually, and, as with the external description, the two descriptions can complement or contradict each other. This particular aspect of characterization allows probably more counterpoint between text and image than any other and allows the authors a good deal of irony.

## Minimal Characterization: *The Twenty-Elephant Restaurant*

Russell Hoban and Emily Arnold McCully's *The Twenty-Elephant Restaurant* (1978) offers the reader an unadorned conception of character. The figures in the story are given no names, simply "the man," "the woman," and "the elephants," and are often identified by number (e.g. "twentieth elephant"). The text focuses on straightforward dialogue, without interpretation or mediation from the narrator—that is, "showing" rather than "telling"—rather than on a description of the action of the story, often in quite specific though objective detail. The illustrations are of two basic kinds, line drawings and full color presentations, and tend toward the symmetrical in that they add little to the information communicated.

The quirkiness and eccentricity of the man and his wife are their dominant features and are in tune with the world in which they live. The wobbly table around which they have sat for fifty years suddenly proves unbearable to the wife, and her whim leads to her husband making a new table. The humorously illogical logic which translates into the couple's creation of the table and ultimately the restaurant is expressed entirely through their conversations. The rationale for making a new table to replace the old one represents this "logic":

> "I've been thinking about it all day," said the woman. "Before we got that
> table you were young and handsome. Now you're old and ugly. . . ."
> "But we've had the table for fifty years," said the man. "It stands to reason
> I'm not as young and handsome as I was fifty years ago."
> "Whether it stands to reason we don't know," said the woman. "All we know
> is how it was before the table and how it is now."

Similarly, the conversation that leads to opening the restaurant begins with the man's observation that the new table he has made is "steady as a rock [ . . . ]. Elephants could dance on that table." The dialogue jumps from this image to the practical details of how one hires elephants to dance on tables, how to pay them, how many tables are needed, and eventually to the outcome of the advertisement: "Elephants wanted for table work. Must be agile. Dancing, cooking and bookkeeping experience helpful."

The whimsy of the characterization is reinforced by the pictures: the shock-headed man with bushy eyebrows, jeans, and red checked shirt is pictured as continually busy with the details of the chaotic venture—cutting trees, sawing, painting, hammering, telephoning—and the busyness is reflected in the actions of all of the others. The elephants share the couple's logic and frenetic pace, though they are rarely individualized except, for example, by the addition of a beret or a chef's hat. Since there is little description, except that of action, the illustrations do provide the only detail about the way the characters appear, as well as the setting in which the action takes place.

But there is little communication of emotion, either in the verbal text or the pictures. The man's dismay when things do not go according to plan is not emphatic, and his wife's response simply undercuts emotion by turning, as usual, to the practical:

> "Nothing goes right for me," said the man. "I start out to have a twenty-elephant restaurant and I wind up being a one-man circus."
> "It's only temporary," said the woman. "Don't do any more until we collect admission and sell some hot dogs."
> The twentieth elephant quickly made a sign.

The accompanying illustration reveals the man, the elephant, and the sign, but does not communicate an affective dimension.

Despite the lack of individualization, the sense of community and of interactive relationships—man and woman, man and animal, man, woman, and animals—are of real significance here. The dialogue above poses a problem, redefines it, and solves it. However, in this book the characters—man, wife, and elephants—tend to be outcomes of the strange and illogical world that Hoban and McCully have created rather than recognizable individuals. Action is driven by the vagaries of language as much as by human decision, and character shaped by the interaction of circumstance and human whimsy.

## Character in Relationship: The Wild Baby Books

The Wild Baby, whose name provides the first clue to his character, is defined very much in terms of his relationship with his mother. One wonders how much of his irresponsible wildness draws its license from the stability and security that his long-suffering parent constantly provides. And the use of the kinship terms, "baby" and "mother," rather than giving them names, underscores the importance of the relationship as well as making the characters more universal.[5]

The first doublespread of the first book (*The Wild Baby,* 1980) immediately sets up the theme of the mother-child relationship and provides the basic information about the two characters. The text says, in a literal translation:

> Once upon a time there was a mother, so kind and mild.
> She had a baby who was so terribly wild.
> He would do all the dangerous things.
> He would never listen to Mama's nagging.

Although the words are quite explicit, and the rhyming pair "mild–wild" ("mild–vild" in Swedish) amplifies the central conflict, the pictures add substantially to characterization. In the verso, the mother is sitting in an armchair, the brown color of which matches her dress (she is "melting" into her surroundings), apparently tired after a long working day, having picked up the baby at day care and done the household chores. Finally at rest, she is still in her apron and worn-out slippers, with a cup of tea in front of her. Since the baby's father is never mentioned, we assume that she is a single mother—a gap that we fill with our extraliterary experience and that can have further psychological implications.

Mama's direct speech in this first spread is conveyed by a speech balloon where pictures are mixed with words: "Don't climb! Mind the staircase! Hit your head—big bumps. Don't eat dangerous things! Tummy ache all day long. Don't cut! Sharp scissors! Blood squirting, blood all over!" The baby has turned his back to the passive mother and is walking in a very determined manner out of the verso into the recto, where he is depicted six times—in a circular simultaneous succession, suggesting recurrent actions—doing all the dangerous things his mother is warning him against. This characterizes him as independent, brave, enterprising. At the same time, the mother, tired as she is, apparently trusts her baby: a more reasonable reaction would be for her to run after him to stop him from hurting himself. So if the baby is wild, much of his wildness depends on the freedom his mother gives him, which reflects the typical Swedish view on infant education at the time the Baby books appeared. The nameless Swedish baby is a happy, liberated child who investigates the world with his mother's blessing.

In the rest of the first book, the character of the baby is simply amplified by more pranks, described more or less symmetrically by words and pictures, while the mother's emotions oscillate between anxiety and admiration, between the natural instinct to protect and the desire to advocate freedom and independence. Most of these emotions are described visually, by mother's posture and facial expression. In every episode, the mother's love ("Baby is the best mother has") and the baby's faith in this love are accentuated. For instance, when the baby runs away, his mother "cried and cried for she could not find him," and he hurries back because he just wants to see "how upset mothers could get"—a testing of boundaries, typical for small children and necessary for their psychological development. In the fire episode, he acts bravely and resolutely, while his mother merely watches the dangerous flames in dismay. In the encounter with the wolf (apparently an imaginary episode), the baby is not afraid, but licks the wolf back. Not one single word of disapproval on the mother's part is to be found in the text, and after almost every episode she is depicted hugging the baby, with a smile on her face.

The second book, *The Wild Baby Goes to Sea* (1982), continues to explore the relationship in a number of ways. From the very first page, when the text tells us that the baby is fond of pranks and likes to get up in the middle of the night and jump up and down, the illustration reveals that it is poor Mama that the baby is jumping on, and that she sleeps with a pillow strapped over her head in an attempt to find some peace and quiet. When the baby decides to "go to sea," he takes his mother's wooden box for his ship, her broom for the mast, empties rolls from her handbag into his "ship," and finally snatches her apron for his sail. Mama cooperates by adding spars for the mast improvised from a coat hanger, and waves good-bye.

The apron is the most obvious stand-in for the mother, since it holds her shape throughout the story. Mama's hovering presence in the baby's imaginary voyage is made even more apparent by her actual representation in two of the pictures. The first is when the text reads, "Yes, someone calls loudly and clearly: BABY COME HOME, IT'S DINNER TIME." The illustration reveals the mother at the door with a plate on which lies a fish. Her second appearance is as part of the baby's fantasy where she sits in an armchair that floats on the sea. As always, Mama smiles, and she has entered into the game, for she is pictured carrying an umbrella and her slippers have turned into little boats. But the text simply tells us that the toys, the rabbit and giraffe, have called her.

Direct speech is used sparsely in the Baby books (in the first book there is no dialogue at all) and is always marked with capitals. The baby's expressions of disappointment and rage over the toy dog, discussed in Chapter 1— "I WANTED A DOG THAT COULD BARK! I WANTED A DOG THAT WAS ALIVE, NOT ONE LIKE THIS! I AM GOING TO SHOOT IT WITH MY GUN!"—certainly offer insight into character, but dialogue is more usually used for communication and plot development. The narrator also gives us some understanding of the feelings of the characters, sometimes overtly and sometimes by implication. For example, in *The Wild Baby's Dog* (1985) we are told that "the baby nags at his mother" (implication: he is stubborn and spoiled; observe, however, that the word "nag" echoes Mama's nagging in the beginning of the first book—the baby pays Mama back), and in *The Wild Baby Goes to Sea* we are given some direct general comments such as "the baby always does what he wants to. He does not like to be quiet," as well as some more-subtle analysis in specific situations such as "the baby laughs to himself HA HA! Because it is now getting really dangerous."

The pictures carry an extensive portrayal of the characters through their body language, gestures, facial expressions, and the like. For instance, when in *The Wild Baby's Dog* the baby has torn down several sheets of the calendar and claims that it is July already and time for his birthday, Mama is very obviously full of admiration for her clever baby, even though her words express the opposite. In addition, almost all of the pictures in the books feature the baby, which naturally emphasizes his central place in the story. In most pictures the baby occupies the central position, surrounded by other characters, reflecting the very young child's centralization of himself.

Clearly, a great deal of the fun of the books derives from the exaggeration of the two characters: the mother's love and patience are beyond sainthood, while the baby's antics are beyond belief! The notion of exaggeration in the characterization is represented both in the text and, even more so, pictorially, as the illustrations develop the text to new extremes. The second page of *The Wild Baby Goes to Sea,* for example, offers the following text: "He flies through the air like an eagle and licks Mama's honey when he pretends to be a bear. Because the baby always does what he wants to. He does not like to be quiet."

While the first few words provide the wildest verbal image ("He flies through the air like an eagle"), the illustration uses the less vivid images to display the baby's wild nature. He is pictured not licking honey from mother's spoon, but on the table, standing on his head, which is completely immersed in the crock of honey. A pool of honey drips from the tablecloth down to the floor where a toy bear lies with its mouth open. The clock tells us it is three, and mother sits at the table in a robe and with the pillow still strapped to her head, which suggests three in the morning. But she does not admonish the baby; instead she sips her coffee peacefully with her eyes closed.

The strength of the bonds of love between Wild Baby and patient Mama is revealed in many ways. Besides her unremitting forbearance, Mama actively involves herself in the games, as mentioned, and is always present when danger threatens. For example, her appearance in the armchair on the sea comes in response to the fears of the toys, an obvious displacement of the baby's sense of peril on his adventure. Even though he does not call her himself, for he is "happy" in the storm, she senses his need of her, and it is interesting that her appearance coincides with the apron losing her shape, which had been so obvious before.

The sense of exaggeration and caricature in the pictorial images of the baby and the mother make an almost ironic contrast to the sensitivity of the depiction of their relationship. Although the baby's facial expressions may be doubled in words (such as "angry," "not happy," "very happy," "the wild baby's wild eyes shine"), the external description is almost entirely visual. The baby's shape and features are cartoonish, and mother is dumpy, as in the picture of her scrubbing the floor on hands and knees with bare feet and her head tied up in a scarf, or as in the welcome-home picture where she wears the same brown dress but accessorized with long black gloves and a cap with huge brim and flap which covers the back of the neck. The humor of the characterization guards against the poignancy and possibile sentimentality of this picture of mother love, which idealizes the relationship while presenting the baby as a little demon.

## Object Characters: *Little Blue and Little Yellow* and *The Egg*

Some picturebooks take on the challenge of inanimate objects as their protagonists and develop them as understandable characters. The tradition of objects as story characters goes back to Hans Christian Andersen, while contemporary picturebooks make wide use of cars, trains, buses, or steam shovels in the central roles.[6] In most cases, the object, just as the animal, is a disguise for a human child.

One of the very few picturebooks that make use of abstract objects as protagonists is *Little Blue and Little Yellow* (1959), by Leo Lionni. The characters are two blots of color; however, they behave like ordinary children and have normal social relationships. Little Blue, like any picturebook character, is introduced in the first page: "This is Little Blue." On the next page, the character is referred to as "he," and thus acquires a gender. It is also specified that he lives with his mother and father—two larger blots of blue, one round and one longish (we refrain from any Freudian interpretations of this fact)—therefore we assume that Little Blue is a child. "Home" is depicted as an uneven brown space with the three blots inside it. From this we can make an inference that Little Blue is the only child. The next page informs us, verbally, that Little Blue has many friends, and we see them in the picture as several blots of the same size (same age?) but different colors. We learn that his best friend is Little Yellow. Since no personal pronoun is ever used in reference to Little Yellow, we have no knowledge of this character's gender. We will choose here to apprehend Little Yellow as female, for ease of interpretation, to keep the gender balance, and to suggest romance elements in the plot. However, it is clear that the color in itself could easily suggest either gender.[7] Little Yellow's social and familial relationships are similar to those of Little Blue: she lives with her mother and father, she likes to play with her friends the colored blots, and she goes to school—which, interestingly enough, is depicted as a black rectangle, as opposed to the uneven brown forms of the homes.

We learn more about Little Blue from his actions: his mother tells him to stay at home, but he goes out to look for Little Yellow. When the two blots hug so hard that they become a single green blot and their parents reject them, they show a normal human reaction by bursting into tears. The parents go through a change when they finally accept the children and their feelings, depicted as a merging of color. Significantly, the parents merge cross-color as well, the implication obviously being that they feel an affection, but not necessarily of erotic nature. This very simple story without one single human or even anthropomorphic character allows substantial characterization by words and pictures. In decoding the iconotext, we "translate" the abstract images into human beings and ascribe them human traits, emotions, and behaviors.

The plot and characterization in the book are heavily dependent on the verbal narrative. Without it, the sequence of white pages with blots of different size and color would hardly make any sense at all, even though with a good deal of imagination it is possible to make out a narrative. The relationship between Little Blue and Little Yellow, though, is easy to understand from pictures alone.

*The Egg* (1978), by Lennart Hellsing and Fibben Hald, is an absurd and slightly sad story about growth, grand visions, and lost chances. The protagonist is an egg, which is a powerful metaphor of the child with its potential yet unrealized. On the first spread, a big bird "thought that life had not really turned out the way it had hoped," so it hatches an egg and flies away. The largest part of the book depicts the egg's fantasies about what it will become when it grows up. The authors use the expressive means of the words and the images, and not least their comical interplay, to the maximum. The egg begins its dreams of the future by imagining itself a "stone egg, which someone could put on a desk or on the window sill or on a shelf [ . . . ] An art egg." The picture shows the egg, displayed and admired in a museum. A reader familiar with contemporary art will immediately recognize Constantin Brancusi's sculpture *The Newborn* in the Museum of Modern Art in Stockholm. To help the viewer, there is an intraiconic text, "Brancusi," on the catalogue that one of the museum visitors is reading. The whole picture is an expanding free association on the verbal image "stone egg."

In the following spreads, the egg literally tries on different identities in its imagination, brilliantly expressed in the pictures. It tries wings and fish fins, two or four legs, two legs and two arms, then wings again. It also tries one or two eyes. Four legs are dismissed, in words, because it will be too expensive to have two pairs of shoes, and too much trouble to polish them. The egg decides on two eyes because spectacles are made for two eyes and not one—"that's why most people have decided to have two eyes." The words are humorous comments on the pictures, while the pictures themselves carry most of the imaginative play. The egg decides that it will need to eat, and therefore must have a mouth and a stomach, big enough to put all kinds of things into: "marbles, a skipping rope and a bed in case one gets tired." This absurd collection of things to carry in one's stomach is just one example of the book's nonsensical elements, visual as well as verbal. The egg immediately realizes that there is no point carrying a bed in its stomach for when it feels tired. Instead, it becomes a bed itself, with "four legs, one in each corner." The polysemantic nature of the word "leg" is accentuated in the picture by the bed/egg having human legs with toes, and by four slippers standing neatly in a row under it. Besides, a round egg can hardly have corners.

In the next picture, the egg fears that if it is a bed, somebody else might come and lie in it. This "somebody else [ . . . ] somebody heavy" of the verbal text is visualized in the picture as a fat man in pajamas. The contemplation about the suitable number of legs, including the polysemy, is developed into a chain of verbal and visual associations about objects with three legs, such as a stool and an antique coffeepot. The egg dreams about having a birthday, riding a bicycle, and playing soccer. It also has nightmares about Easter: "Eggs do not like Easter—you certainly understand why," the text says. The dreams are depicted in thought balloons while the egg is lying still, its facial expres-

Dreams and nightmares in *The Egg,* by Lennart Hellsing and Fibben Hald.

sion changing according to the nature of the dream. The story is thus static and dynamic at the same time, and the protagonist is unchanging but also developing rapidly in a number of different directions.

When the little bird hatches out of the egg, its life suddenly becomes much more predictable. However, the story goes on about the dreams and wishes, most of them expressed visually. The words "It is just like having something, then you immediately want to have something else, something bigger and better" are illustrated by two funny cars, the more fancy one owned by a man with an egg face who appeared in an earlier museum scene, who is never mentioned by words, but apparently is the protagonist's evil demon. He reappears in the next spread, where four short and quite generaliz-ing sentences are illustrated by a series of evocative pictures depicting some milestones in the protagonist's life (a typical "hagiography" found in medieval paintings). The ironic pictorial story presents the protagonist as having both the bird and human nature: it catches worms and insects, builds a nest, and is afraid of cats, but it also goes to school, learns to swim in a swimming pool, has furniture, and travels with a suitcase.

The last spread repeats the first one, with slight changes in tone and color. The grown-up bird hatches an egg and flies away, while the new egg is left to lie and contemplate its future. The circular composition emphasizes the existential message of the book and can be interpreted positively as well as negatively. The character development is followed, in this metaphorical and ironical manner, from infancy to adulthood, with identity crises and other easily identifiable stages; however, the character itself is sufficiently unusual to create an "alienation" effect.

## Animal Characters: Beatrix Potter

Unlike the use of objects as protagonists, which is comparatively rare, the creation of animal characters is a frequent and significant characteristic of children's literature. Although animals are sometimes used as characters in adult literature, often for allegorical or satiric purposes, their popularity in children's literature suggests that little children, from an adult's perspective, have much in common with small animals, and that their behavior is closer to that of animals than of civilized human beings. The fact that many toys for young children are in animal form further reinforces this point of view. But though the child may be seen as having animal characteristics, the animals are usually transformed into anthropomorphic beings with human attributes, including speech, human motivation, and often clothes and social status. To represent main characters as animals or toys is a way to create distance, to adjust the plot to what the author believes is familiar for child readers. This may often be a stereotypical and obsolete attitude toward children.[8] Fables, which represent human faults in animal figures, were considered during certain historical periods to be suitable for children.

The depiction of the picturebook protagonist as an animal (or toy or inanimate object) gives the creator the freedom to eliminate or circumvent several important issues that are otherwise essential in our assessment of character: those of age, gender, and social status.[9] For example, in the case of the protagonist of Virginia Lee Burton's *The Little House* (1942), the irrelevance of age makes it possible to describe a period of many years, which, had the protagonist been a child, would have implied growth and change, while the very essence of the story is that the protagonist does not change, while her surroundings do (cf. the protagonists of Russell Hoban's novel *The Mouse and His Child,* who can spend years at the bottom of a pond, without having to eat or change in age).

The characters of Arnold Lobel's *Frog and Toad are Friends* (1970) or Janosch's Little Tiger and Little Bear books, such as *A Trip to Panama* (1978), are referred to as male, but their age and social status is unclear. They behave like small children, but live on their own; the source of their living, for instance food, is never mentioned. We may say that these characters represent very young children, at the stage where such issues are more or less irrelevant. Both *Frog and Toad* and the Little Tiger and Little Bear books are an endless chain of play and harmless adventure, arcadian by nature.

However, it is not always so. Margret and H. A. Rey's *Spotty* (1945), Russell Hoban's Frances books (*Bedtime for Frances,* 1964, and sequels), William Steig's *Sylvester and the Magic Pebble* (1969), or Ulf Nilsson's and Eva Eriksson's *Little Sister Rabbit* (1983) show animals in easily recognizable family relationships and conflicts. In these books, animals are presented as living in autonomous societies. Often, as in *Sylvester* and the Frances books, it is only from the pictures that we know the characters are animals.

On the other hand, animals can be portrayed within the world of humans.[10] In Charlotte Zolotow and Maurice Sendak's *Mr. Rabbit and the Lovely Present* (1962), the animal has a traditional folktale role of a magical helper and adviser. The boa in Tomi Ungerer's *Crictor* (1958) and the little worm in Barbro Lindgren's and Cecilia Torudd's *A Worm's Tale* (1985) may be perceived as unusual pets, but they are equally children, similar to archetypal orphans, brought up by adult benefactors. The naughty cat Mercury in Sven Nordqvist's Festus and Mercury books (*Pancake Pie,* 1985, and sequels) is definitely a child in disguise. The monkey in H. A. Rey's *Curious George* (1941) and the teddy bear in Don Freeman's *Corduroy* (1968) are young children exploring the dangerous and enticing world of adults. Perhaps one of the attractions in using animals in picturebooks is the rich possibilities of pictorial solutions. Further, in an animal character, one specific trait can be amplified: George's "monkeyhood," Crictor's "snakehood" (for instance, his ability to change shape and make letters of the alphabet), and so on. Animal characters are more easily accepted as "flat," which characters in picturebooks often are, because of their limited scope.

The tension between animal and human traits in the creation of animal characters is especially interesting when a delicate balance between the two is portrayed. The recent popularity of the Swedish Mamma Moo books, which express the irony of a middle-aged female acting in an immature, liberated manner ("Wow, wow, here comes the swinging cow!) is a case in point, for, despite her human attributes, Mamma is pictured plainly as an ungainly cow with a prominent udder.

Beatrix Potter's animal stories accentuate this fluctuating boundary in a variety of ways. Peter Rabbit (*The Tale of Peter Rabbit,* 1902) is one of the most widely known animal characters, exemplifying the naughty boy who values his independence and whose desire to transgress boundaries far outweighs his mother's warnings or his personal safety. Peter is both animal and human: his antisocial impulses are expressed in true rabbit fashion—as a marauding pest in Mr. McGregor's vegetable garden—and Potter's brilliantly accurate anatomical drawings capture the look of the animal in its natural state. For example, Peter is pictured as a true-to-life rabbit when he escapes from beneath Mr. McGregor's sieve; even when his animal body is presented in a more human posture, such as when he creeps under the gate or stands beside the door he cannot open, the representation is exact, offering a striking balance between human and animal characteristics.

The interaction between text and picture in portraying character is exemplified in the spread that pictures Peter entangled in the gooseberry net attended by the sparrows. Here at this tension-filled point in the story, the relationship between text and image is complex. The picture taken by itself could be interpreted as a dead rabbit. Peter's eyes are closed, his position frozen and unnatural. The words tell us the complete story: he is not dead, but imminent death has seized his mind, for he "[has given] himself up for lost."

While the text explains the details—mind-set, tears, exhortation from the friendly sparrows—the picture (to us one of the most poignant in the book) conveys the emotional and physical paralysis of despair. While the words are conventional, "Peter gave himself up for lost," the image provides the emotional dimension the words lack. This contrasts with the sparrows, whose energy is graphically pictured, but to whom the text gives shape, meaning, and motivation: "friendly sparrows, who flew to him in great excitement, and

PETER gave himself up for lost, and shed big tears; but his sobs were overheard by some friendly sparrows, who flew to him in great excitement, and implored him to exert himself.

Peter caught in the gooseberry net from Beatrix Potter's *The Tale of Peter Rabbit.*

implored him to exert himself." It has been noted several times that the phrase "implored him to exert himself" is considered peculiar diction for a children's book, but we know that Potter chose the words deliberately and defended them tenaciously. The Victorian, rather prissy preciseness of language is married to the emotionality of the image, and the effect is both intense and moving. The reader, like the birds, wants to press energy into Peter's lax body, reminding one of the nightmare where one tries to flee from danger but one's legs refuse to move.

The picture of Peter escaping from Mr. McGregor's garden sieve is another instance of restrained words and dramatic image: the "sieve which he intended to pop upon the top of Peter" is a death trap that Peter, flattened against the earth, struggles mightily to evade. "Pop upon the top of" is an offhanded expression that masks the murderous attempt with tea-party words. Again, the characters' motivation is effectively communicated, and the reader's sense of involvement with the animal figure magnified.

This sense of identification with Peter's plight is enhanced by the borderless pictures conveying the sense of a hidden viewer whose perspective, while not the same as Peter's, is often very close. The sieve picture is one such example, as is the picture in the toolshed. We know where Peter is, because we can see his ears sticking out of the watering can, but we too are hiding from Mr. McGregor's search, just as we are right behind Peter and sharing his perspective of the gate to freedom beyond Mr. McGregor hoeing in the garden. This perspectival involvement heightens the reader's sense of peril and Peter's terror, and asserts the human emotions that are depicted as part of this animal's character.

Characterization by means of clothes is of great significance in Potter's work. Besides the notion of clothing an animal as part of the animal/human dichotomy, clothing is also used generally in picturebooks to communicate a great deal of information about the character, including such aspects as social status, age, occupation, and self-image. In terms of the animal/human spectrum, Potter focuses in several of her tales upon the conflict between human, civilized expectations and animal urges.

The ephemerality of the human/animal balance and the fragile veneer of civilization that clothes symbolize are nicely depicted in *The Tale of Mrs. Tiggy-Winkle* (1905), where Lucy's perception of the washerwoman is veiled by the clothes that are the focus of the story. For almost the entire book, Lucy accompanies Mrs. Tiggy-Winkle during her day's round. She learns about the clothes that all the animals wear (little dicky shirtfronts belonging to Tom Titmouse, yellow stockings belonging to Sally Henny-Penny) and about all of the techniques of the professional laundrywoman: clear starching, ironing, and goffering. Mrs. Tiggy-Winkle talks in local dialect, addresses Lucy as ma'am and curtseys to her as signs of respect for her social status, and sits down to tea with her when the work is done. The shedding of the human aspect of this character, created with such careful and authentic detail, is poignantly pictured in the final two spreads of the book.

Facing a picture of Lucy standing on a stile with her laundry on her arm we find the following text: "Lucy turned to say 'Good-night,' and to thank the washer-woman—But what a *very* odd thing! Mrs. Tiggy-Winkle had not waited either for thanks or for the washing bill! She was running, running, running up the hill—and where was her white frilled cap? and her shawl? and her gown—and her petticoat?"

This is followed by an illustration of a hedgehog, and the text, "And *how* small she had grown—and *how* brown—and covered with PRICKLES! Why! Mrs. Tiggy-Winkle was nothing but a HEDGEHOG."

Other Potter stories depict social status and power through clothing: Jemima Puddle-Duck in her bonnet and shawl has no defense against the foxy gentleman dressed in his suit of plus fours, for he is clearly of higher class than she and wins her trust with his fine speech and elegant clothing; and Tom Kitten is unable to live up to his mother's expectations of gentility and the good opinion of her tea-party guests when he and his sisters lose their clothes, which are taken by some passing ducks in their quest for social standing.[11]

## Human Beings in Disguise: The Moomin Picturebooks

The three Moomin picturebooks—*Moomin, Mymble and Little My* (1952), *Who Will Comfort Toffle?* (1960), and *The Dangerous Journey* (1977)—belong thematically to the Moomin novels, in which illustrations play an essential role in characterization. In the novels, the Moomins are a variety of imaginary creatures, half-animals, half-dwarfs or trolls, inhabiting the self-contained world of the Moomin valley. They are clearly human beings in disguise, as Tove Jansson has admitted, and often have prototypes in real life. The core of the family consists of Moominmamma, Moominpappa, and their son, Moomintroll, who can be viewed as the central character of the novels. Otherwise, the Moomin figures function as a collective character, representing different human traits. Thus Sniff is cowardly, selfish, and greedy. Snufkin is an artist who despises material possessions and values his independence most of all. Snork is bossy and pedantic, and his sister, Snork Maiden, kind, vain, and a little silly, a parody on a female stereotype. Hemulen is a bore and a numskull, Muskrat a caricature of a cynical philosopher, and Fillyjonk a neurotic spinster. Little My is a strong and independent female, and so on. The Groke is the only evil, or rather ambivalent, character in the Moomin gallery, who can be viewed as the dark side of Moominmamma and interpreted in terms of Jungian Shadow.

Although described in the text as "trolls," the Moomin figures have no origins whatsoever in folklore, and from their names it is absolutely impossible to guess what the characters look like. When the first Moomin picture-

The Moomin characters would be impossible to imagine without pictures.

book, *Moomin, Mymble and Little My,* appeared, the readers were already familiar with the Moomin character gallery from the novels; moreover, by that time the Moomin figures had appeared widely in newspaper comic strips and the Moomin comic magazines. The only artistic innovation in the picturebooks is the use of color.[12] However, if we treat the picturebooks separately, characterization in them presents several interesting dilemmas.

The three title characters appear in a cumulative plot: the book starts with Moomintroll walking through the woods carrying a jar of milk from the milk store to his mother; he meets Mymble, who has just lost her little sister, My. After several adventures, the sisters are reunited and the trio continues their walk home. The rest of the characters are introduced in a chain plot: Moomintroll and later his two companions meet one character at a time, usually one in each spread: a gaffsie, Hemulen, a fillyjonk, and a household of hattifatteners. Besides these figures, mentioned in the verbal text, there is a variety of anonymous creatures occupied with their own business here and there in the spreads. Since the pages have cutouts, several of these creatures stay along for at least two spreads.

The pictures do not add much to characterization: Moomintroll's changing facial expression reflects the situations he finds himself in; Mymble cries over her lost sister and is happy to get her back; and Little My herself is constantly glad and fearless. Although this book has been interpreted in terms of the main character's exploration of self (the wood being a transparent Jungian symbol[13]), it is plot-oriented rather than character-oriented, which is amplified by the recurrent verbal page-turner: "What do YOU think happened then?" The significant features of the book are humor and nonsense on the verbal side and the intricate layout and elaborate colors on the visual side. Characterization and character development are clearly subordinate.

In *Who Will Comfort Toffle?*, a new character is introduced. In Swedish, the name is "knytt." It is spelled without a capital and used first with an indefinite article—"a little knytt"—and thereafter with a definite article—"the knytt"—which suggests that it is not a proper name but a species. Like most names in the Moomin books, knytt is a nonword, but may give a native reader associations, for instance with "knyte," literally a little bundle, but also used about a little child. Other characters mentioned in the text are the hemulens with their "heavy tread," the groke with her "fierce growl," five fillyjonks riding a horse cart, and eight whompses "in green carriages," the mymble making a lingonberry wreath, a snufkin playing his flute (an interesting detail, since in the novels he usually plays mouth organ), and a variety of other creatures, including the dront, borrowed from Lewis Carroll.[14] Many of the characters are not mentioned in words, but a reader familiar with the Moomin novels will identify most of them. In the end, Toffle meets a female creature, Miffle ("skrutt" in Swedish, associating with little and miserable). Without the supporting pictures, we have no idea about the character's external appearance. Pictures visualize words that have no meaning, that is, words that have no direct connection between the signifier and the signified.[15]

However, the pictures have other functions in characterization apart from the external description. The book describes Toffle's spiritual growth when he changes from an insecure, shy, and frightened little creature to one who finally shows courage and wins his princess. The pictures emphasize the character's traits and moods, mentioned in the verbal text, by depicting him huddled and looking bashfully askance; by placing his tiny figure in the middle of a doublespread, surrounded by tall trees, buildings, and huge creatures that dominate the image; and also by placing him at the edge of a doublespread with an ongoing action to accentuate his outsider position. In confrontation with the Groke, Toffle is still depicted as small when compared to the mountainlike figure of his opponent, but his fierce posture and angry face differ radically from the character presented at the beginning. In the next spread, Toffle and Miffle are portrayed in a close-up, which obviously signifies the characters' higher self-esteem.

*The Dangerous Journey* is the only Moomin book that has a human protagonist and that describes a passage between the real world and the Moomin valley. The book, which came seven years after the last Moomin novel, is very clearly based on the reader's knowledge of the Moomin characters.

Toffle becomes courageous in *Who Will Comfort Toffle?,* by Tove Jansson.

When Susanna meets "a company of the most remarkable creatures [ . . . ] one of them big and stout [ . . . ] one very shy, and two identical," the reader is supposed to recognize them as Hemulen, the melancholy dog Sorry-oo, and the funny little twins Thingummy and Bob.[16] In case the reader is not familiar with the earlier books, the characters are identified on the next spread: "Hemulen, Thingummy, Bob and Hemulen's little dog." Incidentally, the dog is one of the few figures in the Moomin world who is a real animal. Susanna's cat, who reappears in the last doublespread of the book, is a guest from the real world.

Further, the travelers meet Sniff, Snufkin, and a hundred hattifatteners. The pictures help us to identify the figures. Sniff is throughout the story described in the verbal text as grumpy, ungrateful, and selfish, just as he is portrayed in the novels. Snufkin's generosity is emphasized as he offers the travelers warmth and food. Thingummy and Bob are, as in the novel *Finn Family Moomintroll,* where they first appear, characterized by their peculiar speech.

A figure not mentioned by name in the text, but only as "a shadow," is the Groke, whom we see in the picture towering over the freezing travelers. From the text or the pictures, it is impossible to understand the Groke's role in the terrible snowstorm in which the travelers are caught; we need to know from the novels that the Groke represents winter and cold. Too-ticky comes to the rescue in a balloon and takes them all to the happy Moomin valley, where more familiar characters appear. The text mentions Mamma and Pappa, Moomintroll, Little My, Whomper, and Mymble; in the pictures, an initiated reader will also recognize the Snork Maiden, Misabel, Fillyjonk, and the bashful Salome.

The protagonist, Susanna, may seem less important in these adventures than she is in the beginning of the book. The verbal text starts by stating that Susanna is in a bad mood, which is emphasized in the picture by her facial expression. In the next spread, she is confronted, on the symbolical level, with her own aggressions, when her cat turns into a horrible huge beast with sharp teeth and claws. A still more explicit visualization of Susanna's inner landscape in presented in the next spread, when she looks into a pond and instead of her own reflection sees a green slimy monster. However, all the further adventures can also be interpreted as Susanna's exploration of her inner self, where the various characters are projections of her traits and emotions.[17] The changing color scheme of the spreads reflects the evolution of the character. Moreover, Susanna seems to be aware of the fact that it is her aggressions that initiated the dramatic changes in nature: "I am sorry, but it was just me . . . I was sitting in the grass . . ."

Another of the many metafictional remarks that abound in the Moomin suite is also found in *The Dangerous Journey,* when Little My comments on Susanna's appearance in the Moomin valley: "That one is ridiculous, she looks like a figure from some silly picturebook!" The fictional status of literary characters is accentuated. On the other hand, Susanna has been interpreted by some critics as a self-portrait, and her departure from the

The "unmentionable" character: the Groke in *The Dangerous Journey,* by Tove Jansson.

Moominvalley as Tove Jansson's farewell to the Moomins.[18] This adds another metafictional dimension to the narrative.

## Psychological Characterization: *Outside Over There* and *Nightchild*

Portrayal of characters' inner psyches is one of Maurice Sendak's fortes. An especially interesting approach Sendak employs is the manifestation of inner longings, drives, and emotions in external form, perhaps the most famous being Max's Wild Things, which present the child's aggressions and antisocial impulses. As has been pointed out, the beasts are not purely ferocious, for their grotesqueness is moderated by the curved lines and curls with which they are depicted; the child's aggressions, though they appear monstrous to him, are really not so terrible.

A more complex example is *Outside Over There* (1981), where Sendak plays out Ida's distress at the responsibilities placed prematurely upon her by expressing her inner feelings in the outward manifestations of hooded goblins whose macabre dress hides small babies. The emotions, like Max's, are insidious in their first appearance, but quite tameable when recognized. However, unlike the earlier work, where Max's turbulent and rancorous emotions are clearly expressed in the Wild Things whose king he becomes, Ida's inner turmoil is pictured in a more complex and thought-provoking fashion. Sendak's characterization in this book is most concerned with the inner, emotional state of his protagonist, which he expresses not simply in images of and words about the characters, but in metaphoric and symbolic external manifestations of emotional and spiritual states of mind. Both words and images carry aspects of the communication, posing questions and providing information of different kinds.

The second doublespread of the book expresses the emotions of the characters both naturalistically and symbolically. The family group on the right side of the doublespread projects depression: the mother, sitting in a slumped position, gazes woodenly ahead ignoring her children; the baby cries vehemently, and Ida, the protagonist, holds her mother's baby, which is at least half Ida's size and a considerable armful, with her eyes downcast and head turned away. The positioning of her large feet, somewhat apart and pointing outward, suggests the weight she steadfastly bears. To the left of the doublespread, two hooded, faceless figures carry a ladder: they pass before a large dog that sits as family protector but appears oblivious to the strange figures. The text to this scene blandly notes, "And Mama in the arbor," a statement whose serene diction is in clear opposition to the emotions Sendak portrays in his characters' faces and by the presence of the goblins.

Sendak explores Ida's state of mind further through the introduction of the "wonder horn," which Ida plays to soothe the baby, but which soon draws her senses into a realm where goblins replace the child with an ice-baby without her knowing. While the text is brief, it explains the action, while the illustration provides the emotional dimension: Ida's abstracted expression as she is pulled into the music, and her emotions of love and then anger. The activity of the sunflowers, which intrude progressively into the room, supports the growing intensity of Ida's emotions, provoked by the love object melting away. The emotion is also reflected by the appearance of a raging storm and shipwreck through the window, which had before shown first trees and then a ship in full sail.

The sense of penetrating the increasingly symbolic, irrational world of the psyche is expressed verbally and visually through very different modes of communication. One example is the yellow cloak, far too large for the young girl; its intricately presented voluminous folds weigh her down and then sweep her away in the storm. When the text tells us it is "Mama's yellow rain cloak," it asserts Ida's youth, her small stature, and how unready she is to assume Mama's role. But when Ida shakes off the cloak and uses it to pull along the dancing babies, we see her mastering the situation.

The words tell us that Ida "made a serious mistake" climbing backward into the realm of "outside over there," while the pictures provide a pastiche of disconnected scenes with nightmare affect: arches lined with what look like human teeth, a terrified baby carried by goblins, and Ida whirled through the storm, out of control. The words continue the story, including the magical words of Sailor Papa's song, while the images reveal that the goblins are squalling babies. And in the beatific scene, reminiscent of Michelangelo's *Creation of Adam,* where the sisters claim each other in a nonnarrative eternal moment of pure emotion, the words function to provide a narrative context: "Except for one who lay cozy in an eggshell, crooning and clapping as a baby should. And that was Ida's sister."

These strange scenes and multiple images project aspects of character comparable to the inner workings of the mind that psychological fiction attempts to probe. Sendak's techniques are complex and incorporate elements from a variety of styles, surreal, symbolic, and naturalistic.

*Nightchild* (1994), by Inger Edelfeldt, suggests psychological aspects of character through the device of doubling, for the action involves the meeting and interaction of the protagonist of the story, the Princess of Bonaventura, with Nightchild, her dark alter ego. Unlike stories such as *The Prince and the Pauper,* where two characters exchange places to learn about the other side of life, *Nightchild* is the story of self-discovery through self-understanding, or in Jungian terms, the meeting of the "I" with the Shadow.

The Princess realizes quickly that Nightchild is no ordinary child, for she is invisible to all others, and when the Princess spends time in her company, no one realizes she has been away. The sense of the Otherness of this girl is strongly depicted in the illustrations. The Princess wears light, bright colors and is surrounded by sunshine; her hair is curly and blonde, and her skin is fair; her chubby dolls project this golden image, as do their names: Golden-hair, Rosycheek, Sunny-soul, Little Sweetie. In contrast, Nightchild lives in the middle of the forest and is pictured with drab clothes, lank, dark hair, and a pale, sad, sullen expression. We are not surprised to find her dolls with names such as Moss, Chunk, Stoneheart, and Squealing Liza.

The Princess's longing for her dark side is expressed in her "wonder[ing] so much who this girl might be that I could barely sleep. I became pale and tired, and it was not fun to play any more." Their meeting in the forest, after the Princess has spent a dark night perched in a tree for safety, leads to Nightchild's declaration that the Princess is her twin sister. "Your mother is my mother too. But you were born in the daytime, and she liked you at once. *I* was born at night, and as soon as she saw me, she turned away. [ . . . ] She has never seen *me*." "I see you," says the Princess. This statement of recognition and acceptance is echoed in the illustration of the two girls in bed together, where they begin to share each other's characteristics. The shadow child lies peacefully asleep, almost smiling, clutching her own doll, while the Princess, her hair bedraggled, looks solemnly upon her, while her doll sits upon the pillow. A strong sense of vulnerability and trust is communicated by this illustration: the girls are clothed only in wispy nightdresses, and the light and shade are evenly distributed between them. The fox sleeping on the end of the bed reinforces the forest environment, far from civilization.

The Princess brings back tokens from her dark sister in the forest, but cannot bring the girl home. First the Princess must find her true name, Princess Longing, then she injures herself and cannot travel to the forest, and at last she sends tokens that bring Nightchild to the castle. Nightchild becomes literally her mirror image, the dark face scowling from the mirror that she has entered and where she has hidden in a reflected world. Only when the Princess brings together light and dark can the two exist happily together in a world that is "wild and quiet and funny and serious, and [ . . . ] called Castle of Day and Night in the land of Sun and Moon." Nightchild turns on the light inside the mirror and smiles. The two aspects of character have been resolved.

The notion of the division of the self into a daytime and a shadow persona carries by implication not only the rejection of the dark side, but also the distortion of the acknowledged aspect of the self. This implied distortion is not suggested in the verbal narrative, but is expressed in the illustrations, particularly those that picture the Princess's home and parents. While the external view of the castle in which the Princess lives is old and traditionally turreted with high, narrow windows, the views of the inside are very different. The windows are double paned and modern in appearance, and the rooms are intimate, cozy, and furnished with a traditional stove and rather ordinary furniture. Furthermore, the breakfast table offers just bread, rolls and jam, and

The Princess and Nightchild begin to take on characteristics of each other in *Nightchild,* by Inger Edelfeldt.

boiled eggs, and mother and father come in their housecoats looking rumpled, and, in the mother's case, in her curlers. It is also clear, in the evening scene when mother, in her slippers, brings hot chocolate and warm scones, that this "castle" has no servants, and no pomp and circumstance. Rather it seems just like an ordinary home with ordinary parents. In fact the only regal touch is the breakfast mugs, which bear fun pictures of people wearing crowns.

The notion of the distinction between the real world of the castle and the fantasy world of the forest (where the breakfast table in Nightchild's house holds mugs and bowls shaped into sad, grotesque faces) is thus subtly altered to suggest the spawning of two fantasies—the world of the castle and the world of the forest—with the real world serving as the springboard to both. The characterization of the girl is thereby made even more complex and true to the psychological dimension: an ordinary girl who likes to dream that she is special, a Princess, and who makes herself the focus of an elaborate

Nightchild as the Princess's reflection.

fairy tale where the division in the self is articulated and resolved through fantasy.

## Setting as Support for Characterization: *The Tunnel*

Setting can strongly illuminate or comment upon characters. For instance the description of a character's room can give us clues about the kind of person we are dealing with. Max's cold and empty room in Sendak's *Where the Wild Things Are* (1963) is a telling indication of his mother, though she never appears in the visual text. Similarly, the contrasting change of setting in Anthony Browne's *Piggybook* (1986) from a tidy home to complete disorder communicates the metamorphosis from people to pigs. In *Sylvester and the Magic Pebble,* the character is literally integrated into the setting as he is transformed into a rock.

Anthony Browne's *The Tunnel* (1989) employs a fascinating use of setting to provide insight into the characters of a brother and sister, though we must accept that there is considerable gender stereotyping in this book. The two facing pages of the front endpaper depict the walls of two rooms, both in

brown and green tones, that reveal completely contrasting styles. The first is
papered in a large and intricate plant and leaf pattern in shades of green, with
a white baseboard and brown carpet. The second is papered in brick pattern
and color, with white baseboard and a green carpet. On the brown carpet lies
a leaf-patterned book. The green carpet is the color of grass. On the first two
pages of the book we are introduced to the characters who live in these
rooms: the girl, dressed in a pastel pink-and-blue-patterned sweater, stands
before the leafy wallpaper; her brother, dressed in a vivid blue, red, and yellow striped sweater with white stars, stands before the brick. The accompanying text, which tells us they "were not at all alike. In every way they were very
different," is almost redundant, as is the following description of their activities, which are displayed in the pictures.

If the book continued in this way, it would hold little interest. But the
brick wallpaper is echoed in additional ways: a brick wall serves as backdrop
to the boy's play; one stands outside the window where the children sit;
another where they walk outside, the girl with her book, the boy with his ball;
and a segment of brick appears through the broken plaster of the wall edging
the area that has become a dump. Finally, the tunnel through which the boy
enters the other world is edged and walled in brick. In similar manner, the
leafy wallpaper and the book, which the girl abandons to follow her brother,
prefigure the dense leaves that surround the tunnel entrance, and the world
beyond is one of trees and grass, though these are supernatural and surrealistic in the shapes they take on. Nonetheless it is clear that the children have
moved from a brick-dominated environment, one in which the boy felt at
home, to a realm of nature and magic, one that was encapsulated in the girl's
book, which we see was a book of fairy tales.

When she finds her brother, he has lost all color and turned to stone,
clearly unable to function in this other world in which his sister, though
afraid, retains her color, her warmth, and her power to humanize. By putting
her arms around her brother she is able to bring him back to life and to color,
and his first act is to turn around and address her for the first time by her
name: "Rose! I knew you'd come." Simultaneously, the setting is transformed
from a bare plain covered with tree stumps to a grassy forest with a ring of
flowers. Until this point in the book, neither child has been named by the narrator, but referred to as "sister," "brother," and "boy," and the sparse dialogue
has offered only "baby" as a pejorative term used by the brother for his sister.
When the two return home, we find that the narrator now refers to each of
them by name: "Rose smiled at her brother. And Jack smiled back." In the
back endpaper, the two wallpapers still stand adjacent, but the girl's book has
moved over to the brick room and is joined by the ball with which the boy has
been playing.

Two of the most emotionally affecting settings are those that support the
portrayal of Rose's emotions as she follows her brother. The words express

her state of mind as she prepares to look for him: "His sister was frightened of the tunnel and so she waited for him to come out again. She waited and waited, but he did not come. She was close to tears. What could she do? She *had* to follow him into the tunnel" (author's emphasis). But it is the setting itself, portrayed both in words and illustrations, that reveals her sensations: her fear is communicated to the reader by the description of the tunnel, which was "dark, and damp, and slimy, and scary." This use of the surroundings to echo the emotions is reinforced by the reader's sharing of the experience pictorially, watching Rose literally disappear into the darkness as her feet catch the last of the light, and then her laborious progress through the tunnel, which emphasizes the sense of claustrophobia.

The second depiction of high emotion through setting is in the presentation of the trees Rose passes on the other side of the tunnel. As the verbal text describes her feelings—"She thought about wolves and giants and witches. [ . . . ] By now she was very frightened and she began to run, faster and faster [ . . . ]"—the growing sense of fear is projected onto the metamorphosis of the trees. They change from an everyday appearance to gnarled, twisted, knotted trunks that take the shapes of increasingly grotesque animals. Undifferentiated limbs, tails, and eyes seem to stretch out to grasp her as she passes, or, in the form of snaky roots, to trip her, and the incipient transformation takes the shape of bears, wolves, boars, weasels, snakes, and gorillas emerging from the trees. The depiction of how it feels to Rose, in which her figure blurs out, leaving a trail like a photograph where the figure has moved, further presents her terror in a way that the simple statement "she was very frightened" cannot, and communicates the sense that it is the terrors in her mind, spawned of her imagination, that are of great significance here. The notion of a stone brother becoming human further offers a metaphorical or even allegorical insight into Rose's thoughts and feelings.

The illustrated characterization-by-setting is infinitely more effective than the rather straightforward and ordinary verbal text, and provides a much greater sense of individualization, growth, and interpersonal relationship. Besides the contributions to character development, the details of the illustrations expand the interpretation of the story by means of a number of devices, for example the "quotations" from and references to other stories, a feature that will be considered in later chapters of this book.

## Gender Construction: *Mina and Kåge*

Among the various aspects of picturebook characterization, the question of gender is of interest. It is easy to state that many picturebooks discussed in our study have boys as protagonists, and in those that have girls, the protagonist's gender is in many cases not essential. Apparently the reason for this is that picturebooks usually address the reader at an age when gender identity is not relevant yet; Sendak's Max, Lindgren and Eriksson's Sam, and the Wild Baby are not really boys, while Burningham's Shirley or Jansson's Susanna are not really girls—rather, they are merely children, genderless and often ageless. This does not mean, of course, that gender stereotypes cannot be prominent in certain picturebooks; besides *The Tunnel,* one may recall the naughty Peter Rabbit and his well-behaved sisters. Similarly, the psychological tension of the father-daughter relationship in Anthony Browne's *Gorilla* (1983) or Pija Lindenbaum's *Else-Marie and Her Seven Daddies* (1990) presupposes that the protagonist is a girl. However, picturebooks seldom make use of the gender-specific (and stereotypical) character traits, described, for instance, in John Stephens' essay "Gender, Genre, and Children's Literature."[19] The protagonist's gender is more likely to be emphasized by external features, such as clothes, than by psychological traits.

Many picturebooks are based on fractured fairy tales, subverting gender stereotypes, such as Robert Munsch and Michael Martchenko's *The Paper Bag Princess* (1980), or Babette Cole's *Princess Smartypants* (1986) and *Tarzanna* (1991), the latter also a severe criticism of modern civilization. Fam Ekman's *Red Cap and the Wolf* (1985) makes Little Red Riding Hood into an innocent young boy who goes visiting his grandmother from the idyllic countryside to the dangerous big city, where he meets a cunning female wolf disguised as a shop assistant. Anthony Browne's *Piggybook* is perhaps the most overt parody on stale gender behavior. Exciting as these stories are in their own right, they are basically symmetrical in characterization devices, that is, both words and images equally interrogate gender stereotypes. Unfortunately, quite a few picturebooks confirm the stereotypes, explicitly, in words and pictures (for instance, in *Babar,* 1931, extremely conservative in its gender roles), or implicitly, mainly in pictures. The latter may be illustrated, for instance, by P. C. Jersild and Mati Lepp's *German Measles* (1988), where the boy's pajamas are blue, and the girl's pink with frills; the boy is listening to his Walkman and reading comics, while the girl is playing with her Barbie doll. Even though this is not in any way essential to the story, the implicit ideology is disturbing.

We have found it difficult to locate picturebooks where words and pictures tell different stories from the gender point of view: for instance, the verbal story being "feminist" and the pictures more conservative in their gender construction, or the other way around. One example analyzed by Anita Tarr is Howard Pyle's *King Stork* (1973), illustrated by Trina Schart Hyman, whose very male-oriented story is subverted by its illustrations. While the text describes the male protagonist who evades death, passes the tests, and wins the King's daughter by answering her challenging riddles, he and the King are depicted in the illustrations as liquor-swilling louts, while the Princess is beautiful and intelligent. The "hero" follows the flying Princess, discovers her witchy mother, who is responsible for the riddles and the Princess's power, and destroys the witch. Thus he defeats the feminine principle and deprives the Princess of her supportive mother and of her power. Nonetheless, in the final picture we see that, although apparently defeated, the Princess is regaining her power, although not a word appears in the text. She gazes out of the window, oblivious to her coarse husband, and we see the beginnings of small wings sprouting from her back, wings which will once again enable her to fly.[20]

*Mina and Kåge* (1995), by Anna Höglund, is an unusual picturebook in that it has two verbal texts: one is the omniscient narrator's text, placed over or under each picture, the other, the characters' text, placed in speech balloons inside the pictures. Since the two verbal texts are contradictory, they also produce different kind of counterpoint with the pictures.

Mina and Kåge are two bears, perhaps two teddy bears, which is never mentioned in the verbal text. The verbal text tells us that the characters "lived together in the same house," but there is no mention of their actual relationship: Are they just friends, a brother and sister, or lovers/spouses? By the end of the story we see them sleeping in the same bed, that is, the visual text alone suggests that Mina and Kåge are two adults living together. Their gender is emphasized by their clothes: Mina's checkered dress and Kåge's brace trousers and a bow tie. In the beginning, the verbal text states: "In the morning they usually had coffee," which is in most places associated with adult behavior. Kåge also smokes a pipe. The characters seem to have enough economic means to travel around the world, but no work or other sources of income are mentioned. The book is thus quite ambivalent about the social status of the characters, which is a frequent occurrence in picturebooks (as well as novels) involving animals. In his travels, Kåge meets "other bears who speak foreign languages: Swahili, Finnish, Mandarin . . ." It is also mentioned that he is in Vietnam, where there once was war. The universe of the book is a curious mix of imaginary and real. This creates uncertainty as to how we should interpret the gender roles presented in the book.

In all the initial pictures, Kåge is depicted smiling, his head raised high, his pose speaking of self-assurance. Mina, on the other hand, has her head lowered, her facial expression gloomy and solemn. The verbal story tells us that one day Kåge decides to go traveling, packs his suitcase, orders Mina not to forget to water the flowers, and when Mina asks him to take her along, says that it is too far away and that he only has one ticket. So far, the pictures more or less support the verbal story. While Kåge is packing, Mina, a tiny figure in the background, watches him with a resigned pose. Kåge gives her a patronizing hug and leaves with a high-handed gesture, while Mina rushes after him—the motion lines emphasize her speed—with her arms stretching after him.

The next picture shows furious Mina having just thrown the flowerpot on the floor—again, the motion lines convey this act. The narrator's text placed over the pictures states in a neutral tone: "He is gone now." The narrator's text placed under the pictures focalizes Mina in a sentence that can be interpreted both as direct speech and as FID (Free Indirect Discourse): "Stupid Kåge." The speech balloon carries the text (in handwritten block letters): "I am not going to water the silly flowers! I hope he drops dead!" The message of the balloon is much closer to Mina's rage as expressed in the picture. The narrator's neutral, "male" discourse seems to suppress Mina's true feelings, which is especially clear in the next picture, in which Mina looks desperately and forlornly at the broken pot, while the text comments: "I am ALONE, Mina thought."

The plot progresses showing Mina hiding from loneliness under the table day after day—a marvelous visual depiction of depression. The narrator conveys her thoughts in indirect speech, which we, after the initial pages, have learned to distrust. After the first letter from Kåge, Mina pulls herself together, cleans away the broken flowerpot, bakes a cake, and washes up the dishes. Her inner "text," expressed by the balloons, is silent. She has been totally muted after the first fit of rage.

When Kåge comes back, Mina is first overwhelmed by joy. Kåge unpacks his suitcase, taking out the presents he has brought for Mina and chatting away happily. His choice of presents is very revealing: a silk dress and a little statue of Buddha. The pictures show Mina standing in her usual pose, hands behind her back, head lowered, watching Kåge. But as he gives her the silk dress, explaining, in words and in pictures in a speech balloon, where silk comes from, Mina explodes once again in rage. The narrator's text continues quietly: "You talk too much, Kåge. You've had fun, Mina said. But how could you leave me!?" The balloon repeats the last phrase, with big

Mina's visualized emotions in *Mina and Kåge,* by Anna Höglund.

block letters and a different punctuation: "HOW COULD YOU LEAVE ME!!" Mina now behaves in a way women are often expected to behave: first she rages, but immediately after she starts crying, and the narrator's text conveys her "female logic": "The flowers got broken! It's your fault, Kåge, that I threw them!" Kåge also behaves as males are expected to do and comforts Mina: "I've been inconsiderate, said Kåge. Poor Mina, you must have been very upset." This condescending tone—he talks to Mina as one would talk to a child, not a spouse—is supported by his pose in the picture; however, for the first time, his broad smile is gone. He is fully determined to get things right. For instance, he plants some new flowers in a new pot, and when Mina, in another fit of rage, jumps on her new silk dress, he irons it and puts it up on a hanger (which may be considered a deviation from the stereotypical gender behavior). These actions are only narrated visually: Mina holds the dress in front of the mirror, apparently gets furious again, jumps on it crying, and lies on the floor while Kåge is ironing. The narrator's comment to all this is overtly didactic: "Although Kåge was rather stupid, he understood that Mina must be allowed to be angry . . . for a long . . . long time." The happy reconciliation is depicted by the two bears sharing a bed, Mina firmly holding the Buddha statue in her hand.

The splendid line in the end, when Mina announces that she is now going away traveling, in a way spoils the subtle character development of the book, making Mina's growth unnecessarily obvious. However, this announcement is made in a speech balloon, which is an intricate way to show that Mina's suppressed "text" has now come forward. Since Kåge's reaction is only expressed visually—he drops his pipe in amazement—the picture accentuates the female character's final mastery of the articulated, ordered "male" language.

## Complex Characterization through Dialogue and Action: *Granpa*

John Burningham's *Granpa* (1984) makes an excellent contrast to *The Twenty-Elephant Restaurant,* with which we began this chapter, because it uses some similar techniques—dialogue, line drawings, and color pictures— and focuses upon relationship, in this case between a grandfather and his granddaughter. Like *Restaurant,* the characters are not named, but the familial relationship is strong in affect and (unlike the "man-woman" nomenclature of *Restaurant*) precisely identified. Despite these initial similarities, it is clear that *Granpa* offers an example of what we might term an uncertain iconotext, for it challenges the reader at every level and offers a variety of possible interpretations.

The relationship is explored not simply in the snippets of dialogue that accompany all but one of the illustrations, but also in the wealth of information pictured visually. In addition, unlike *Restaurant,* where time is always in the present, *Granpa* includes much information from the past, representing Granpa's memories of his own childhood and adding a rich dimension to the communication and miscommunication between the generations expressed both in the text and in the illustrations. The counterpoint between the dialogue, the line drawing, and the full color picture produces a multidimensional sense of the characters and their relationship.

A good example is the triad of dialogue, drawing, and picture that centers on games and sport. In the color spread, Granpa is playing with his granddaughter's skipping rope while she looks on from her bicycle with its training wheels. The illustration, which pictures Granpa's beatific smile and closed eyes, shows us that he is really enjoying himself with the child's toy, and the dialogue lets us know that the play has brought back memories of his own boyhood: "When I was a boy we used to roll our wooden hoops down the street after school."

This verbal prompt brings other memories with it. The line drawing presents the paraphernalia of a range of sports: a cricket bat, ball, bail, one pad and glove; a tennis racquet in an old-fashioned press; and croquet mallets, one of them broken, with hoops, ball, and post. Accompanying them is a chest with address label and imprinted name, and the whole picture is adorned with dead leaves and a large spider's web that reinforce the passage of time. Since the line drawing presents the sports equipment as old, broken, and missing significant parts (for example, only one of the required pairs of bails, pads, and gloves), the memory cannot be of Granpa's boyhood, when the equipment would have been in working order, but is either a later memory or simply a representation of the acknowledgment of time passing.

The triad technique communicates a good deal of information about Granpa's character: we know how he looks; we know that he is young in body and in spirit and delights in playing with his granddaughter; and we know something of his past and the world he remembers. His granddaughter's response to his sharing of his boyhood memories is humorous: "*Were you once a baby as well, Granpa?*" While Granpa is reliving his boyhood and sharing his memories with his granddaughter, she is trying to understand that this old man was once a child like her. Besides exploring their relationship, the book also limns the dimensions of each character as an independent being.

The subtlety of Burningham's presentation of this relationship derives in great part from his capturing the essence of communication between the generations, presenting the special love between the two characters but also understanding that miscommunication is a fundamental part of this relationship. This might be quite trivial, as when Granpa, playing that the mud pie is chocolate ice cream, is corrected to understand that it is in fact strawberry.

But in other cases, we see that the conversation is not a dialogue, but two monologues.

In the gardening scene at the beginning of the book, Granpa is planting out a box of seedlings into individual pots and says (in response, one would imagine, to a question such as "Why are you doing that Granpa?", "There would not be room for all the little seeds to grow." The girl's nonresponsive comment is *"Do worms go to Heaven?"* On the following page we find the two singing together, but they are singing different songs, and the line drawing shows that Granpa is drawn again into memories of the past where he sang his song before. The relationship is given additional dimension by the later doublespread that puts each character on a separate page, backs to each other, and faces and stances depicting negative emotions, while the text informs us, "That was not a nice thing to say to Granpa." This event provides an element of verisimilitude in a relationship that could be sentimentalized and provides an opportunity to question the "not a nice thing" that the child has said. Her crossed feet, slightly hunched shoulders, and arms akimbo suggest that she is dogged in her assertiveness, and Granpa looks hurt and even sulky. But other readers may interpret this scene differently, according to their own empathy with the characters.

This juxtaposition of pure dialogue and illustrations, without any descriptive or explanatory narrative, leaves a great deal to the reader, who must look carefully and sensitively at what unfolds in order to understand the nature of the characters and what is happening, and not happening, between them. The format itself also raises some questions, especially the nature of the line drawings. In some cases, for example the singing scene and the sports equipment drawings described above, they clearly represent Granpa's memories. In other cases they are giving additional current detail, for example the pills, hot water bottle, and thermometer that appear when Granpa is unwell, or the box of seedlings and the pots that accompany the gardening scene already described. In yet other cases they are pure imagination, for example the humorous drawing provoked by the comment, *"What if you catch a whale, Granpa?"* and the sea drawing accompanying *"Tomorrow shall we go to Africa, and you can be the captain?"* The final line drawing is simply the girl, sitting alone, with a color picture of Granpa's empty chair on the facing page.

Another challenge is raised by the format of the verbal text. We have already noted that the dialogue may often be considered two monologues, where the characters miscommunicate, or talk around rather that directly to each other. But even this interpretation can be challenged. The (usually) two sets of words on each doublespread are set in contrasting type, one of which is in italics. The first page gives the reader an immediate clue to the speaker, for the words are in regular type only and ask, "And how's my little girl?"

which certainly sounds like Granpa. From this point on the reader takes the italicized type to represent the words of the girl, and the book makes sense this way. However, the reader is assuming that the words are indeed spoken, for there is no narrator to interpret, nor are there quotation marks around any of the words, so it is possible that some of the statements or questions are unspoken comments. One could hypothetically take this to extremes and wonder whether in fact all of the words belong to one person imagining the other's response, but this is unlikely. The absence of words in the last picture actually reinforces that the dialogue, though it may not always seem truly interactive to the reader, is a real communication to those involved, and that when one of the partners is gone, so are all the words.

Nonetheless, there are some real puzzles in terms of characterization, and the ambiguity of some of the spreads is extremely challenging. One that we find endlessly intriguing is the doublespread with the words (in regular type) "I didn't know Teddy was another little girl." At the most obvious, this is Granpa reacting to something that the child has said, although this is one of the occasions on which there is only one speaker (if we assume the words are spoken aloud). But the line drawing of a bear prettifying in front of a mirror carries an uncertain relationship to the dialogue and picture, and multiple interpretations of character offer themselves. The bear is not a girl but a woman, wearing high heels and powdering her face. Is this Granpa's vision of a toy (and the granddaughter) as incipient woman? The girl's face in the picture is colored redder than it usually is. Does that mean she is blushing, or is it just a quirk of the printing? If she is indeed blushing, then the look on Granpa's face also requires interpretation; he is looking at his granddaughter out of the corner of his eye, not directly. What is he thinking of ? Or is this just a simple innocent comment, because teddy bears are genderless or perhaps male. In this case, the primping bear in the line drawing could be a statement of Granpa's surprise and his humorous conjuring of a very female bear, or even a humorous comment from the narrator on the notion of gender stereotypes.

Another picture that incites discussion is the doublespsread that involves a picture of the two fishing, a fantasy line drawing of Granpa catching a whale and the statement and question: "If I catch a fish we can cook it for supper. *What if you catch a whale, Granpa?*" Once again we wonder where the humor is focused: Is the child fantasizing Granpa catching the whale with her help? Is Granpa laughingly visualizing what the scene would look like (intrepidly he reels in the giant fish while his granddaughter clutches his leg to be sure he doesn't go overboard)? Is this a shared vision? Or is this the narrator's humorous comment on the irony of the situation and the delightful imagination of children? Without knowing the answer, the reader cannot tell much about Granpa's sense of humor—whether it is well developed or an unimportant aspect of his character.

More evident is the final doublespread of the book, already alluded to, where the line drawing of the girl faces the picture of Granpa's chair. The child sits on a straight chair with her feet beneath her, face resting on one hand, and looks toward the empty chair and table. There are no words, for the conversations are over. The fact that the girl is represented only in the line drawing and not in the colored picture conveys a sense of complete separation. The sparseness of detail suggests a bareness and coldness, and the loss of Granpa's presence is overwhelming.

While it is perhaps dangerously academic to overinterpret the possibilities, we do want to assert the complexity of this nonnarrated picturebook (again, "showing" without "telling") with its various elements in fascinating counterpoint. What is certainly true is the degree of involvement demanded of the reader, not simply in interpreting what the book is conveying, but, because of the ambiguity, in empathizing with the characters and injecting elements of one's own emotions and experience into the work. In drawing the readers into the process of characterization, Burningham makes them feel like participants in the relationship he depicts.

## Notes

1. Lawrence R. Sipe, "How Picture Books Work: A Semiotically Framed Theory of Text–Picture Relationships," *Children's Literature in Education* 29 (1998) 2: 97f.

2. John Stephens, *Language and Ideology in Children's Fiction* (London: Longman, 1992): 164.

3. On static vs. dynamic and flat vs. round orientation in children's fiction, see Joanne M. Golden, *The Narrative Symbol in Childhood Literature: Exploration in the Construction of Text* (Berlin: Mouton, 1990): 41–52.

4. See further William Moebius, "Introduction to Picturebook Codes," *Word and Image* 2 (1986) 2: 141–158.

5. It is interesting that the British and American translations of the Swedish original provide names for the baby, Bodger and Ben, respectively.

6. Cf. Joseph H. Schwarcz, *Ways of the Illustrator: Visual Communication in Children's Literature* (Chicago: American Library Association, 1982): 150–168.

7. Interestingly, all our Finnish students did not hesitate to pronounce Little Yellow a female, whereas our American students were divided on the gender interpretation.

8. Cf. Joseph H. Schwarcz and Chava Schwarcz, *The Picture Book Comes of Age* (Chicago: American Library Association, 1991): 9.

9. Cf. Sonja Svensson, "Barnböcker utan barn." In *Barnkultur—igår, idag, imorgon* edited by Ann Banér, 73–102 (Stockholm: Centre for the Study of Childhood Culture, 1999).

10. Cf. Margaret J. Blount, *Animal Land: The Creatures of Children's Fiction* (New York: Morrow 1974); Mary Rayner, "Some Thoughts on Animals in Children's Books," *Signal* 28 (1979): 81–87.

11. For a more detailed discussion of the function of clothes in Beatrix Potter see Carole Scott, "Between Me and the World: Clothes as Mediator between Self and Society in the Works of Beatrix Potter," *The Lion and the Unicorn* 16 (1992) 2: 192–198.

12. Some scholars have noticed a possible influence of Matisse, see, e.g., Lena Kåreland and Barbro Werkmäster, *En livsvandring i tre akter* (Uppsala: Hjelm, 1994): 138.

13. See Kåreland, op. cit.: 26ff.

14. It is interesting to observe the author's use of definite and indefinite articles with her creatures' names; it may seem incoherent, but apparently signifies whether the creature is unique (the groke) or one of many (a snufkin). In the Moomin novels, Tove Jansson is also inconsistent in capitalizing the names.

15. For a contemporary native reader, the coinages from the Moomin books have become a natural part of the language; therefore the words *knytt* and *skrutt* are immediately associated with the characters rather than with any of the original connotations.

16. Different hemulens appear in all Moomin novels. Sorry-oo is portrayed in *Moominland Midwinter,* and Thingummy and Bob are introduced in *Finn Family Moomintroll.*

17. Cf. Lena Kåreland's and Babro Werkmäster's Jungian interpretation of the book, in Kåreland, op. cit.: 87–123. See also Boel Westin, "Resan till mumindalen. Om Tove Janssons bilderboksestetik," in *I bilderbokens värld,* ed. Kristin Hallberg and Boel Westin, 235–253. (Stockholm: Liber, 1985). Both studies draw clear intertextual lines from *The Dangerous Journey* back to *Alice in Wonderland.* It may be of interest to know that Tove Jansson has illustrated a Swedish translation of *Alice).*

18. Kåreland, op. cit.: 139.

19. John Stephens, "Gender, Genre, and Children's Literature," *Signal* 79 (1996): 17–30.

20. This analysis has been presented by Anita Tarr in her paper "Trina Shart Hyman's Subversive Reading of Howard Pyle's King Stork: A Woman-Text" at the 1995 ChLA Conference at the University of New Hampshire.

# CHAPTER 4

# Narrative Perspective

## Some General Remarks

Perspective, or point of view, presents an extremely interesting dilemma in picturebooks, which once again has to do with the difference between visual and verbal communication, between showing and telling, between iconic and conventional signs.

In narratology, the term "point of view" is used in a more or less metaphorical sense, to denote the assumed position of the narrator, the character, and the implied reader (or narratee, to keep the symmetry). There is also a distinction between the literal, or perceptional, point of view (through whose eyes the events are presented), the figurative, or conceptional, point of view (conveying ideology or worldview), and the transferred, or interest, point of view (how does the narrator benefit from telling the story). All three types of point of view can be fixed or variable in a verbal text. With pictures, we can speak of perspective in a literal sense: as readers/viewers, we behold the picture from a certain fixed point of view imposed on us by the artist. Even though we can by eye movement "read" the picture left to right or right to left or in a circular pattern, the basic point of view is unchanged. It can, however, change within a sequence of pictures, both in direction and in distance ("zoom"). Pictures cannot *directly* and immediately convey ideology or serve someone's purpose in narration, although they have their own indirect means to accomplish this.

Further, narratology makes an essential distinction between point of view ("who sees") and narrative voice ("who speaks"). While this distinction is somewhat metaphysical in a novel, in a picturebook we should probably treat the words as *primarily* conveying the narrative voice, and pictures as *primarily* conveying the point of view. We stress "primarily" because the verbal text can in itself have a point of view (that is, use various types of focalization), while pictures can at least in some sense be "narrated."

Most narratologists agree that all verbal texts are narrated, even though the narrator can be covert. The author may deliberately give an impression of a nonnarrated text, for instance, by including actual or fictional documents, reports, newspaper clips, or tape-recorder transcripts. Since these elements are by definition verbal, it may seem that they are irrelevant for text–image interaction in picturebooks. There is, however, a unique feature in picturebooks that we have so far, for lack of a better term, named "intraiconic text," that is, words appearing inside pictures and in some way commenting on or contradicting the primary verbal narrative (e.g. Maurice Sendak's *In the Night Kitchen,* 1970, and *We Are All in the Dumps with Jack and Guy,* 1993, Colin Thompson's *Looking for Atlantis,* 1993, or Inger and Lasse Sandberg's *Yes, You May, Dusty Said,* 1993). These words should probably be apprehended as "nonnarrated," which, however, does not mean that they are not part of the narrative. On the contrary, very often they provide a metafictive comment on the primary narrative and/or an interpretive strategy.

The four most prominent features of the narrator's presence in the text are the description of setting, the description of character, the summary of events, and the comments on events, or the characters' actions. While the two last elements are *predominantly* verbal in picturebooks, the first two, as already shown, can be both verbal and visual, agreeing or counterpointing in various ways.

Dialogue is generally regarded as a nonnarrated form, and indeed, pictures cannot convey direct speech. They can, however, make use of different devices to suggest speech, for instance, the visual speech balloons in Barbro Lindgren and Eva Eriksson's *The Wild Baby* (1980), partly duplicated by the verbal text. In most picturebooks, dialogue alternates with narrated text. It is, however, unusual to have visual close-ups of the speaking characters, like those in film or comic strips; that is, dialogue is most often limited to the verbal level. In John Burningham's *Granpa* (1984), dialogue (or arguably two sets of inner monologue) is the only verbal text of the book. Since pictures cannot directly convey dialogue, the discrepancy between verbal and visual levels is especially palpable.

While verbal texts can be nonfocalized (which is often referred to as "omniscient, omnipresent perspective"), externally focalized (following one character's perceptional point of view only; "objective, dramatic, perspective"), or internally focalized (penetrating the character's thoughts and feelings; "introspective"), pictures for obvious reasons lack the possibility of internal focalization, at least in a direct sense—the character's feelings may naturally be conveyed by facial expression, position in the page, tone, color, and other graphic means. While the introspective narrator has, together with the first-person narrator, become one of the most common narrator types in contemporary psychological children's novels, the picturebook is essentially restricted in its use of introspection. It does, however, have its specific ways of conveying a "subjective" point of view.

On the other hand, pictures have unlimited possibilities of conveying literally an "omnipresent" perspective by giving a panoramic view of the setting, such as depicting several parallel events or several characters at different places, that is, expressing something that the verbal text only can express indirectly, for instance by saying: "At the same time . . ."

Since only the verbal narrative can comment on the events and the characters or address the reader immediately ("Now I will tell you . . ."), visual narrative excludes all forms of intrusive and authoritative narrators, which we often associate with traditional children's literature. Pictures can only be didactic indirectly.

However, pictures have their own expressive means. For instance, a character gazing from the picture straight at the reader/viewer may be apprehended as an "intrusive" visual narrator. The use of mirrors can create a sense of a first-person perspective, comparable to a self-portrait in painting. By placing the characters below the level of the viewer's gaze, the picture creates a sense of superior narrative position, and so on.

One of the most interesting questions arises from the notion of ironical and nonironical (or unreliable) narrators. Since irony is a rhetorical figure based on a deviation from the dictionary meanings of words, pictures in themselves cannot convey irony. However, pictures can provide an ironic counterpoint to words, showing us something different from what the words say and revealing the narrator either as naive or a deliberate liar. Since most picturebooks use or pretend to use a child's perceptional point of view, the discrepancy between this visual point of view and an adult, didactic or ironic narrative voice can become the most significant point of tension of the book. This is perhaps the best illustration of the phenomenon that Barbara Wall calls "double address,"[1] even though she applies the notion only to purely verbal texts.

Because of the limited volume of picturebooks, we seldom meet in them complicated narrative structures with several diegetic levels. However, we should not exclude such possibilities and should consider what happens if words and pictures tell stories on different diegetic levels and with several narrative frames. Normally, both the verbal and the visual narrator in a picturebook will be extradiegetic-heterodiegetic ("omniscient" and not participating in the story). We assume that this narrator is an adult, which means that there is a deliberate distance between the narrator and the implied reader. However, an ever growing number of picturebooks use a intradiegetic-homodiegetic (first-person child) verbal narrator, apparently in an attempt to bridge this distance. The visual perspective in these books can be quite complicated and ambivalent, either reflecting a child's "naive" perception, which in itself is a daring device, or offering an authoritative adult point of view.

From our earlier argument it should be clear that we are mostly interested in the various patterns of interaction between word and image, which in this case means, for instance, that the verbal and visual point of view contradict each other, or that the visual point of view contradicts the verbal narrative voice. However, since the whole area of narrative perspective in picturebooks is practically unexplored, we feel obliged to start with some basic discussion.

## Omniscient Perspective

Let us begin by considering a book normally classified as having an omniscient, omnipresent perspective, H. A. Rey's *Curious George*. The cover of the most common edition shows the tiny monkey being rather firmly led by the arms by two police officers, who are about three times as high as George: the power position is clear. The cover repeats a picture inside the book, with a significant difference. In the book, George is distressed, which is shown by the downturned corners of his mouth, and his whole posture suggests fear and submission. The figure on the cover is smiling broadly, and his posture almost suggests dancing rather than being dragged. This notwithstanding, the point of view on the cover is omniscient and does not take sides with any of the agents in the picture.

The cover of the standard Swedish edition (1967) is different. It also repeats, at least partly (without the background setting), a picture inside, portraying George the monkey flying with a bundle of balloons. As viewers, we are positioned at almost the same level as George, slightly below him, and the houses on the ground are depicted from ours and George's shared perspective. Thus the visual perspective of the cover immediately manipulates us to share the protagonist's point of view. The title, however, contradicts this, since the epithet "curious" is not the protagonist's evaluation of himself, but the didactic narrator's disapproving attitude.

The endpapers show George walking the electric wires, allowing us to behold him at a distance and again slightly from below, which, as in the cover, accentuates George's superior position and his high self-esteem.[2] The point of view reinforces our identification with the protagonist (suggested by the Swedish cover, and implied by the title), who is featured and centered both visually and verbally. Although the character is an animal, we unmistakably recognize him as a naughty and stubborn child.

The establishing page of the book shows George in an omniscient, but "neutral" (portrayed at the same level) perspective, which is confirmed by the words: "This is George. He lived in Africa." Note that the change in tense immediately signifies a distance between the narrator and the narrative. The following three sentences of the original 1941 edition distort the verbal narrative perspective: "He was very happy. But he had one fault. He was very curious." The statement "He was very happy" has an ambivalent perspective. It may equally be an internal focalization of the protagonist (= "George considered himself happy"), an omniscient narrator's statement (= "I know that George was happy"), or an objective narrator's inference (= "I believe that George was happy"). Since the picture shows George indeed smiling happily as he is swinging from a branch and eating a banana, the last interpretation is the most plausible. The statement "But he had one fault. He was very curious" amplifies the didactic perspective. Thus the one simple picture and five short sentences of the original establishing page present several different points of view, none of which are in complete accord. In the revised edition of *Curious George* from 1969, the text has been changed to: "He was a good little monkey and always very curious." Unlike the original version, this statement very clearly comes from an omniscient, didactic narrator. The change eliminates the ambiguity of the verbal perspective, making the text more consistent and in harmony with the omniscient perspective of the picture. This is just another example of how different versions of picturebooks reveal the importance of text–picture interaction, too often neglected by publishers and especially translators.

The verbal text on the next page says: "One day George saw a man. He had on a large yellow straw hat." The words "George saw" express the character's literal point of view: we share his perspective and "see" the man in the yellow hat together with him. The visual perspective of the picture is reverse: although slightly shifted, we share the man's literal point of view, looking at George from a considerable distance. This corresponds to the next sentence: "The man saw George too." Thus the picture reinforces the change of perspective from the focalized child character on the cover through the omniscient— presumably adult—narrator over to the adult man, a bearer of civilization, an interpretation amplified by his carrying a gun, a camera, and binoculars, symbols of power and knowledge. Moreover, we are also immediately allowed to share the man's internal point of view, his thoughts: " 'What a nice little monkey,' he thought." By sharing the man's thoughts, we are also involved in his plan to capture George; thus as readers/viewers, we have "betrayed" our earlier identification object and are now on the adult, civilized man's side.

The next two spreads, in which George is caught, bring us back to the character's perceptional level, especially as we only see one foot and the hands of the man. However, since we are aware of the man's conspiracy—we have been given his thought "I would like to take him home with me"—and see through George's carelessness and naivete, the identification is impeded. Instead, we share the authoritative, ironic perspective of the adult narrator. Although the rest of the verbal text in the book focalizes the character both externally and internally (mentioning George's feelings of curiosity, fear, or joy), and the pictures mostly duplicate the words, the overall sense of the omniscient, didactic perspective is persistent. Not even the final sentence— "What a nice place for George to live!"—is persuasive enough and is still apprehended as the narrator's conceptional, or ideological, point of view (= "I know that George liked the Zoo because it was a nice place"). The naughty child is socialized, and the adult narrator expresses his content.

## Focalization in Words and Pictures

In Maurice Sendak's *Where the Wild Things Are* (1963), the verbal perspective is limited omniscient, that is, Max is consistently focalized throughout the book, both externally and internally. The point of view is practically fixed; however, the didactic verbal narrator is revealed in one single statement: "made mischief," which is hardly Max's own evaluation of his behavior, unless we regard it as Max's ironic quotation of his mother's usual attitude. The literal visual perspective is omniscient, except for one picture in which Max has turned his back to us, and we thus share his point of view. However, if we interpret Max's adventures as imaginary, the visual text is narrated from his conceptional ("subjective") point of view. He is the king of all wild things, and we are forced to accept it. Moreover, in many pictures, Max is staring

Contrast between adult and child points of view in *Look There, Dusty Said,* by Inger and Lasse Sandberg.

right at the viewer from the picture, expressing anger, sadness, but more often joy, perhaps the joy of a storyteller—he is, in other words, the visual intrusive narrator of the book.

*The Wild Baby* also has a limited omniscient verbal narrator, focalizing the baby in almost every episode, accentuated by the childish vocabulary. The perspective may, however, shift to the mother, for instance when she is searching for the baby, who has hidden or run away. The visual perspective is consistently omniscient, and no attempts are made to reflect the child perspective by means of any graphic devices.

There are several picturebooks specifically based on the difference in the literal point of view between characters, notably adults and children. In *I Don't See What You See* (1976), by Simone Cederqvist, the facing pages of every spread are contrasted by the shift in perspective from the father to the little girl. In Inger and Lasse Sandberg's *Look There, Dusty Said* (1983), the illustrator makes use of frames to reflect the limited literal perspective of a young child. Both books are "symmetrical" and "redundant" in that the perspective shifts in pictures are meticulously duplicated by words. However,

41

while words can only indicate this shift by describing it, in *Dusty,* by alternate focalizing of the boy and his grandparents externally, the pictures have a means of directly conveying the perceptional point of view. The effect of both iconotexts would have been much stronger if the words had not overclarified what the pictures express clearly enough.

A more sophisticated use of the diverse perspective is to be found in Ulf Stark and Eva Eriksson's *When Daddy Showed Me the Universe* (1998). The father takes his son on a walk out of town, past shops, parks, and factories, intending to show him the universe. The boy is uncertain about what the word "universe" means, but with a child's curiosity he keeps his eyes open and registers many details in the surroundings. While the father is looking up at the starlit sky, stating proudly that this is the universe, the boy notices the small things: pictures conveying his point of view are close-ups of a snail on a little rock, a green straw, a thistle, and a puddle. "All this was universe! I thought these were the most beautiful things I had ever seen," the verbal text comments. The father makes fun of his son: "Don't be silly [ . . . ] Look up." He points out the constellations for the boy, talking in a high-flown manner about the universe. The panoramic pictures, contrasting the close-ups, emphasize how small the boy and his father are in this big world. However, the story is abruptly brought back to earth and the everyday as the father steps into dog's dung because he has not been watching the ground. The child perspective turns out to be as important as the adult's in some respects.

In Ilon Wikland's *Where Is My Puppy?* (1995), the whole plot is based on the discrepancy between the verbal and the visual point of view. A little boy is running through the pages of the book, both indoors and outdoors, looking for his dog. The verbal text focalizes the boy externally ("he sees . . .") and internally ("he is upset"). The visual text has an omniscient perspective that allows us to see the dog hiding from the boy in every picture. To help us grasp the narrative device, the dog is fully visible to us in the first few spreads, while it is obscured from the boy by an open wardrobe door or by a blanket cast over a chair. In the subsequent spreads, we are trained to look for the dog, and so just a tail, an ear, or a paw are shown. This is a good example of how the contradiction in verbal and visual point of view provides the real action of the story.

## The Dilemmas of a First-Person Perspective

In his essay "The Eye and the I: Identification and First-Person Narratives in Picture Books," Perry Nodelman points out some problems arising from the double narrative in the picturebook medium. The verbal narrative in a picturebook may use the first-person, or autodiegetic, perspective. Pictures, on the other hand, as Nodelman remarks, "rarely convey the effect of an autodiegetic first-person narration,"[3] which he finds odd, and we cannot but agree. Picturebooks are supposed to be addressed to a young, inexperienced audience, yet they use within the same story two different forms of focalization, which puts very high demands on the reader. While identification with the "I" of the verbal text in itself presents a problem for young children, the contradictory perspective of the visual text is rather confusing.

A consistent first-person narrative in the visual text would imply a correspondence to "subjective camera" in film: the point of view of the protagonist/ narrator and that of the reader/viewer coincide. One of the very few movies in film history acknowledged as consistently making use of "subjective camera" is *Lady in the Lake*. The narrator, who never appears on the screen, is a detective, that is, in fact not the protagonist, but an observer.

In a picturebook, a first-person narrator would mean that, while we share his point of view, we never see him appear in any picture. For an unsophisticated reader, this would present considerable difficulties. But also generally speaking, the convention of visual communication, be it painting, film, or picturebook, creates in us the expectation of seeing the protagonist in the picture, and this convention is valid even though the author has chosen to tell the story from the first-person perspective. However, there are certain ways to let the reader share the first-person narrator's point of view and yet portray him in the picture.

In the first spread of Stefan Mählqvist and Tord Nygren's *Come Into My Night, Come Into My Dream* (1978), we share the literal, or perceptual, point of view of the young boy—as viewers, we are positioned straight behind him (cf. *Where the Wild Things Are*). But we equally share his conceptional point of view: we see the adults from below, from an oppressed position. Moreover, the mother's head is cut off so that she lacks a face, there is no eye contact with her, while the father is too far away in the background for us to see his face clearly. The subject position is clear: the reader, identifying with the protagonist/narrator, feels small and powerless. The verbal text supports this: "They looked at me, as if I had peed on the carpet in the sitting room, as I did when I was a baby." Before the story even starts we share the protagonist's sense of guilt and of being unfairly treated.

On turning the page, the perspective is twisted 90 degrees. We are still positioned below the adult level of perception, seeing only the mother's arm as the boy tugs at her, but we no longer share the narrator's point of view. We are outside observers, while in the verbal text the narrator continues to refer to himself as "I."

In the next spread, the point of view is from above. While the verbal text accentuates the emotionally charged perception of a frightened child awakening in the middle of the night, the visual text contemplates the picture in an almost vertical perspective. Moreover, the roof of the house is removed, and we have the awkward sense of peeping intrusively into someone's life. The visual narrator has taken an omniscient, omnipresent, almost godlike position. The verbal text, "I went to the door leading into the sitting room," is in total contradiction with the visual perspective. And although the next spread brings us back to the same level as the boy, still the first-person visual perspective is not restored. The scene describes the boy's encounter with the Other: from the seed he planted in the carpet during the daytime, an elf has grown. Identifying with the boy, it is natural for us to apprehend the elf as the Other, the mystical and frightening. The verbal text describes the "I" cautiously peeping into the room. However, the picture forces us to see the boy from outside, almost sharing the stranger's point of view (much like the man in the yellow suit watching Curious George). True, as adults we can suggest many psychological interpretations of this scene, such as the elf being a subconscious part of the boy's mind. The endpaper illustration supports this interpretation, as a number of images and symbolic figures seem to be emerging from the boy's head. A little further on in the book, it is hinted that the elf may be dreaming the boy, just as the boy may be dreaming the elf—a clear echo of Carroll's *Through the Looking Glass,* but perhaps a too-sophisticated intersubjective interpretation.

As earlier stated, internal focalization is impossible in a visual text, that is, pictures cannot directly express thoughts and feelings. However, the visual text can, for instance, elaborate with symbols and images in order to convey the inner world of the character. The boy wonders whether the strange crea-

Visual first-person perspective in *Come Into My Night, Come Into My Dream,* by Stefan Mählqvist and Tord Nygren.

ture is a frog, and the creature gets irritated: "Why should I be a frog?"—
"You are green," I tried to explain, "frogs are green."—"There are many
things which are green," the creature says. The visual text is the boy's
response to this utterance, depicting a variety of green animals: a grasshopper,
a spider, a lizard, a frog, a beetle—and a tangle of green plants. The visual
text is, in other words, the boy's internal point of view, a representation of his
thoughts, a visual counterpart to a stream of consciousness, initiated by the
word "green."

In the next spread, the nightmarish picture corresponds to the verbal
statement: "In the night, loneliness comes stealthily, like a hungry cat hunting
for mice." Again, the picture is an inner image, internal focalization. This is a
remarkably sophisticated narrative technique as a verbal simile is transformed into a concrete visual image. Generally, the pictures in the book are
stylistically heterogeneous, thus reflecting the mosaic of the child's mind.

In the penultimate spread, the boy meets his own reflection: "I took several steps forward. The mirror was like air. As soon as I turned and looked
back, I was alone." In a "subjective camera" narrative, showing the narrator's
reflection in a mirror is the only way to let us see him, much like a self-
portrait in painting. However, here again we watch the movement of the boy
and his double from the side, and the verbal and visual point of view are dis-
placed 90 degrees. In the very last spread, the boy takes off his clothes, in a
soft slow-motion, and crawls into his parents' bed, in a fetal position. In the

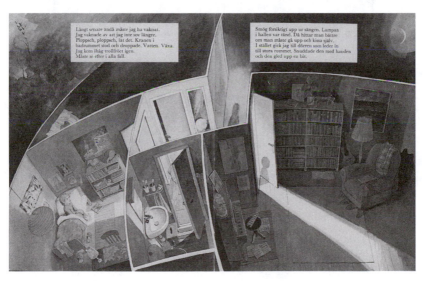

Omniscient visual perspective contradicting the first-person verbal narrative in *Come
Into My Night, Come Into My Dream*.

Endpapers of *Come Into My Night, Come Into My Dream* support
the "objective" interpretation of the journey as a dream.

verbal text, this is a positive resolution after a nightmarish journey, conveying
the boy's perception: "I have to be close, very close now." But the point of
view of the visual text is ambivalent. Once again, we view the scene from outside and slightly above. The subjective sensation conveyed by words is counterbalanced by the objective rendering of a fact in the picture. Actually, the
phrase "I have to be close now" expresses the boy's wish and hope, while the
picture leaves it for the reader to decide whether the desired reconciliation
has taken place. The cold bluish color of the picture emphasizes the coldness
of emotion and the boy's body does not touch that of either parent.

There is a clear discrepancy in this book between the immediate and
naive voice of the child narrator of the verbal text and the detached and

sophisticated adult narrator of the visual text. The title manipulates the reader to interpret the story as a dream. Otherwise, as readers we are free to choose our interpretation: the boy's journey may have been a dream or a game ("objective" adult perspective), but it may have been real as well ("subjective" child perspective). The reason we insist that the visual narrator is an adult lies in the abundance of adult allusions present in the visual text, or at least allusions that are deliberately addressing the adult coreader. In the third spread of the book, we meet several significant details that may escape our attention at first reading, but that prove to be important in the development of the story. A little metafictional detail is an earlier book by Mählqvist and Nygren lying on the floor, *I'll Take Care of the Crocodiles* (1977), which also uses the first-person narrative and has supposedly the same protagonist. This self-allusion may address children and adults equally. Another detail from "reality" without a specific addressee is the jigsaw puzzle on the floor in the boy's room, which also turns up in his dream. None of these are of course mentioned in the verbal text. However, the paintings the parents have hung on the nursery walls, among them Picasso's *Guernica,* are meant to be recognized in the first place by adult coreaders. Incidentally, these are not exactly the paintings one would normally hang in a child's room, and it is no wonder the boy has nightmares (a good example of indirect pictorial didacticism). The images from the paintings indeed appear during the boy's journey, most notably in the only wordless spread, a goldmine for an art critic as well as a psychoanalyst: we see a variety of experiences transformed into nightmares. The function of the picture is the same as in the three wordless spreads in *Where the Wild Things Are*. The visual text reflects the child's daydreams and nightmares, his fright, and impressions from the adult world, all of which he lacks words to describe. Thus the wordless spread illustrates Jacques Lacan's notion of the imaginary stage in the child's psychological development, when the child's inability to express his fear and his feelings with words makes him instead convert them into images.

On the other hand, the illustration is full of interpictorial allusions, which only work for the adult coreader. As noted by many critics, René Magritte seems to be one of the favorite sources of quotations in contemporary picturebooks.[4] At best, young readers may have seen reproductions of artwork alluded to. The naive child narrator does not make any connection between his dream and the paintings in his room. The adult visual narrator is playing a game with the adult coreader at the child's expense.

## The Detached "I"

It seems that few picturebook creators are aware of the aesthetic problems discussed above. Against all common sense, first-person narratives in picturebooks for young children are used more and more extensively. We say against common sense because all empirical studies show that small children, whom these books allegedly address, have not yet developed a clear sense of an "I" and have problems identifying themselves with the strange "I" of the text. We are usually trained to identify with focalizing characters or do this by intuition. When the "I" of the story lacks a name, as do the narrators in Mählqvist's book, in *Poor Little Bubble* (1996), by Inger Edelfeldt, or in *Aldo* (1991), by John Burningham, the identification is strongly encumbered.

In *Poor Little Bubble,* the first-person narrative pattern is still more complicated. Mählqvist's book starts *in medias res* and is therefore perceived as if happening "here and now," with no distance between the reader and the narrator. *Poor Little Bubble* starts: "Once upon a time I made a snowman." The narrator does not say, "Once upon a time when I was a little girl," but a narrative distance is immediately created by the fairy-tale–like initial formula and confirmed later in the text when the narrator says, "I know what happened out there in the garden; I understood it later." The temporal index "later" is indefinite; it may imply the next day, but is more likely many years. Anyway, from this moment, the first-person narrator is no longer autodiegetic, telling her own story and focalizing herself. Instead, the little snowman becomes the focalizing character, and the narrator becomes omniscient, entering his mind and conveying a whole scale of emotions, from joy through sorrow to anger. The spread shows Bubble in the verso vignette *en face,* smiling happily as he thinks about the pancakes that the "I," his adopted mother, has promised him. This part of the verbal text matches the wordless recto: a plate with pancakes and jam in a comiclike thought balloon. The verbal text "He saw me through the window as I was eating pancakes" is reinforced by the 180 degree change of perspective. In fact, we share Bubble's literal viewpoint in this picture. What prevents us from identifying with Bubble is the round frame of the picture; frames, as we have repeatedly shown, effectively create a distance between the viewer and the scene. In Mählqvist's book there are no restricting frames, as though we were invited to enter the described universe. Maybe the frame in *Poor Little Bubble* is another clue that the story is told in retrospect. Anyway, we have lost the perceptional, literal viewpoint of the narrator, and we have difficulties sharing the conceptional viewpoint of the character. Since the character is not human, the identification is still more problematic.

In the next spread, the perspective is omniscient, from above. The verbal text says, "He looked at the lighted window," but we no longer share the snowman's literal viewpoint, the visual perspective contradicting the verbal one. The visual narrator in this scene is obviously an adult, telling her story long after the fact. The "I" of the verbal text is an extradiegetic narrator, detached from the events.

The next two spreads show Bubble going up to the house, knocking on the door, entering the house, and walking along the corridor toward the little girl's room. The level of perception changes between verso and recto: first we see somebody's legs and feet from below (Bubble's perspective), and then Bubble in the corridor from above (omniscient perspective). Further, since the girl is in her room—it is the mother who opens the door—neither of the two pictures can possibly convey her point of view. The omniscient visual perspective continues through the story, when the girl takes the melting snowman out in the garden, pats him soothingly, contemplates a solution, and finally implements her plan, making a snow mother for Bubble. In the penultimate recto, which depicts Bubble in his snow mother's arms and still retains its detaching frame, the perspective can perhaps be the first-person narrator's, both the autodiegetic girl in the story and the extradiegetic, retrospective, adult narrator. A figure not mentioned in the verbal text, the grown-up snowman, little Bubble's potential father, can equally be ascribed to the child and adult perspective. However, the verbal text of the last spread clearly brings us back to the naive point of view: "And I could go away and do whatever I wanted, without having to think about poor little Bubble. What a relief." The girl's position in the verso does not allow us to share her point of view. Neither does the recto, showing her "doing whatever she wants," for instance dressing up and playing with her toys in a crowded room painted in bright, warm colors, which contrast sharply to the cold bluish colors of the outdoor scenes. The evaluation "poor little Bubble" may be equally a child's and an adult's, but the character's happy countenance rather suggests that she does not feel sorry for the snowman.

The ambiguous narrative perspective in this book is rather disturbing. Since the middle part of it, focusing on the little snowman both in words and pictures, encourages us to empathize, if not identify, with him, the closure, in which he is abandoned, leaves the reader deeply dissatisfied. The detached

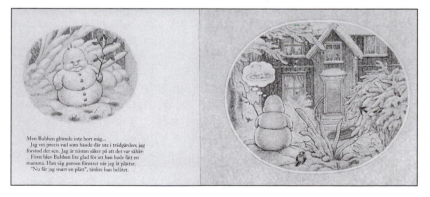

Change of visual perspective between verso and recto in *Poor Little Bubble,* by Inger Edelfeldt.

position of the first-person narrator impedes identification with her, which is invigorated by her obvious coldness of emotions and her neglect of the little snowman. In the beginning of the book, she says casually: "I had to go into the house and eat pancakes. And when I had eaten pancakes, I had to go and take care of my dolls. So I forgot all about Bubble." Even though this thoughtlessness is psychologically characteristic of a young child, the reader can easily get frustrated. The girl has actually promised to be Bubble's mother, which is a bond most readers will easily relate to. The double narrative perspective also reflects the double moral of the storyteller: from her own childish viewpoint, the girl is right; however, from the adult perspective her careless, irresponsible attitude is dubious. On the other hand, the dilemma she is faced with is impossible, as the verbal text expresses: "Bubble couldn't stay inside with me, and I couldn't stay outside with him! I had promised to be his Mom, but what could I do? I wish I hadn't promised." The psychological dimension of the book leaves many questions unresolved.

A way to deal with such obvious aesthetic discrepancies would be to say that the books we have been discussing are not addressed to small children, but this approach has its own problems. Picturebooks are traditionally regarded as reading matter for small children; it is also assumed that child readers prefer stories about characters of their own age or slightly older. While the two picturebooks we have discussed certainly appeal to adult coreaders, as well as critics and jury members of literary awards, presumably evoking their childhood memories, preschool children would find them perplexing, while older children would find them too childish. Although we are not primarily interested in the way children "understand" picturebooks, we cannot avoid noting how the books consistently address two parallel audiences.

## Contradiction and Counterpoint in Perspective

While in the above-mentioned books the verbal and visual perspective seem to be in conflict, a number of recent texts seem to explore, maybe unconsciously, the possibilities of creative counterpoint in narrative perspective, albeit cautiously and on a rather modest scale. In *My Sister Is an Angel* (1996), by Ulf Stark and Anna Höglund, the verbal narrator is Ulf, seven years old. He tells us a story about his dead sister, who is an angel and comes to visit him. Nobody in the family but Ulf can see her. A natural interpretation is that the sister is an imaginary companion, just like Aldo in Burningham's book. The picturebook medium, however, creates a problem. From the first-person child narrator's "objective" perspective, his story is true: he has a sister who is an angel and comes to play with him. The information we receive from the pictures is somewhat ambivalent. For instance, Ulf says that his sister trips his brother up, or hoses water on the father, while we see clearly that Ulf himself is the culprit. The sister illustrates the way a young child commonly transfers his faults and mistakes onto an imaginary friend. This is, however, an adult inference and judgment. The visual narrator is an adult, since pictures present an adult's conceptional point of view. It is conceivable that the visual narrator is the grown-up Ulf (identical with the author, Ulf Stark) telling the story of his childhood many years later, seeing through the faults of the seven-year-old Ulf, but still pretending to share his point of view. For an adult writer/illustrator, such a perspective may seem a daring narrative device, but it can be confusing for a young child. Either the verbal or the visual text is insincere—a sophisticated adult reader would probably say ironic.

*Little Sister Rabbit* (1983), by Ulf Nilsson and Eva Eriksson, has a first-person narrator who is a young male rabbit. Animals have always been popular characters in picturebooks, and among the many different animals portrayed, mice and rabbits have had the leading position. The book, with its nice, well-behaved, loving rabbit boy, who obeys his parents and takes care of his little sister, may be seen as a clear intertextual response to Beatrix Potter's *Peter Rabbit* (1902).

Using an animal as a first-person narrator creates an identification problem. Apparently, the authors believe that the readers will identify with the "I" of the story, accepting him as a substitute for a human child. However, the very first sentences set up a distance: "This is where we live, my sister and I. Right here. On the sunlit hill [ . . . ] Here is our burrow." The characters are anthropomorphic animals, but not fully as humanized as in *Peter Rabbit.*

Further, as in many earlier mentioned examples, there is a discrepancy between the point of view of the verbal and the visual narrative, except for the first two establishing pictures. In the first page (verso) we see a general panorama of the hill, and in the second picture (recto) the view is zoomed into the burrow and the long, narrow passage to the door of the rabbits' home. Both pictures have the first-person perspective, that is, we share the point of view of the narrator, who is thus placed outside the pictures and in front of them.

In the next spread and consistently to the end of the book, the visual perspective is omniscient, while the first-person narrative voice is somewhat confusing: "This is me. I am sleeping and breathing deeply." The present narrative tense and the colloquial tone of the narrator ("This is my little sister. She is sleeping and . . . oh, well!") suggest that the events are taking place here and now, and that the narrator is naive and unsophisticated. The omniscient visual point of view contradicts the voice. However, for a more trained reader, the contradiction produces an ironical effect. While the pictures tell the story in a neutral and "objective" manner, the narrator/protagonist presents himself as brave, capable, and clever, trying all the time to hide his

Här bor vi, min lilla syster och jag. Vi är alldeles ensamma hemma
och ligger och snusar i sängen. Mamma och pappa är ute just nu,
ute på jakt efter morötter.

Här är jag. Jag sover och snusar... Här är min lilla syster.
Hon sover och ... Nähä!

Contradiction in visual and verbal perspective in *Little Sister
Rabbit,* by Ulf Nilsson and Eva Eriksson.

irritation and fear. In a well-disguised intertextual allusion to Beatrix Potter, it
is the parents, and not the naughty child, who are "hunting" for carrots at
night—an apparently dangerous and definitely illegal enterprize.

Although most of the story is "symmetrical" and "redundant," there are
several details in the visual text that add to the ironical counterpoint. In a
visual flashback, the narrator tells his sister about a distant relative ostracized
for sucking his ear. Although the picture merely "expands" the words, its
humor is obvious and most probably beyond young readers' understanding.
Another visual detail, not mentioned in the verbal narrative, is the stuffed tro-
phy over the hearth, being, as the intraiconic text says, "Carrot found in 1898

by Uncle Fig." Both are apparently the products of the adult omniscient visual narrator.

In Pija Lindenbaum's *Else-Marie and Her Seven Daddies* (1990), most pictures portray the visual omniscient perspective at odds with the first-person verbal narrative. Many of the pictures featuring the tiny daddies have a perspective from above, which is logical; however, this device is not consistently applied throughout the book. In the picture portraying Else-Marie read-

Omniscient visual perspective contradicting the first-person verbal narrative in Pija Lindenbaum's *Else-Marie and Her Seven Daddies.*

ing in bed, the visual narrator is swaying high over the room, thus being superior both to the daddies and the girl. Also, when Else-Marie is all alone resting on a sofa, the same perspective is used, for no obvious reason. One picture
is especially contradictory in its point of view: the small daddies waiting
impatiently outside the bathroom. The verbal text says, "I hear them moan
and sigh outside the bathroom door," though the point of view is definitely
omniscient, since the narrator is on the other side of the door, reading comic
magazines on the toilet (depicted in the next spread). There are, however, several pictures that convey the narrator's perceptional point of view, notably her
inner visions of what might happen if the daddies come to take her home
from day care. The scenes are painted in sepia tone, signifying the internal
focalization. There is also an "objective" spread in which the daddies have
actually come to fetch Else-Marie and are depicted in a perspective that may
be omniscient as well as first-person, since the narrator is not present in the
picture. However, we suggest that the perspective is omniscient because the
viewer is suddenly positioned on the same level as the tiny daddies.

The book may seem dynamic in its constantly changing visual perspective, but there is no logic or consistency in these changes, and all the pictures,
except the above-mentioned inner visions, contradict the first-person verbal
perspective. Further, let us consider the conceptional point of view, that is,
interpret the humorous plot as the girl's imaginary story. Presumably she has
no father at all and compensates for this lack by inventing her seven little daddies. The conceptional point of view is exclusively that of a child, since
nobody in Else-Marie's surroundings seems to react to her unusual family,
least of all her mother. Bearing this in mind, it is all the more strange that the
pictures subvert the overall meaning of the iconotext by using the omniscient
perspective.

Another picturebook where the subjective child perspective is the prominent part of the plot is John Burningsham's *Aldo*. The autodiegetic narrator's
imaginary friend, who appears when she is lonely or maltreated, is in itself a
commonplace, and it is the perspective that makes the book worth mentioning. In the depiction of Aldo, the words and pictures are in accordance, and
nothing reveals the "objective" viewpoint, unlike the similar situation in *My
Sister is an Angel*. However, in the initial episodes, the narrator is presented
as either naive or insincere. She says that her mother often takes her to the
park, while the picture shows the mother pulling her daughter behind her, the
girl looking sorrowfully at the playing children. Similarly, she says that it is
nice to eat in a restaurant with her mother, while we see her envious glances
toward other children who have friends with them.[5]

*The Big Brother* (1995), by Ulf Stark and Mati Lepp, is told from a naive
perspective, where the principal narrative device is the "filter," that is, the
shift in point of view between the focalizing character and the reader. In this

book, we as readers understand that the narrator's big brother is nasty to him, for instance letting him stand tied to a tree for a whole day. The narrator says he has enjoyed it, because from his point of view, his big brother has been kind to him and let him participate in the game of Red Indians all day, in the role of a captive. However, there is nothing in the visual omniscient point of view that amplifies or contradicts the verbal irony. Possibly, we can note the picture where all the leaves have fallen from the tree, expressing the little boy's subjective sense of time: he has been standing there for such a long time that it will soon be autumn.

All the books we have discussed in this chapter exemplify the narrative dilemmas arising from the fact that the verbal and the visual perspective in picturebooks can never fully coincide. Among other things, we have tried to show how books that use the child perspective in the visual narrative often impose the adult ideology on the reader by means of the extradiegetic narrative voice. On the other hand, it should be evident from the discussion that the equally disharmonious combination of a child focalizer in the verbal text and the omniscient visual perspective is the most common in picturebooks, and that few authors seem to be aware of this.

However, our examples also reveal the unlimited and so far seldom exploited possibilities in complementary and contradictory perspective, which result in humorous and ironic effects.

## Notes

1. Barbara Wall, *The Narrator's Voice: The Dilemma of Children's Fiction* (London: Macmillan, 1991).

2. Cf. William Moebius, "Introduction to Picturebook Codes," *Word and Image* 2 (1986) 2: 141–158.

3. Perry Nodelman, "The Eye and the I: Identification and First-Person Narratives in Picture Books," *Children's Literature* 19 (1991): 2.

4. See, e.g., Joseph Stanton, "The Dreaming Picture Books of Chris Van Allsburg," *Children's Literature* 24 (1996): 161–179.

5. Cf. Clare Bradford, "The Picture Book: Some Postmodern Tensions," *Papers: Explorations in Children's Literature* 4 (1993) 3: 10–14.

From *The Tunnel,* by Anthony Browne.

# CHAPTER 5

# Time and Movement

Picturebooks present a unique challenge and opportunity in their treatment of spatiality and temporality. This area—the picturebook chronotope[1]—is also an excellent illustration of word and image filling each other's gaps, or, of even greater significance, compensating for each other's insufficiencies.

Two essential aspects of narrativity are impossible to express definitively by visual signs alone: causality and temporality, for the visual sign system can indicate time only by inference. In general, the flow of time can be expressed visually through pictures of clocks or calendars, of sunrise and sunset, or of seasonal changes (the best example of the latter is perhaps Virginia Lee Burton's *The Little House,* 1942), that is, through a *sequence* of pictures. However, in most cases, the verbal text serves to extend meaning by creating a definitive temporal connection between pictures and to reveal time's progress.

## Temporality and Movement within the Individual Static Picture: Simultaneous Succession

Unlike film, the picturebook medium is discontinuous, and there is no direct way to depict the flow of movement. However, unlike decorative art, the picturebook medium is narrative and sequential, and intends to convey a sense of movement and of duration. There are a number of techniques used in pictures alone, as well as a variety of options employed in the interaction of words and pictures, to imply movement and changes that take place over time.

In the studies of picturebooks, we find various examples of how movement can be depicted by purely visual means.[2] Different graphic codes, many borrowed from comics and photography, have been adopted by picturebook authors. These include such features as blurs, motion lines, and the distortion of perspective. Movement is further implied by the depiction of action in progress, actions not yet completed, such as characters with one foot raised, characters poised in midair at the high point of a jump, or characters leaning over to pick up an object. Scott McCloud's comprehensive study of comics contains many useful tools for picturebook analysis.[3] In each case, the reader's interpretation that movement is involved depends on prior knowledge, gained either from real life experience or from earlier reading.

However, the most often used and the most successful device to express movement within a single picture is what art critics call *simultaneous succession;* a technique widely used in medieval art. It implies a sequence of images, most often of a figure, depicting moments that are disjunctive in time but perceived as belonging together, in an unequivocal order. The change occurring in each subsequent image is supposed to indicate the flow of time between it and the preceding one. In medieval painting, it is used in hagiographies, each separate image within the picture portraying a single episode in the life of a saint. The "narrative time" of the whole painting may thus cover many years. In picturebooks, a depiction of the same character several times on the same page or doublespread suggests a succession of separate moments with temporal—and occasionally causal—relationship between them: one image precedes another and may cause it. Usually, the temporal span is much shorter than in pictorial hagiographies. Like blurs and motion lines, simultaneous succession is a narrative convention that has to be decoded by the viewer.

Perry Nodelman, following Joseph Schwarcz, uses the term "continuous narrative."[4] The term "simultaneous succession" (or simultaneous picture) is widely used by the German picturebook critics,[5] who often exemplify it by citing the magnificent transformation scene in Binette Schroeder's *The Frog King* (1989). It has also become an established picturebook concept in Sweden.

One of Nodelman's examples is the spread from Wanda Gág's *Millions of Cats* (1928), showing the little kitten growing "nice and plump." According to Nodelman, small children have problems identifying the sequence as simultaneous succession and instead apprehend it as individual pictures of different cats. We have heard Fibben Hald, the illustrator of *The Egg* (1978), commenting of his simultaneous succession—the egg starting to fly—that children "of course" do not understand that this device implies movement. However, although we have done no empirical research, our experience leads us to believe that it is unusual for children to be unable to interpret this technique. The ability to read simultaneous succession, like other learned skills, is a matter of possessing the right code to understand it. Just as the viewer of a medieval painting became accustomed to reading its sequence, children are similarly trained to decode a series of pictures, though some may be able to do it spontaneously.

A metatextual illustration of reading and misreading simultaneous succession is presented in Rudyard Kipling's story "How the First Letter Was Written." The little girl, Taffy, draws a succession of events on the same piece of birch bark, while her mother interprets the drawing as portraying several men at one single moment. The child in this case appears a more sophisticated picture reader than the adult: "There wasn't lots of spears. There was only one spear. I drawded it three times to make sure [ . . . ] you are just the stupidest people in the world." However, the story also problematizes the issue of visual versus verbal decoding: "At present it is only pictures, and, as we have seen to-day, pictures are not always properly understood. But a time will come [ . . . ] when we shall be able to read as well as to write, and then we shall always say exactly what we mean."

A good example of simultaneous succession is found in the first spread of Barbro Lingdren and Eva Eriksson's *The Wild Baby* (1980), where the baby is depicted six times in a wild circular motion corresponding to the verbal text: "[ . . . ] he always disobeyed her, he was reckless, loud and wild." The circular composition emphasizes that the events depicted here are repeated again and again over a long period of time, and illustrate one method of conveying the iterative frequency by visual means. We can start reading the picture at any point and continue clockwise, several times, even though the baby is depicted in the bottom right corner moving on toward the next spread (a "singulative" event). When the baby is depicted climbing on the clothes rack, he has just lost a shoe. In the next shot (clockwise) he has no shoe. This little detail can help us establish the order of events, even though the clockwise reading of a static picture comes naturally to Western readers (see Figure 1).

**Figure 1.** *The Wild Baby.*

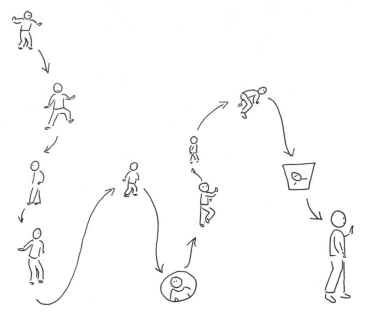

**Figure 2.** *Come Into My Night, Come Into My Dream.*

A similar semiclosed composition is found in the "dream" spread of *Come Into My Night, Come Into My Dream* (1978), by Stefan Mählqvist and Tord Nygren. It is impossible to determine where the movement starts, although our reading strategy suggests that we start in the upper left corner and cross the spread diagonally. A Chinese or Hebrew reader would probably read it otherwise. But the position of the boy, in profile and turned right, enables us to read the temporal order of events, at least where he enters the picture and where he is about to leave it. We thus apprehend the movement as linear and singulative (see Figure 2).

Both in the beginning of the book and in the end, there is a linear movement depicted by means of simultaneous succession. We read the picture left to right, and the logical development, supported by the verbal text ("I woke up [ . . . ] crept out of my bed [ . . . ] went to the door"), helps us to establish the temporal sequence.[6] On the last spread we see four separate temporal moments in a sequence: the boy enters the pictorial space, takes off his pajama top, takes off pajama pants, is naked. The verbal text is a summary: "I take off my pajamas." It is impossible to determine how long the sequence takes, but it is depicted in a kind of slow motion, accentuating that the boy is careful not to wake his parents with an abrupt movement.

One of the many contemporary picturebook authors who consistently make use of simultaneous succession for a variety of purposes is Sven Nordqvist. In most cases, he uses it to convey a single, quick and dynamic linear movement, for example where Mercury the cat moves rapidly in a wild trajectory across the spread and is shown at several stages of the movement. The trajectory is clearly marked by motion lines. In most cases, the movement is visual only. In *Pancake Pie* (1985), the words merely state that "Mercury rushed away like a comet with the red-and-yellow curtain flashing from his tail" (see Figure 3). Mercury actually leaves the spread in the bottom right corner (pageturner), and the trajectory is continued on the next spread.

In *Wishing to Go Fishing* (1987), the cat's impatient movement is partially duplicated by words, but nearly half the movement is described only visually (see Figure 4). In *Merry Christmas, Festus and Mercury* (1988), Mercury's surfing over the floor is accurately duplicated by words (see Figure 5). It is surprising that in later books, Nordqvist abandons the successful visual dominance, perhaps not trusting his reader to enjoy the picture by itself.

Simultaneous succession is also used to convey less violent movement, and in these cases the repeated figures of Mercury are placed closer to each other, even though the cat's poses and the motion lines around him in no way

**Figure 3.** *Pancake Pie.*

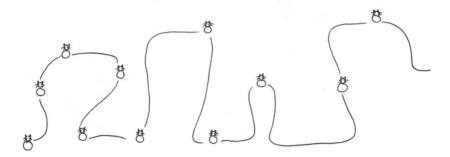

**Figure 4.** *Wishing to Go Fishing.*

suggest a static picture. Finally, old man Festus is occasionally depicted several times in the same spread, though this does not imply any rapid movement, since his posture is quiet and relaxed. The repeated figures merely indicate several temporal moments, and the span of time between them is indefinite and may even be quite long. In *Ruckus in the Garden* (1990), for instance, he is depicted inspecting his field, digging, raking, and kneeling down to plant. In the same book, he is depicted three times on the same spread, chasing the cows in an endless circular movement (see Figure 6).

Colin Thompson provides an excellent example of a combination of techniques in one doublespread of *Looking for Atlantis* (1993), where we find both simultaneous succession together with the blurs and motion lines depict-

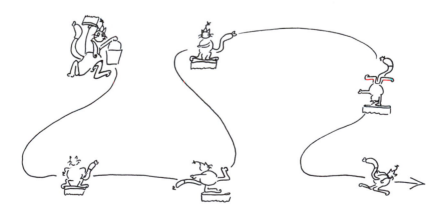

**Figure 5.** *Merry Christmas, Festus and Mercury.*

**Figure 6.** *Ruckus in the Garden.*

ing movement in time. Carrying the text "I looked in every dark corner and in every book," the spread reveals the boy looking in the fireplace on the left-hand side of the picture, while his second representation simultaneously reaches for a book on the right-hand side. His path from fireplace to book-shelf is mimicked by the path of a train, which is disappearing into a tunnel next to the book the boy is reaching for. The train has clearly emerged from the fireplace, as its trajectory is marked by a smoky band it has traced through the air (a band that, incidentally, serves as the text-holder). This smoky or blurry band suggests incredible speed, for the second coach of the train is almost swallowed by the blur, suggesting that it is faster than the eye can easily see. And, interestingly, this single image of the train covers the boy's arm in the right-hand representation, passing between it and the reader's eye. If the train moves at surreal speed, the boy must have moved even faster, for he is reaching for the book before the train has passed through its tunnel. Thus Thompson simultaneously communicates movement in time and in no time, challenging each concept with the other.

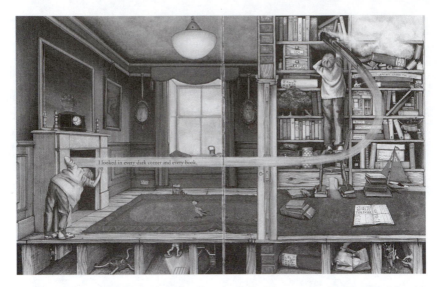

Simultaneous succession and motion lines in Colin Thompson's *Looking for Atlantis.*

## Temporality and Movement on One Spread with a Sequence of Pictures

Another way to convey movement and thus the flow of time in picturebooks is by means of a sequence of pictures. If the same figure is first depicted under a tree and in the next picture in the tree, we read this as meaning that the figure has climbed the tree, which we know from experience takes some time. The sequence thus conveys the flow of time. If this is in addition explicitly stated in the verbal text, the information becomes redundant, which weakens its overall impact. Many wordless picturebooks make use of sequences to convey temporal relations; let us once again consider Jan Ormerod's *Sunshine* (1981) and *Moonlight* (1982). Since the shots are framed and clearly delineated, we have no problems following the temporal development of the story (see Figure 7).

Several pictures on the same doublespread encourage us to apprehend a temporal—and often causal—relationship between them. Two spreads in *The Wild Baby* consist of a series of shots with a clear temporal order. In the first, the baby climbs from a stool up to the kitchen sink, dives into it headfirst, sits in leisurely fashion on the edge talking to his mother, and finally walks out with an aggravated expression on his face. The words that accompany this sequence are deliberately atemporal, even though they contain the temporal index "then": "When Mama was washing up after dinner, rattling with cups and saucers, she almost fainted because the Baby dived in the sink to take a

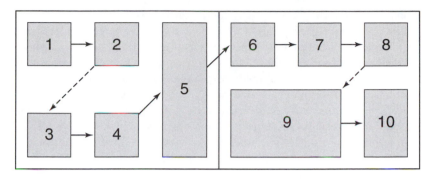

**Figure 7.** Ormerod's *Moonlight.* Dotted lines indicate implied connection.

swim. There was a terrible rattle when he dived. Then he was not allowed to swim any more in Mama's kitchen." The sequence of pictures is read top to bottom, left to right, and the connection between shots two and three is implied (see Figure 8).

In another spread, the words on the verso say, "The baby is the best thing Mama has, but he gives her a scare every day. One Thursday at one o'clock he plunged into the toilet." The four shots show the baby kicking at his potty, climbing up the toilet, trying to balance on it, and falling in. They are read left to right in two rows (see Figure 9). In the three shots on the recto of the same spread, Mama rushes to save the baby, he shakes off the water, and Mama washes him in a tub. The words say, "But he re-emerges again after a while and shakes like a real dog. *Then* the baby must wash for many days, until his Mama has no water left" (emphasis added). The words here lack clear

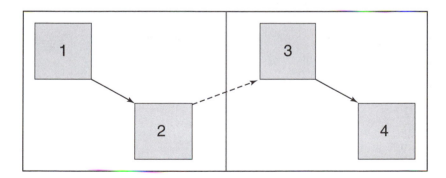

**Figure 8.** *The Wild Baby.*

temporality. Moreover, they express the iterative frequency, suggesting that the last shot takes place repeatedly, "for many days." The three shots are read top to bottom, clockwise in a semicircle (see Figure 10). The movement of the whole spread becomes thus quite complicated (see Figure 11). However, since the temporal and causal relations between the shots are unambiguous, we choose the correct order automatically.

In *Pancake Pie,* two pages depict successive shots in which Festus and Mercury are looking for lost objects. In the first picture, the text says, "They looked three more times [encouraging the viewer to do the same] in the larder, in the stove, in the wardrobe, and in the kitchen bench [ . . . ]" (see Figure 12). The second picture says verbally, "They looked in the hen shed, behind the tool shed, in the garden, in the woodshed, behind the sofa and in the larder" (see Figure 13). In both cases, if we follow the order of shots prompted by the text, we must start in the upper right-hand corner of the page and continue counterclockwise in a semicircle. Counterclockwise is not a

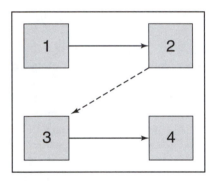

**Figure 9.** *The Wild Baby:* Verso.

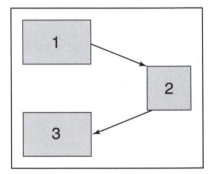

**Figure 10.** *The Wild Baby:* Recto.

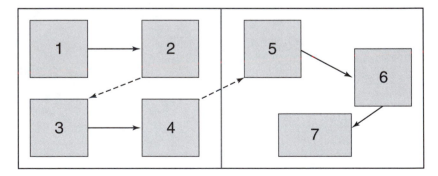

**Figure 11.** Temporal and causal movement in a picture sequence: A doublespread from *The Wild Baby.*

natural direction for Western readers to follow, and neither is starting in the upper right-hand corner. To what extent the order is deliberate is impossible to say, but the words undoubtedly manipulate the viewer to choose this order. In the same book, a simultaneous succession (Festus mending the bicycle, going to the store, and baking the pancake pie) is presented in the same counterclockwise pattern (see Figure 14). In *The Fox Hunt* (1986), a simultaneous succession starts in the upper left-hand corner of the verso and continues counterclockwise across the bottom of the page into the recto, which is a slight magnification of the scene. Apparently we must acknowledge this composition as part of Nordqvist's poetics. Interestingly enough, no later Festus and Mercury books use the counterclockwise movement.

**Figure 12.** *Pancake Pie.*

**Figure 13.**

**Figure 14.**

Nonlinear order of events in *The Egg,* by Lennart Hellsing and Fibben Hald.

Finally, there are pictures where the correct order of individual shots is next to impossible to determine. In Lennart Hellsing and Fibben Hald's *The Egg,* seven shots are placed on the same spread. We may intuitively start in the top left corner, and it is quite natural to end in the bottom right corner, where the bird is about to leave the page (pageturner). However, it is hard to say in which order the rest of the shots are to be read. The words give no guidance. They do say, "It learned to eat and walk and fly and swim," which may help us to identify some episodes, but the rest of the verbal statement is as ambiguous as the pictures: "It learned all possible other things as well. It grew bigger—but not much better—and not at all cleverer." For instance, the school episode precedes the swimming in the picture (if we read top to bottom), while it obviously corresponds to "all possible other things," following the swimming in the verbal text. Since the shots partly merge it is not even possible to determine which detail belongs to which episode. Apparently, this iconotext is not intended to create a clear temporal or causal relationship.

## Temporality and Movement in the Interaction of Verso and Recto

Unless the doublespread in a picturebook is a single picture, there are also different possibilities in relationship between verso and recto. Too many picturebooks neglect this important compositional detail, resulting in two pages facing each other that neither cooperate nor contradict, but seem to be arbitrarily placed on the same doublespread. In a good picturebook, the creator uses the tension between verso and recto to imply movement as well as temporal and causal relations.

Perry Nodelman exemplifies this once again with *Millions of Cats:* the verso shows a pond and thirsty cats, on the recto all water is gone; on the verso there is grass on the hill and hungry cats, on the recto all grass is gone. This is clear and simple causality. Nodelman does not, however, point out that both spreads are symmetrical: the pictures repeat exactly what the verbal text says.

The verso of the second spread of *The Wild Baby* shows the mother looking into the baby's empty bed, expanding the words: "He hid from his Mama every day. And when she looked in the baby's bed he was never there." Both the words and the picture encourage the viewer to look at the recto for explanation. And indeed we get it at once: "He had jumped up into the clock, or somewhere else. She never really knew where he was!" The reason we claim that the pictures expand the words rather than duplicate them is that both word and image have substantial gaps in temporality. "He hid from Mama *every day*" implies the iterative. The picture illustrates merely one of many similar situations. The continuation "in the clock, or somewhere else" is a verbal gap that the picture leaves open, since it only shows the baby sleeping inside the clock, while the indefinite number of other options is left for the viewer's imagination. In fact, the baby might be hiding under the bed in the verso picture. The temporal and causal relation between verso and recto is not as immediate as in *Millions of Cats.*

In the next spread, the verso shows the baby hanging in the lamp. The text may seem redundant, but it only says that the baby "got up [ . . . ] and hung himself on the lamp." The picture shows how he has done this: the open drawers and a stool on the chest allow us to follow the implied movement. The recto picture is a direct effect of this action, and the words are still more open: "Poor Mama woke from the crash. But the baby managed of course and ran away to hide at tremendous speed." In the picture, the baby is indeed running toward the edge, into the next spread and next piece of mischief.

Since *The Wild Baby* has an episodic plot, almost every spread has a similar composition, with the verso showing a prank and the recto the result or outcome of it. The repetition of the pattern is a pedagogical as well as aesthetic device, training the viewer to make the temporal and causal connection between the facing pages.

Some scholars have suggested the notions of "home page" (or secure page) for verso and "away page" "adventure page" for recto.[7] This is not an absolute rule, but quite often the verso establishes a situation, while the recto disrupts it; the verso creates a sense of security, while the recto brings danger and excitement. Consider the first spread of *The Wild Baby:* the verso shows the mother nagging at the baby, who has already turned his back to her, heading into the recto where he is doing all the dangerous things his mother warns him against.

## Pageturners

Perry Nodelman makes a point of picturebook pictures being different from works of art in their composition, since every picture in a picturebook (except perhaps the last one) is supposed to encourage the viewer to go on reading.[8]

We have already used the term "pageturner" in different contexts, assuming it to be self-explanatory. Pageturner in a picturebook corresponds to the notion of cliffhanger in a novel. In the novel, a detail at the end of a chapter creates suspense and urges the reader to go on reading; in a picturebook, a pageturner is a detail, verbal or visual, that encourages the viewer to turn the page and find out what happens next. As we consider this dynamic design feature of the book, we see an escalation of the degree of reader involvement in bringing a sense of movement to the book.

In symmetrical books, pageturners are most often verbal. The most primitive pageturner is used, for instance, in flap-books: "Where is the dog?"— (open the flap)—"The dog is under the table" (e.g. *Where's Spot?,* by Eric Hill, 1980). In *Where Is My Puppy?* (1995), by Ilon Wikland, the question is only asked in the title, but the whole book is based on the boy's searching for his dog. The pageturner is the dog, who is hiding from the boy. While the verbal text states that the dog is not in the living room, not in the boy's room, not in the bathroom, not in the bedroom, and so on, the visual text allows the viewer to see what the boy does not see: the tip of the dog's tail, an ear, a paw, or even the whole dog fully visible from our perspective.

In many books pageturners are symmetrical, the visual and verbal aspects being mutually redundant. In H. A. Rey's *Curious George* (1941), George sees a girl buying a balloon and stretches his hand to take one himself, "but—" says the verbal text, while the picture shows George snatching the whole bunch of balloons, and we can easily anticipate what happens in the next spread.

The thread in *The Story About Somebody* (1951), by Åke Löfgren and Egon Möller-Nielsen, and in *The Red Thread* (1987), by Tord Nygren, are visual pageturners since they urge the viewer to search for the continuation of the thread in the next page. In the wordless *Do You Want to Be My Friend* (1971), by Eric Carle, the mysterious green line running through the book, which appears to be a snake, is the obvious visual pageturner. In fact, most pageturners in picturebooks are visual. The recurrent figure of the wild baby in the lower left-hand corner of the spread, running toward the edge and into the next spread, is a visual pageturner, never doubled by words.

In Jan Lööf's *Peter's Flashlight* (1978), every two spreads are connected by an iconotextual/symmetrical pageturner. The boy, who is afraid of the dark, sees monsters around him, but as he flashes his flashlight at them, they turn—in the subsequent spread—into a backhoe, a pile of barrels, or a tree. The plot is based on the apparent contradiction, verbal as well as visual, in the two connected spreads. As the book progresses, the plot becomes predictable; there are, however, details that add to the suspense. There is a visual sign that is important for the narrative but does not appear in the verbal text—the dog. It is present on all pages throughout the book, but it only emerges in the verbal text in the very last sequence, when the uncle asks the boy, "Have you seen my dog?" The boy says that he has not, but the dog is an additional visual pageturner that keeps the plot going. The viewers are expected to notice it and to correlate the verbal question "Have you seen my dog?" with what they have read from the pictures.

In *White and Black and All the Others* (1986), by Inger and Lasse Sandberg, the pageturner is both verbal and visual; however, it is implied rather than explicit. After the wall between the two countries has been pulled down, the white butterflies fly into the white country, and the black butterflies fly into the black country. The natural reaction, prompted by the words and pictures equally, is "But they will be invisible there!" And this is exactly what happens on the next spread. Unfortunately, the symmetrical iconotext creates a redundancy.

## Episodic Development and Direction Decoding

In discussing the reading of individual pictures, we suggested that the "natural" way to decode movement is left to right, the way we read words. Visual pageturners placed in the bottom right corner support this reading, since they prompt the reader to continue at the bottom left corner of the next spread. Most picturebook authors seem to have accepted this convention when they arrange the book in a single movement from left to right. Pat Hutchins's *Rosie's Walk* (1968), one of the favorite texts of many picturebook scholars, is the simplest and most consistent example of such a movement.[9]

Ivar Arosenius's *Journey with a Cat* (1908) is based on a sequence of similar episodes ("chain plot") that we assume take place one after another. It is supported by the verbal repetition of the temporal index "then" ("Then they met a cock," "Then they met a pig," "Then they met a goose," "Then they came to a river," and so on). In almost every picture, the girl riding the cat is placed on the left while the creatures they meet are placed on the right, so that the implied movement is left to right. There are, however, several exceptions. When the girl and the cat come to the city, they are portrayed from behind, so that we share their point of view. The line of sight thus moves away from the viewer and into the picture. In another page, the girl meets the king and accompanies his carriage for a while, moving from right to left. However, returning home, the girl and the cat continue to travel from left to right.

In *Millions of Cats,* Perry Nodelman notes, the man's journey takes him from left to right even when the return journey home is depicted.[10] This is not really true, since in the spread depicting the actual homecoming, the man and the cats move from right to left, from the "adventure page" into the "secure page." This seems to be another convention in many picturebooks: safe homecoming is accentuated by the right-to-left movement.

Conventional left-to-right visual narrative in Ivar
Arosenius's *The Journey with the Cat.*

However, a much more sophisticated book, such as Anthony Browne's
*The Tunnel* (1989), is also very clearly based on the left-to-right movement.
After the first establishing spread, in which the two characters are presented
first in close-ups and then in their respective settings (indoors for the girl, outdoors for the boy), the first, very cautious "adventure" is depicted when the
boy leaves his bedroom (his "own" space, security, in the verso) to frighten
his sister in her bedroom (alien space, recto). After that the brother and sister
are sent out—very promptly by the mother's hand pointing to the right—into
the next spread and into the awaiting danger. The scared sister is always
depicted to the left of her brother, closer to the security of home. In fact, in the
breakfast scene, he is pointing left with his hand—in sharp contrast with the
mother's gesture—suggesting that the sister's place is at home. The only significant deviation from the left-to-right movement is presented in the two pic-

tures in which first the boy and then the girl crawl into the tunnel: away from the reader, into the unknown and dangerous. Otherwise, the journey goes consistently from left to right, which is also accentuated by the sequence of framed pictures on some spreads, alternating with a little framed picture on the verso and a full-page picture on the recto ("expanding" space), a frameless, wordless doublespread (further expansion of space), and a little framed picture on the recto against a black background. The narrative tempo created by this variation is disturbing, which conveys the psychological charge of the book. The temporal relationship is especially tangible in the sequence of pictures where the stone figure is turning back into the boy: his static, awkward pose with a wide-open mouth and face distorted by horror is changing into a "softer and warmer" figure, as the verbal text suggests. The words also claim that the transformation happens "very slowly," "little by little," and the sequence of four pictures with very little movement conveys this slow and painful process. Interestingly enough, the color of the surrounding landscape changes as well, becoming more bright and vivid. However, the homecoming (logically right to left) is only depicted by words: "They ran back, through the forest, through the wood, into the tunnel, and out again."

The movement in Maurice Sendak's *Where the Wild Things Are* (1963) is quite complicated as compared to *Journey with a Cat* or *Millions of Cats,* and similar to that of *The Tunnel.* However, the two sea voyages, to and from the wild things' country, are portrayed as moving left to right, and right to left respectively. Conventional as it may be, these directions are based on the way we perceive certain visual patterns as harmonious or disharmonious, well-described in art criticism (see Figure 15).[11]

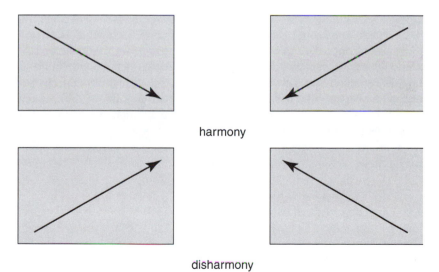

harmony

disharmony

**Figure 15.**

Homeward movement in *Journey to Ugri-La-Brek,* by Thomas and
Anna-Clara Tidholm.

A picturebook author may either deliberately or subconsciously subvert
harmony by breaking the convention of movement. In *Journey to Ugri-La-
Brek* (1987), by Thomas and Anna-Clara Tidholm, the movement on almost
every spread goes from left bottom to right top corner, in a diagonal that
according to art critics creates uneasiness. Even in the spread where the two
children do not move but rest beside a fire, the smoke from the fire continues
the diagonal. The sense of discomfort is amplified because the children are
going away from the viewer, into something unknown and frightening. This
is of course the theme and the message of the book (they are searching for
their dead grandfather). However, the viewer feels detached from the characters and may apprehend this as disturbing. On returning home, the children
still move left to right, however, they follow a more harmonious diagonal, left
top to right bottom, which perhaps reestablishes a sense of security.

It is once again apparent that reading pictures left to right is a convention
that has to do with our reading words, in a linear movement, left to right. We
will illustrate the conventionality with two brief examples.

*There's a Nightmare in my Closet* (1968), by Mercer Mayer, is a banal
story, obviously inspired by Sendak's *Where the Wild Things Are.* There is,
however, something strange in the spatial organization of the pictures. While
in most picturebooks, for instance *Wild Things,* danger appears from the
right, from the "adventure page," in this book the monsters appear from the
left, the "home page," and the secure bed is placed to the right." In the second

spread, the verso picture shows the boy getting out of bed on the left side, and in the recto picture he is closing the closet door, which both in the previous and in the subsequent doublespreads is situated *to the left* of the bed. The whole movement of the plot, including the direction of the boy's gaze and the page-turners, is oriented right to left, contrary to logic. The only possible explanation is that the book was originally produced for copublication in Israel. Since the Hebrew text is read right to left, the pictures were made to support this movement. In the Hebrew edition, the flow of words and pictures are in full accord. However, for a Western edition, it would have been prudent to reverse the pictures.[12] The publishers must have been at least partially aware of the problem, since the cover picture is indeed reversed in the Hebrew edition as compared to the American one; in both cases, the movement of the cover is "correct," that is, following the direction of the print and leading the character into the book.

In the Arabic translation of *The Wild Baby,* the text is also read right to left. However, the publisher was obviously unaware of the significance of visual reading. Instead of being reversed, the pictures merely change place. As a result, the baby on the recto walks out of the picture, back into title page, while on the verso he walks back from the dangers of the hall into the security of his mother's drawing room. The movement becomes illogical and completely out of balance (see page 158).

These examples prompt all kinds of experiments possible today through various technical means: What happens if we reverse pictures or whole spreads in picturebooks? The importance of balanced movement becomes all the more evident. Anyone who has given lectures on picturebooks accompanied by slides has at some time experienced the discomfort that occurs when pictures get reversed in the projector. In nine out of ten cases you notice this even if there are no words to reveal the mistake.

## Temporal Duration in Words and Pictures

While the verbal text, even though it may contain temporal ellipses, is somewhat continuous and linear, pictures are always discontinuous. From the visual text alone these is no way to judge how much time has passed between the two pictures.

Further, the duration of a verbal text—that is, the relation between story timespan and discourse timespan—is relatively determinable. It can be more or less identical "isochronical"; in narratology this pattern is called a *scene*. If the story time is longer than the discourse time we are dealing with a *summary*. The extreme form of summary is an *ellipsis*: discourse time is zero. However, discourse time, can be longer than story time, for instance by means of descriptions, deviations and comments. When story time is zero while discourse time goes on, we are dealing with a *pause*.

Antithetical movement: In the Arabic version of *The Wild Baby,* with reversed right-to-left verbal text, the pictures are unchanged.

Determining the duration of a visual text presents considerable difficulty: How long time does the action in a picture last? And it is hard to assess the discourse time: How long does it take to narrate a picture? Since a picture is static, we might suggest that its story time is zero, while its discourse time is indefinitely long. That is, in narratological terminology, the duration pattern of a picture is a pause.

On the other hand, if a static picture conveys motion (for instance, through simultaneous succession), its story time may be shorter (rapid movement) or longer (slow movement), but more than zero. Its discourse time may be equal to story time, especially with slow movement, resulting in a visual scene. It can hypothetically be shorter, if the succession depicts a period of many years, as in medieval hagiography, or at least many days, resulting in a visual summary (the kitten in *Millions of Cats* growing "nice and plump"). Finally, it can be longer—a pattern so seldom observed in narrative prose that it lacks a special term. It is, however, close to a descriptive pause.

Dealing with a sequence of pictures, either on the same spread or different spreads, we encounter various forms of ellipses. Verbal ellipses can be either definite (when it is specified that two hours, five days, or ten years have passed) or indefinite ("He walked a long, long time," *Millions of Cats*); explicit (when the text specifies that some time has passed) or implicit. Without devices such as the image of a clock to communicate the passage of specific time, visual ellipses can only be indefinite and implicit.

Let us return to the wordless picturebook *Moonlight*. The story time is perhaps two or three hours, beginning with the family having supper and ending with their falling asleep. The compact story time means that ellipses between individual frames are apprehended as very short, sometimes as short as the few seconds it takes the girl to turn her head. Other ellipses may last from several minutes—between being in the bath and having just got out of it—to the half hour or so between the mother falling asleep and the father waking up.

By contrast, in the episodic *Wild Baby* the temporal ellipses between spreads are indeterminably long, lasting from several hours (from day to night or the other way around) to several months. The words do not supply any information, as they only say "One day" or "One night" or "Another day."

In *Rosie's Walk*, the very fact that the verbal text consists only of one sentence makes us apprehend the visual ellipses as practically nonexistent. Similarly, we might assume, the first three spreads of *Where the Wild Things Are*, held together by one sentence, would be perceived as having no ellipses between pictures. However, the duration is more complicated. The verbal statement "made mischief of one kind/and another," divided between two spreads, leaves a substantial gap. The two spreads show us two of many possible mischievous acts. Both pictures are dynamic, implying motion and temporal duration, but it is impossible to say how much time each piece of mischief takes and how much time passes between them. In the third spread, there is a temporal ellipsis that is required for the mother to discover what Max has done, confront him, and send him to bed. In the previous picture we see a staircase, apparently leading to Max's room, but he may have climbed the steps slowly and reluctantly, or rushed up chased by his angry mother.

The ellipsis between this and the next spread, although intensified by the temporal index "That very night," also is indefinite. The whole book reflects a tension in the subjective time perception of a child, living several years in his imagination, and the objective adult time, which may take just a few minutes, before the mother comes upstairs with the boy's warm supper. The repetition of the words "grew/and grew—/and grew," again divided between three spreads, and intensified by the magical transformations in the room and by Max's changed facial expression and bodily position, creates a sense of a very quick motion, but the sequence can equally convey a longer duration, with slow, gradual changes. The boy's subjective sense of time is expressed verbally by "through night and day and in and out of weeks and almost over a year," while the two pictures illustrate only two episodes of this long journey. The visual ellipsis is thus filled by words. The most obvious ellipsis, verbal as well as visual, occurs in the three wordless spreads depicting "the wild rumpus." The transition from night to day, as well as the changed phase of the moon, implies a longer timespan, at least within the fantastic secondary time.

In John Burningham's Shirley books (1977–78), there is a discrepancy between the short duration of the "realistic" verso pictures and the long time of the adventure. While in both narratives there are visual ellipses between individual pictures, we apprehend the ellipses of the realistic level as short and the ellipses of the fantastic level as long.

The different duration patterns determine the tempo of the text. Alternating scenes and summaries speed up or slow down the narrative. Pauses stop the plot development altogether. Ellipses allow quick progress in time. In a picturebook, verbal and visual duration patterns most often conflict. The most common temporal combination is verbal summary (story time longer than discourse time) and visual pause (story time zero, discourse time indefinitely long). While the words encourage the reader to go on, the images demand that we stop and devote a considerable time to reading the picture. In this, the picturebook medium is radically different from film, where discourse time is predestined. Film critics are often obliged to study the composition of individual shots by "freezing" the narrative, but this is not the normal way to perceive the film.

Whether an individual picture is static or conveys motion, the more details there are in a picture, the longer its discourse time. The common prejudice is that children do not like descriptions, preferring scenes and dialogue.

This must be an acquired preference, imposed on children by adults, since all empirical research shows that children, as well as adults, appreciate picture-book pauses and eagerly return to them.

## Movement: Direction and Counterdirection

We have earlier argued that we normally read pictures left to right, just as we read words. However, considering a picture as a narrative pause, we must now interrogate this statement. If a picture is totally symmetrical with the words, that is, it functions as mere decoration and does not contribute any new information, we may indeed read it left to right and quite quickly. For instance, in a spread from *Strit* (1943), by Grete Janus Hertz and Bengt Janus, the words "Here are Per and Ola" accompany a picture of two boys. Reading the picture left to right, we assume that the boy on the left is Per and the boy on the right is Ola. In the more complicated but still symmetrical *Millions of Cats,* the verbal description of the old man's journey is accompanied by the visual description, which we are supposed to read left to right. However, we are not as bound to this as in reading words (which we after all cannot read backward). We may identify the figure of the old man on the recto first, follow his route to the right edge of the page, return to verso and the picture of his house, and then follow the whole journey left to right. Yet the clear linear movement of the picture invites us to follow it.

In pictures without a persuasive linear pattern and with many details, our reading is arbitrary. The artist may deliberately or unconsciously place a detail in the picture that will attract our attention and compel us to start reading the picture from this point. Since individual readers fill visual gaps differently, the actual pattern of reading a complicated picture can vary indefinitely. However, if the words, even though they may be few, are well balanced against the images, they will prompt the reader's decoding of at least the most essential elements of the visual text. Notably, intraiconic words have exactly this function (for instance, "Brancusi" in *The Egg*).

While many picturebook illustrators actively promote left-to-right decoding of their pictures, often as a way of developing reading readiness by teaching the conventions of the book (at least in the Western tradition), others may challenge this. Two such examples are provided by Tord Nygren's *The Red Thread* and Colin Thompson's *Looking for Atlantis*. While *The Red Thread* offers a metafictive approach by making the direction of decoding and the notion of linearity a subject of his work, Thompson sharpens the visual acuity of his readers by challenging their powers of perception and their ability to decode often surreptitious detail in a nonlinear fashion. From the beginning, *The Red Thread* demands that the reader/viewer consider circular and linear patterns. The front endpaper juxtaposes the carousel's circular movement

Challenging the linear reading: *The Red Thread,* by Tord Nygren.

with the flight of the runaway carousel horse, broken from its moorings, which follows the path of the red thread from left to right. Yet the following title-page spread sets the horizontal line of the thread and of the horizon against the view of the child and the reader; like the path of the boat, the horizontal lines cross the transverse ones. As we are made aware of our tendency to perceive beginnings and ends (the hatching egg toward the beginning, the bee's funeral toward the end of the book), we are also alerted to the atemporal and nonlinear nature of creativity and mocked for our need to find order even when it is not inherent in what we see.

The doublespread featuring the joyful chaos of creativity defies any left-to-right decoding. While the red thread may carry our eye from the left to the right margin in its meandering path, it can carry it back in the other direction just as well. Better still, the eye is free to roam in any direction, catching the effervescence of music and color depicted. While a man in a checkered outfit kicks an ink bottle to the right of the spread, forming an ink blot in the shape of a witch heading for the edge of the page, a contrasting surge of movement runs from right to left as a band of rainbow-color characters run from their paint boxes toward the center of the picture. The ten rainbow strips (several of which are led by butterflies), emerging from the flute, French horn, and bass trio, travel in arcs that point left, right, and straight up. The recorder player facing bottom right is balanced by the boy rolling a big red *C* toward the left. As a boy emerges right from a sketchbook, a cat slips out to the left. And pen, pencil and brush, engaged in the creation of the woman's gown, all point left, as does the slant of the drawing board on which the fanciful creatures perch.

Besides these directional balances, the nature of the relationship between groups on the page is primarily independent. Two observers are present, the girl in white at the bottom left and the man at top right. They are completely unconnected. The figures create a collage rather than a picture, though a pencil sketch lying on the drawing board suggests a design. A fuzzy rabbit chews on an unpleasantly surprised crescent moon. A boy plays with a truck and his ABC. A green witch with a long nose sweeps musical notes off a sheet of music into a heap at the bottom. A woman and two children rendered in black and white except for the flowers they carry stand adjacent to a tin lid holding a dead bee, which is in color and in different proportion. Even the group of musicians seem to come from different traditions. The bassist performs in traditional conservative evening dress, with bow tie and high collar; the French-horn player is still in process of design, but her hair is spangled with stars or flowers; while the flute player, with conical hat, billowy tunic, and doll-like red patches on the cheeks, appears to be in costume. Finally, the drawing board itself is set against a discontinuous background: day and night, beach and city are all represented.

While some of the doublespreads use different conventions, including the definitive left-to-right motion of the last page and back endpaper, Nygren clearly alerts us to the variety of ways in which a picture may communicate to us. The pictures can be read in as many directions as the only words that appear in the book: "sator/rotas, opera/arepo," and "tenet" reads the conjurer's board, which can be decoded backward, forward, up and down, though we must turn the book on its head to see this!

The American edition of *Looking for Atlantis* is advertised at <amazon.com> as a book for four-to-eight-year-olds, and the inside cover suggests that children can search the book in order to count the number of fish, doors, books, mice, birds, stairs and/or ladders, boats, and trees. In addition, another exercise is recommended: "How carefully do you look at people around you? Take five seconds to look at the next person who enters the room. Then close your eyes and see how much you remember." As these pedagogical applications (which are not in the original British edition) turn the book into a puzzle or game, they also countermand the usual notion of reading a narrative as a sequentially developing series of actions or events, and of decoding the pictures in support of this narrative.

Whatever the possible applications, the book itself stands as a developing narrative, and the illustrations advance the theme of the story that the search for Atlantis, or whatever imaginative and inspirational image for "hopes and dreams" one prefers, will be successful if one can "learn how to look." Nonetheless, the notion of "learning how to look" is episodic, with each picture offering a new and different environment and opportunity. Although in most cases where there is narrative text it appears on the left side of the doublespread, the illustrations themselves do not support a left-to-right movement. Rather, they suggest a nondirective motion, a deliberate scanning for detail with humorous rewards and reinforcement in the amusing minipictures, word play, in-jokes, and unaccustomed juxtaposition. As such they present a counterpoint to the narrative text, not only by means of intraiconic text, but through images whose relationship to the narrative is most often just a reference to water.

While the penultimate three doublespreads are clearly directive in their use of arrows and staircases, they are strongly outnumbered by the others. The bathroom picture is a good, simple example: the bath balanced by the washbasin and toilet; the mouse entering the pipes on the left balanced by the lizard entering on the right; a left arrow above a right one; steps at the bottom right balanced by those reflected in the mirror on the left. The detail below the bathroom floor draws the eye down below the main picture, so that any tendency to move in one direction is counterbalanced by its reverse.

More complex is the kitchen scene with its intriguing verbal and visual images. The mice's store, which includes a box of "spare squeaks," "tail tonic," and "2nd user teabags," provides some verbal fun, while the mousetrap, which is about to be eliminated by sticks of explosive set by the mice, rewards the eye searching for images.

The Grandfather's chest holds among a multitude of objects cannonball cream, macho mariner biscuits with extra weevils, a saxophone full of flowers, a porthole window, a plate of egg and fries, and a Swiss navy knife with a paintbrush and a mushroom included among its folding blades. There is no order nor prioritization among these objects—one is as fascinating as another and the eye wanders aimlessly and distractedly among them seeking new treasures. (See illustration on page 22.)

"You Have/ To Learn How/ To /Look" states a series of book titles on the shelf of the television room. Through a crosssection of the armchair facing the boy one sees a complete mouse residence with bunk beds, hammocks, staircases, and cozy balls of upholstery stuffing, while on the shelf are books entitled "Romeo and Jellyfish" and "Prawn Free." Supporting the watery theme are various aquariums and bottles and screens with sea scenes.

While Nygren's book is much more sophisticated than Thompson's, particularly in its studied and thought-provoking visual commentary on cultural and artistic traditions, both provide a strong counterthrust to the narrative linear movement that drives many picturebooks.

We can thus conclude that in their duration patterns, picturebooks are contradictory by definition. This does not, however, prevent symmetrical books from duplicating pictures with words. The effect of the visual pause is then disturbed, and a fixed discourse time is imposed on the reader.

## More Complex Temporal Relations

The various deviations from straight, chronological narrative order, the so-called anachronies, are traditionally regarded as unsuitable for children, and have only recently become prominent in children's novels.

Complex temporality is often limited in picturebooks because of their compact nature, which excludes long time spans. The vast majority of picturebooks have a short story time, often just one day or even less. We would, however, like to give some brief examples of anachronies, all the time bearing in mind the counterpoint of the visual and the verbal aspect.

### *Analepses*

An analepsis (flashback, switchback) is a secondary narrative that precedes the primary one. The verbal expression of analepses does not differ from that in a novel. However, in the interaction between word and image, several solutions are possible. In Sven Nordqvist's *The Hat Hunt* (1987), Grandpa finds himself remembering his childhood, prompted by the sight of some objects he owned as a little boy: a tin soldier, a watch chain, a pocketknife, a magnet, and a whistle. The process of remembering itself may be an allusion—on the sophisticated reader's level—to Proust. The words mark an explicit temporal change: "Now he saw [ . . . ] He was only seven years old then [ . . . ]". The two doublespreads depicting the memory are divided into two distinct pictorial spaces, the analepsis represented by a kind of a thought balloon, with yellowish colors reminiscent of old, faded, photographs. The first scene is static, while the second is presented in simultaneous succession, read in a semicircle clockwise. The style is deliberately different from the boisterous primary story, not only in the soft colors, but in a much more "realistic" manner, imitating contemporary picturebooks set in the past. The analepsis is explicit. However, both scenes are more or less symmetrical to the verbal text.

Analepses in John Burningham's *Granpa* (1984) are much more sophisticated. They are not marked as anachronies in the text. In fact, the verbal text has two parallel stories, both in direct speech. Granpa's speech is printed in ordinary typeface, while the little girl's is in italics. In the spread portraying the girl and Granpa singing, she is creating her own, rather nonsensical song, while Granpa is singing a traditional children's song. We have already considered this spread in terms of characterization; let us now consider it in terms of temporality. The colored drawing on the recto—which represents the primary story—features them both singing, with an array of toys around them.

Explicit visual analepsis in Sven Nordqvist's *Hat Hunt*.

The line drawing on the verso is an implicit analepsis, describing a scene from Granpa's childhood, clearly depicted by the children's clothing. The memory is obviously prompted by the song.

In the spread depicting a winter scene, the recto shows the girl and Granpa on a slope, while the line drawing of the verso shows Granpa as a little boy, going down the same slope on a sled, together with some friends. His words duplicate the picture: "Harry, Florence and I used to come down this hill like little arrows," while the girl says: *"You nearly slipped then, Granpa,"* bringing the narrative time back to the primary story.

In both spreads, there is a delicate balance between the verso and the recto, where the words emphasize the two stories. In the rest of the book, the verso illustrations either comment upon the recto in some way or else represent a fantasy or a dream (contrary to Shirley books, where the dream pictures are in full color and placed on the recto). However, while the two analepses clearly focalize Granpa, the rest of the verso pictures may equally be the girl's or Granpa's visions, and the very last picture of the girl, facing the empty chair, may equally be interpreted as an omniscient narrator's point of view or the girl's. Visually, it can only be the omniscient perspective, because we do not share the girl's literal point of view. However, metaphorically, it can be the girl's.

Note that in both books, visual analepses are used in conjunction with old people's memories. They also lie outside the primary story, the so-called external analepses. The reach of analepses is beyond the implied (child) reader's experience, but well within the experience of the protagonists.

In the last spread of *The Wild Baby,* the baby's encounter with the wolf is told visually in the form of speech balloons. This is an internal analepsis that is part of the primary story. It may also be called a completing analepsis, filling an earlier ellipsis. The reach of the analepsis is short, for the baby is just telling about something that happened to him some hours before. The visual analepsis is duplicated by words, which creates redundancy.

### Prolepses

A prolepsis (flashforward, anticipation) is a secondary narrative that is moved ahead of the time of the primary narrative.

A visual prolepsis can be illustrated by *The Egg*. Two thirds of the book involves prolepses describing the protagonist's visions of the future. It is, however, only by means of words that we can know we are dealing with a prolepsis: these include verbal reminders, such as "the egg thought," or metafictive/extradiegetic comments, such as "I have never seen / . . . / but I haven't seen anything else either—yet."

### Paralepses

One of the most interesting types of anachrony in children's fiction at large is a paralepsis, a secondary narrative the time of which is independent of the time in the primary story. In his analysis of Sendak's *Outside Over There* (1981), Stephen Roxburgh maintains that the whole story takes place between the two steps taken by Ida's baby sister.[13] The temporal paradox of *Where the Wild Things Are* has been discussed by many scholars. In the paralepsis, Max travels "through night and day and in and out of weeks and almost over a year" and then back "over a year and in and out of weeks and through a day and into the night" while primary time stands still, and when Max comes back he finds his supper warm and waiting for him. The flow of the secondary time is indicated verbally, while the primary time is only implied by the warm supper. However, the visual signs contradict the "objective" primary time: there is a new moon in one of the first pictures in the book and a full moon in the last.

Most picturebooks describing an imaginary journey involve paraleptic temporality, since the magical journey cannot possibly be fitted into the short timespan of the primary narrative. However, very few books make extensive use of visual means to convey this temporal feature.

In *The Wild Baby Goes to Sea* (1982), the pictures show both day and night seascapes, while the words repeat the temporal index "then." The journey is concluded at twelve o'clock, which is indicated verbally and visually, by the picture of a clock. In the picture, fantastic and real space merge. Half of the picture is light, the other dark with a full moon, so both words and picture are ambivalent as to whether "twelve o'clock" implies noon or midnight. The next picture, however, leaves no doubt: it is broad daylight, so the journey has not taken more than a few hours of primary time.

In *Journey to Ugri-La-Brek,* the journey involves a change of day and night, which is depicted visually and occasionally supported by words: "It is now evening and dark [ . . . ] Now [ . . . ] the sun has risen." Furthermore, autumn changes into winter, and the words state: "They travel for a thousand years, and they become a thousand years old [ . . . ] their shoes are worn out, and all the cakes are eaten up." Also, travel back takes "a thousand years, but much quicker, because it is homeward." The picture of traveling home is a simultaneous succession and has both a night and a morning scene.

### Achrony

Achrony implies that the temporal deviation from the primary story cannot be placed in any given moment within the scope of the story. While achronies are extremely rare outside purely experimental prose, we may claim that all pictures are achronical. Pictures by definition cannot have a direct temporal relation to words or to other pictures; they are not directly connected with any given moment of the verbal or visual narrative. We apprehend the individual spreads of *Come Into My Night* as having a temporal-causal order because we expect narratives to have it. However, several spreads in the middle of the story can easily change places. Most episodes in *The Red Thread* are achronical, even though a potential narrative line in the book is ironically implied.

### Syllepses

A syllepsis is an anachronical narrative connected to the primary narrative by any other relation than temporal, for instance spatial or thematic. Jane Doonan uses the term "running stories" for visual narratives introducing minor characters not mentioned in the verbal text.[14] A good example of visual syllepses is provided by the wordless narratives told by the small creatures in the foregrounds of Festus and Mercury books. These creatures, never mentioned by words of the primary narrative, seem to live totally independent lives of their own. However, in their actions they are influenced by the events in the primary narrative or at least are thematically connected to it. Another example is *Hey Presto! You Are a Bear!* (1977), by Janosch, in which the child and father's play is accompanied by the various pranks and adventures of a cat and two mice in the foreground.

In *I Can Drive All Cars,* by Karin Nyman and Tord Nygren, which in itself is a very simple story, the illustrator, like Nordqvist and Janosch, puts small figures on every page, mostly musicians playing violin, cello, flute, clarinet, harp, concertina, guitar, and so on. Apparently, when the readers get sufficiently familiar with the primary story they are encouraged to "read" the syllepsis, discovering the musicians on subsequent pages, sometimes well disguised in the landscape. There are also some other stories, or rather allusions to stories, and famous figures, for instance Santa Claus flying a helicopter, Nils Holgersson on a goose, and Thumbelina on a swallow, as well as details and characters that are definitely out of place in the setting of the primary story.

Some picturebooks are deliberately constructed in sylleptical patterns. Mitsumasa Anno's *Journey* (1977) has been analyzed by many critics without making use of the notion of syllepsis.[15] In this wordless picturebook, the viewer is encouraged to find tiny characters in every spread (including the protagonist and implied narrator) and follow their separate adventures throughout the book.

*Charlotte's Piggy Bank* (1996), by David McKee, is apparently derivative from *Journey,* but it takes the whole idea of a sylleptical narrative one step further. Unlike *Journey*, there is a verbal story in the book, but a rather primitive one, with a strange and unsatisfactory resolution. It may even feel frustrating, but it is perhaps a deliberate device from the author used in order to draw the reader's attention to the other aspects of the narrative. The story of Charlotte and her animated piggy bank is accompanied by basically symmetrical pictures, but these pictures are minor details on every spread. Around

Sylleptic visual narrative in Sven Nordqvist's *Pancake Pie* (detail).

Charlotte made a stall in the street and sold the toys that she didn't want any more. "You're nearly full," said Charlotte as she put the money in the pig. The pig said nothing.

Sylleptic visual narratives in David McKee's *Charlotte's Piggy Bank.*

Charlotte's rather unimaginative everyday activities, dynamic and extensive life is going on, and on close examination, as in *Journey,* figures or groups of figures with stories of their own can be pursued through the book. The most prominent is an elderly couple with identical heart-formed marks on their T-shirt and shopping bag. The lady spies out the man, follows him, manages to attract his attention, and they get into conversation and apparently discover common interests, dancing happily on the pavement in the last spread. Other stories are probably slightly more difficult to trace, since the characters do not always appear on subsequent spreads. Two young people walking their dogs and constantly getting tangled in the leashes seem to have found each other too, as have the two roller skaters. A man on a bicycle buys a bunch of flowers and finally arrives safely at his sweetheart's door. The priest choosing a postcard in the first spread is carrying it, written and with a stamp attached, in the last. Each story apparently has its own duration independent of the primary verbal-visual narrative, which takes at least some weeks.

Some scenes demand a keen eye to be perceived as scenes in the throng of other figures, for instance two female flight attendants waving to each other across the page, or a man and a woman obviously waiting for each other at different corners, looking impatiently at their watches. Some people just seem to be walking around purposelessly, reappearing from time to time: a man talking on his mobile phone, a motorcyclist, and others. A variety of single episodes adds to the general commotion: thefts, car accidents, lovers meeting, ladies gossiping, tourists taking pictures. On the last spread, just as Charlotte's piggy flies away on its magically acquired wings, a boy is given a similar pink spotted piggy bank and the first coin to put into it, suggesting that the story goes on beyond the last page. In the same spread, McKee has a self-quotation portraying two children from his picturebook *I Hate My Teddy Bear* (1982).

With the enormous richness of detail, the primary story loses its interest. This is probably supposed to demonstrate the image's superiority over the word. The distorted perspective of each spread adds to the humorous effect.

To conclude our discussion of temporality in picturebooks, we would like to point out once again that books that do not make use of the picturebook medium's special ways of conveying time and movement are often those we apprehend as "complementary," where pictures merely "illustrate" one static episode of the verbal narrative.

# Notes

1. A chronotope as a literary notion, introduced by Mikhail Bakhtin, implies an entity of temporal and spatial relationships expressed in a text. See Mikhail Bakhtin, "The Forms of Time and Chronotope in the Novel," in his *The Dialogic Imagination* (Austin: University of Texas Press, 1981): 84. See further Maria Nikolajeva, *The Magic Code: The Use of Magical Patterns in Fantasy for Children* (Stockholm: Almqvist & Wiksell International, 1988). On the specific nature of the picturebook chronotope see Maria Nikolajeva, *Children's Literature Comes of Age: Toward a New Aesthetic* (New York: Garland, 1996): 133–136.

2. See Joseph H. Schwarcz, *Ways of the Illustrator: Visual Communication in Children's Literature* (Chicago: American Library Association, 1982); William Moebius, "Introduction to Picturebook Codes," *Word and Image* 2 (1986) 2: 141–158; Perry Nodelman, *Words About Pictures: The Narrative Art of Children's Picture Books* (Athens: The University of Georgia Press, 1988); Ulla Rhedin, *Bilderboken: På väg mot en teori* (Stockholm: Alfabeta, 1993); Jane Doonan, *Looking at Pictures in Picture Books* (Stroud: Thimble Press, 1993).

3. Scott McCloud, *Understanding Comics* (Northampton, MA: Tundra, 1993).

4. See Nodelman, op. cit.: Schwarcz, op. cit.: 23–33. Schwarcz also offers some psychological explanations of the ways in which readers perceive motion in a static picture that we find ambiguous and therefore prefer not to consider at this point.

5. E.g. Alfred Clemens Baumgärtner, "Erzählung und Abbild. Zur bildnerischen Umsetzung literarischer Vorlagen," in *Aspekte der gemalten Welt: 12 Kapitel über das Bilderbuch von heute,* ed. Alfred Clemens Baumgärtner, 65–81 (Weinheim: Verlag Julius Beltz, 1968); Alfred Clemens Baumgärtner, "Das Bilderbuch: Geschichte - Formen - Rezeption," in *Bilderbücher im Blickpunkt verschiedener Wissenschaften under Fächer,* ed. Bettina Paetzold and Luis Erler, 4–22 (Bamberg: Nostheide, 1990); Dietrich Grünewald, "Kongruenz von Wort und Bild: Rafik Schami und Peter Knorr: Der Wunderkasten," in *Neue Erzählformen im Bilderbuch,* ed. Jens Thiele, 17–49 (Oldenburg: Isensee, 1991).

6. Cf. Joseph H. Schwarcz's remark that "the continuous narrative causes the visual text to become linear to some extent," Schwarcz, op. cit.: 30.

7. E.g. Rhedin, op. cit.: 178–182.

8. Nodelman, op. cit.:126.

9. See more examples in Nodelman, op. cit.: 163ff.

10. Nodelman, op. cit.: 163.

11. See, e.g., Rudolf Arnheim, *Art and Visual Perception* (Berkeley: University of California Press, 1974).

12. Cf. a similar argument in Schwarcz, op. cit.: 30.

13. Stephen Roxburgh, "A Picture Equals How Many Words? Narrative Theory and Picture Books for Children," *The Lion and the Unicorn* 7–8 (1983): 20–33.

14. Doonan, op. cit.

15. E.g. Nodelman, op. cit.: 188f.

# CHAPTER 6

# Mimesis and Modality

## Mimetic and Nonmimetic Representation

This chapter will focus upon the contrasts between mimetic, or literal, and nonmimetic, or symbolic, representation, that is, statements we interpret as a direct reflection or imitation ("mimesis") of reality as opposed to statements we know we must interpret on different levels, for instance as symbols or metaphors. We will be examining the ways in which picturebooks' word–illustration dynamic presents narratives that embody contradiction between the two modes of apprehension involved in the mimetic and the nonmimetic.

The essence of this opposition can be conveyed by the concept of modality, a linguistic notion covering categories such as possibility, impossibility, contingency, or necessity of a statement. Modality enables us to decide on the degree of truth in the communication we receive. Mimetic interpretation means that we decode the received communication as true ("this has happened," which is termed "indicative modality"). Symbolic, transferred, nonmimetic interpretation encourages us to decode texts as expressing a possibility ("it may have happened"), an impossibility ("this cannot have happened"), a desire ("I wish it happened"), a necessity ("it should have happened"), or probability ("I believe that it has happened"), and so on. As empirical research often demonstrates, unsophisticated readers tend to interpret texts mimetically, identifying with protagonists and sharing their individual perception.

We have chosen to speak about modality rather than genre, since picturebooks, more than any other kind of children's fiction, effectively blur the common distinction between genres, doing so by verbal as well as by visual means. We find that the concept of modality enables us to examine the intricate ways in which picturebooks convey the apprehension of reality, which always involves subjective aspects, without resorting to the rather artificial division of narratives into fantasy and realism. As we will show, the word–image interaction creates a significantly broader spectrum than this binarity

As always, the dual narrative of picturebooks presents us with an additional interpretive challenge. We believe that drawing the term "modality" from its linguistic context provides a complex range of subjective expression. This use of the term differs from its earlier use in picturebook criticism to refer to the apprehension of images alone and the ways in which they can convey a sense of reality. This latter, visual approach, developed by Gunther Kress and Theo van Leeuwen, depends rather on a simple spectrum that ascribes photography a higher degree of modality ("closer to the truth") and abstract or surrealist art a lower degree ("far away from truth").[1] While pictures alone can communicate this simpler spectrum, they are limited. Artists have means, based on conventions, to influence interpretation. For example, pictures of mythical creatures or unfamiliar or distorted objects are automatically apprehended by us as unreal, while photographic and other true-to-life images are apprehended as real. Unnatural colors, for instance red sky and blue glass, will also prompt us to interpret the picture as imaginary. But there are limitations to what can be communicated: in pictures without words, it is hard to tell whether what we see is real or unreal, a dream, a wish, a prescription, a permission, or a doubt.[2]

A sequence of visual images immediately creates a potential for the more complex kind of modality that we are discussing. And by adding verbal statements, the author can further force the viewer to adopt a particular interpretation. For instance, a landscape in a painting titled "A Dream" will most probably be interpreted as imaginary, even through the picture itself may be true-to-life.

Complex modality can be achieved through the interaction of words and images in picturebooks, so that the reader can decide whether to apply mimetic or symbolic interpretation. While the verbal story is often told from a child's point of view presenting the events as true, the details in pictures may suggest that the story only takes place in the child's imagination. The pictures thus subvert the verbal narrative's intended objectivity.[3] In all picturebooks with fantastic elements, as in fantasy novels, there can be at least two possible interpretations of the events. They can be accepted as having actually taken place, which means that as readers we accept magic as part of the fictional world created by the author; or the magic adventures may also be accounted for in a rational way, as the protagonist's dreams, visions, hallucinations, or imaginative experiences caused, for instance, by fever or psychical or emotional disturbance.[4]

In this chapter, we will explore the various ways the reinforcement and subversion of mimesis works in picturebooks. A symmetrical picturebook may permit the reader choice in deciding whether the story is intended as true or as play, dream, or imagination. But when verbal and visual texts are contradictory, there is a variety of options. For example, although the verbal and the visual text may support each other in general, a minor detail can be inserted that subverts the other's credibility: the detail may suggest that what was presented as true is in fact a dream, or vice versa (what we call the "Mary Poppins syndrome"). The verbal and visual texts may also offer quite different perspectives on events: for example, where the child describes a ghost in the verbal narrative, the pictures present the image of a curtain or a sheet so that the modality of words and pictures is contradictory. In the most dramatic cases, the verbal and visual texts contradict each other consistently, creating considerable ambivalence.

In our discussion, we will focus on three modalities: "indicative" (presenting the events as true), "optative" (expressing a desire), and "dubitative" (expressing a doubt). We have chosen a number of picturebooks with fantastic elements because the clash between mimetic and nonmimetic representation is more obvious in them; however, books with seemingly realistic settings and events can also contain elements of modality with words and pictures in counterpoint.

## Symmetrical Indicative: Verbal and Visual Narratives Both Present the Events as True

Let us start with some relatively simple cases. *Journey with a Cat* (1908), by Ivar Arosenius, does not problematize modality through words or through pictures: that is, the story is presented as true on both the verbal and the visual level (indicative modality). It is not a traditional fairy tale taking place in an imaginary realm, since the protagonist is an ordinary child. The text tells us that Lillan walks along a road and meets a cat who starts talking to her and offers her a ride on his back. There is no explanation of the cat's ability to talk, but Lillan is not astonished at this ability and takes it for granted. Literary conventions compel the reader to accept both the cat's supernatural quality and the further events, in the course of which the two adventurers meet all kinds of creatures and finally come to the king's palace. They are treated to a royal dinner, and the cat eats so much that his belly bursts and has to be sewn up. In the end, Lillan and the cat come back to the mother and, typically, are so tired that they go immediately to sleep.

Since the pictures are very simple, without backgrounds or details besides the essential, there is nothing in them suggesting either a mimetic or a symbolic interpretation. The initial agreement between the storyteller and the reader—that within its own fictional frames the story is true—lasts throughout the book. However, an adult, or objective, interpretation will prompt us to view the story as the child's imaginative play. The characters the girl and cat meet during their journey are all borrowed from a child's everyday experience: domestic animals (or perhaps toys) such as a cock, a pig, and a goose; some fish in a pond; some more dangerous animals, such as an aggressive cow and a crocodile; and some funny creatures, such as a horse wearing boots and a flowery waistcoat (mostly for the sake of the rhyme: "häst" with "väst" in Swedish). They also meet some people: an old man, a police officer, and a fine lady. Although the king is depicted as a fairy-tale character, wearing a crown and a fur coat, for a young Swedish reader the meeting is not totally implausible. This episode, including gluttony and its inevitable consequences, is also a commonplace in many early Swedish picturebooks;[5] thus for a child reader, the story carries intertextual links. But in order for the whole story to subvert its own credibility, we must step outside the text, into a didactic metatextual space (in which we as sophisticated readers know that the events described do not normally happen), since the iconotext itself creates an illusion of being mimetic. In terms of modality, words and pictures are consonant in suggesting the indicative nature of the narrative.

Another Swedish picturebook originating from almost the same time as *Journey with a Cat* is Elsa Beskow's *Peter's Voyage* (1921). A number of Elsa Beskow's picturebooks describe a fantastic journey,[6] usually employing the same unproblematical approach as Arosenius. *Peter's Voyage* is one of the interesting exceptions. The text and the pictures describe the boy and his teddy bear sailing away in a realistically depicted sailing boat, the mother waving from the shore. The setting is realistic too, but the voyage follows a typical fairy-tale development: they meet a gigantic fish, which the teddy bear bravely defeats; they get into a storm, come first to Africa and then to China, where the emperor offers the boy his daughter's hand in marriage. The boy, however, decides to go home, bringing as trophies a boatful of bananas and a little monkey from Africa. In the last picture, repeating the composition of the first one, the mother is happily meeting them on the shore. Nothing in the story suggests any ambivalence in its interpretation. The evidence, in the form of bananas and the monkey, is not questioned. The main iconotext thus establishes the modality as indicative.

However, in the cover illustration, the boy is shown steering a cardboard boat over a striped rug, with a makeshift mast and a handkerchief for a sail. The round frame of the picture accentuates the detached nature of the story. Thus, although the story itself, in words and pictures, suggests that the voyage is true, the cover subverts the indicative modality. Since we normally start reading picturebooks with the cover, the illustration manipulates the reader from the beginning to apprehend the story as play, establishing its modality as improbable. It is the metafictive detail of the visual text, commenting on the narrative mode, that determines our reading. The book is therefore slightly more complicated in its modality when compared to *Journey with a Cat*.

The cover of Elsa Beskow's *Peter's Voyage* contradicts the story.

## Symmetrical Optative: Both Verbal and Visual Narrative Present the Events as Desired

Inger Edelfeldt's *Through the Red Door* (1992) features an explicit boundary between reality and the imaginary world: the red door in the stone wall that the nameless girl protagonist discovers as she stands alone in the street while her father buys a newspaper. Over the door, which the girl is sure was not there a few moments earlier, we see a bronze mask of a man wearing a crown whose face resembles her father's and that anticipates the Weeping King she will meet in the dream realm. The female symbolism of the red color is transparent in the book: the color of blood, or more precisely, menstrual blood, is featured not only in the door, but in the red caravan of the fun-fair, the red horse of the merry-go-round, and the Red Country that lies beyond the fair. The verbal and the visual stories are symmetrical in their symbolism. Throughout, the prevailing visual imagery of the book compels the reader to choose a symbolic interpretation.

The images of the landscape beyond the red door are those of abandonment and desolation: the fun-fair is in ruins, and there are no friends to share the girl's adventure. There is a metafictive, self-commenting detail in the picture that is easy to miss: the puppet theater shows the likeness of the girl together with the Lion Boy she will meet later in the story. She rides the merry-go-round, until the red horse comes alive and runs away. The circular movement of the merry-go-round (childhood) is exchanged for linear progress (adolescence). The girl arrives "in the red forest where all trees bear fruit," but in this country the girl meets the Weeping King, the father's double, who intends to keep her forever in the eternity of childhood. The change in the girl's mood is conveyed by her facial expression and posture: happy and free when riding her red horse, she is pictured as depressed when locked in the King's castle or dancing for him.

The door to the world of the imagination in *Through the Red Door,* by Inger Edelfeldt.

When she meets the young male, Lion Boy, she can be happy again, but her loyalty is torn between the young man and the King, her father substitute, who applies emotional blackmail: if she leaves him, he will cry so much that his tears will flood the whole world. This threat is envisioned in a powerful picture where the King's face hovers over roaring waves, while the girl is depicted in the corner, with her head lowered and her hands hanging exhaustedly down. Lion Boy gives her a red apple to taste and she decides to escape with him, but when they reach the wall they must separate. However, he promises that "if you can find the red door again we shall meet once more!" As she finds her father waiting outside the wall, the door is pictured fading away in a reddish blur.

On the last page, the girl sits at her desk drawing pictures of a red horse and of a princess in a yellow dress. These visual details, together with images of a string doll reminiscent of the Lion Boy and the core of a red apple on her desk, support the interpretation of an imaginative adventure, something she has invented while waiting for her father in the street (desire, optative modality). But the verbal text gives no direct clues, referring only to the girl's determination to find the red door again and never to listen to the Weeping King.

Although the implications of the book are quite transparent as compared to many of the texts we are going to discuss later, the female author/illustrator's depiction of a female character's imaginary quest is of particular interest. The father-daughter relationship and the girl's transition from the father to a male companion demand a different type of story from most of those discussed below, and the book seems less structured on both the visual and the verbal level than the stories involving a male or gender-neutral child.

## Verbally Provoked Dubitative: A Few Statements Undermine the Credibility of the Iconotext

The most primitive way of subverting the indicative modality is to make an explicit verbal statement that the events are untrue, such as at the end of the famous Danish picturebook *Paul Alone in the World* (1942), by Jens Sigsgaard and Arne Ungermann. After breathtaking adventures, the protagonist wakes up to discover that his experience has only been a dream. Some readers might feel cheated since they have been applying the wrong modality through the text.[7]

A more subtle way to interrogate the credibility of the narrative would be to put the reader in doubt. In Tove Jansson's *The Dangerous Journey* (1977), the sudden transformation of reality into a magical world is accounted for in the verbal text: it is a pair of magical glasses that enable Susanna to enter the world of Moomins. The magic agent is similar to the door in Edelfeldt's *Through the Red Door*. The real and the magical worlds are clearly separated, and the presentation in words and in pictures is symmetrical. The cat from

Susanna's real world is transformed into a monster. Apart from that, there are no tokens of reality in the magical world. For an unsophisticated reader, the iconotext is constructed in the indicative mode, conveying the protagonist's subjective perception of her experience. For a sophisticated reader, the book invites psychoanalytical interpretations with its many powerful images, and the journey is thus treated as an exploration of self—the fears, aggressions, and other dark sides of the psyche.[8] In this reading, the modality of the iconotext is desire, and again words and pictures are symmetrical.

However, in the end, Susanna and the happily retrieved cat are going home, and the narrator says, in a metafictive comment, "She never discovered whether everything has been real, but as far as one understands, it does not matter." Thus the credibility of the story is touched upon, in words, but the reader is left with the same doubts as the protagonist. There is nothing in the pictures to support either interpretation. Since there is no home and no parents or other adults depicted, the border between reality and fantasy in the visual text is just as vague as in *Journey with a Cat*. It is only the words that express doubt (dubitative modality).

## Interplay of Visual and Verbal: Words and Pictures Vie with Each Other to Create a Shifting Spectrum of Modality

One of the most famous dream journeys in picturebook form is obviously Maurice Sendak's *Where the Wild Things Are* (1963). Much has already been written about the objective-subjective interpretation of this text, but a few points can be reiterated.

As in *Journey with a Cat,* neither the words nor the pictures directly suggest that the story is true (indicative) or imagined (desired), and the reader is free to assume either of the two positions. However, two details manipulate the reader to take either the one or the other viewpoint. As pointed out by many critics, the verbal statement at the end of the story that the supper is "still hot" supports the objective, adult interpretation: the actual duration of the story has probably been no more than ten minutes, during which Max has lived through two years of his imaginary life among the Wild Things. Apparently neglected by unsophisticated readers, this detail is the strongest argument for interpreting Max's story as an expression of his imagination. But a visual detail subverts this conclusion. In the early pictures of Max's bedroom, we see a half-moon, while in the last picture, the moon is full. For an observant reader, this detail creates doubt. It is quite significant that the detail supporting symbolic reading is verbal ("symbolic" in Lacanian terms), while the detail supporting mimetic reading is visual ("imaginary" or "imagistic").

A comparative analysis of *Where the Wild Things Are* and *The Wild Baby Goes to Sea* (1982) reveals how visual aspects of plot, setting, and characterization take the iconotext in different directions despite similarities in verbal narrative. The plot summary of both books is indeed quite comparable: an imaginary journey full of dangers and adventures that, however, is traumatic and compensatory in Max's case since he has just had a major conflict with his mother, but for the Wild Baby is a normal, conflict-free act of liberation and maturation. This purely thematic difference is magnified by pictorial modality, that is, by visual details contributing to our interpretation of the narrative as possible or impossible.

Wild Baby's experience, conveyed mostly by pictures, is indeed much more playful and enjoyable, totally lacking Max's strong feelings of abandonment, longing, and guilt. The baby's journey is initiated "on a day when it is quiet and a bit boring," that is, the child uses his vivid imagination to give color to his everyday life.[9] Both books start in the mimetic mode with a description of the boys' mischief. These first pages establish an expectation of modality contrary to the cover pictures' suggestions of fantastic adventures, and are therefore necessary as a contrast to the modality of the coming plot. The recto of the first doublespread of *The Wild Baby* amplifies the sense of mischief-making, as does the second spread of *Wild Things,* with the words "and another." The omission of this doublespread in the American version of *The Wild Baby* dampens the characterization of the baby. While Max's make-believe games are clearly aggressive, the baby's are relatively innocent and humorous.

Max's mother is absent from the pictures, and the cold and empty room to which Max is exiled stresses the coldness of his mother's emotions (further emphasized by the chilly greenish colors). We may wonder whether this is a child's room at all, especially given the size and shape of the bed. However, the picture may convey Max's inner landscape rather than the actual view of the room, in other words, his subjective apprehension of his temporary prison. This room is already a transitional space. By contrast, the pictorial setting of the first spread of *The Wild Baby* accentuates the mother's casual attitude to tidiness and order, as well as her friendly and liberal attitude to her child. If Max is exiled from the adult space, the baby has invaded the adult space—both Mama's bedroom and the living room—with his toys. Max is emotionally absent from reality, while the baby never actually leaves it. Thus both the initial setting and character constellation in *The Wild Baby* are radically different from Sendak's book, creating not only a different point of departure for the two protagonists' journeys, but also different modality expectations.

As in *Wild Things,* there is nothing in the verbal text of *The Wild Baby* suggesting that the journey is only play. But the pictures stress the modality very promptly. While Max's imaginary boat is waiting for him, ready with sails up and his name on the bow, the baby must create his vessel from whatever his surroundings provide. The wooden crate is the only detail mentioned in the verbal text, while the pictures feature a broom-and-clothes-hanger mast and spar, an apron-sail, and tools scattered on the floor that suggest the baby's construction efforts. The buns that the baby takes from his mother's handbag are, for a Swedish reader at least, a clear allusion to Moominmama and her cornucopia of a handbag. While the baby takes provisions and his toy friends, Max is sent to bed alone and without supper. The baby's toys serve as projections of the baby's persona, and as objects for the transference of his fearful emotions, so that he can be brave and strong.

The mother may be perplexed by her baby's initiative (her face in the picture shows apparent amazement as she views the boat), but she does not stand in his way; moreover she supports his imaginative play by waving "full or sorrow" from the shore and calling "Take care!" In this picture, the blue rug is turning into sea waves, while the boat is still a crate and the mast a broom. This makes an illuminating comparison with the cover of *Peter's Voyage,* which contradicts the reality of the story. In *The Wild Baby* this picture captures the very moment when reality and imagination meet, and also when modality becomes ambiguous.

During Max's journey, there is nothing to remind him of home or to serve as a link back to security, that is, to subvert the indicative modality. Like

On the border between real and imaginary: *The Wild Baby Goes to Sea,* by Barbro Lindgren and Eva Eriksson.

the baby, he creates his imaginary landscape from his real surroundings, "the ceiling hung with vines and the walls became the world all around." In the pictures we see the gradual transformation of the few objects in Max's room and their total dissolution in the fantastic landscape. By letting the boat-crate retain its original form while depicting the sea as real, the illustrator of *The Wild Baby* emphasizes that the journey is only play, as does the inclusion of other transformed objects: a pot and pan become two more ships, the saltcellar acts as a lighthouse, mother's creamy curtains and red armchairs turn into a whale's open jaws, and the two oval portraits on the wall (shown on the penultimate spread when the journey is over) metamorphose into the monster's eyes. Perhaps even the mother's black rubber gloves, which she is wearing in the penultimate picture, have stimulated the image of the black octopus. The child is really using imagination during his play, but none of these visual details is mentioned in the verbal text, which is presented from the child's viewpoint and therefore as a real adventure. The modality of the verbal text is thus indicative, while the visual details remind us all the time that the actual modality of the text is desire.

The pike is an especially interesting detail. It appears from the waves as a huge sea monster threatening to eat up the baby and his companions and is defeated when the baby attacks it with the buns he has taken with him. This episode evokes one of the most central motifs in children's fiction: the dilemma of eating or being eaten, which is also extremely prominent in *Wild Things*.[10] Max's longing for his mother is directly connected with the food she provides: "from far away across the world [he] smelled good things to eat." "From far away" has a double implication here. On the objective level, Max is in his nursery on the upper floor of the house, while the kitchen with the food must be on the ground floor (we see a staircase in one of the pictures). It is indeed very far away for a little child. And secondly, in terms of feelings, he is emotionally "far away" from the world of reality.

In *Baby,* the mother calls her child for lunch almost immediately after he defeats the fish. With her call the imaginary world dissolves, the sea dries up, and the monstrous fish appears cooked and served on a platter in a symbolical reversal of eating and being eaten. This picture again reveals the place where reality and imagination meet. But because the baby knows that his mother is patient and will wait with the food, he lets imagination take over again; the journey continues, and the mother joins in. While the words never actually mention the mother's participation in the adventure, the picture is quite explicit. This is essential for the unsophisticated reader's choice of modality: if an adult is taking part in the adventure, then it must be real! When the American edition deletes the mother from the picture (illustrations in Chapter 3), the ambivalence in modality is reduced: that is, the reader is manipulated toward a more certain interpretation. While the Swedish text is also ambivalent, saying that the mother is happy that "they" have come home safely, where "they" may include herself, the American version says, "Mama was delighted too/to see her baby and his crew," stressing that she has not been part of the adventure.

Nonetheless, the "Mary Poppins" evidence, which the mother can see as well as the baby—the rooster rescued from the sea—declares that the journey was real and implies a probability that contradicts the otherwise improbable modality of the whole book. The final modality will therefore remain in doubt. In *The Wild Baby's Dog* (1985), there is similar evidence of the adventure being true: the dog has lost his tail. This is, however, only present in the visual text.

The last picture of *The Wild Baby* shows a joyful meal scene in which, once again, adult territory, the dining room, is invaded by the baby's army of toy friends. The former enemy who in the fantasy world threatened to eat the travelers is now itself eaten up, the bones resting neatly on a plate. Unlike Max, who is still obliged to eat his supper, albeit hot, all alone in his bare room, the baby is enjoying a shared meal with his mother and faithful companions.

The comparison between the two books shows that in *Wild Things,* the visual and the verbal modality are equally indeterminable, and the reader is free to choose an interpretation. In *The Wild Baby,* on the other hand, the words primarily express the indicative mode, presenting the baby's experience as true, while the pictures offer a variety of modal counterpoint, making connections between fantasy and reality. Thematically, *Wild Things* creates a sense of insecurity, despite its happy ending, while *The Wild Baby* depicts a harmonious child who uses his creative imagination and learns through play to be independent, while all the time feeling supported by his mother. This harmony and security is in the first hand conveyed by pictures. Thus modality contributes significantly to the meaning we extract from the iconotext.

## Visually Provoked Dubitative: Pictorial Details That Undermine the Credibility of the Iconotext

It is obviously much more gratifying for picturebook creators to subvert the modality of the story by visual means, which are implicit rather than explicit, therefore allowing a wider range of interpretations. Such subversion means that while the iconotext encourages or manipulates the reader to adopt a certain modality, some visual details will lead to doubt.

We will discuss three examples with slightly different patterns of subversion. The initial bedtime situation of *I'll Take Care of the Crocodiles* (1977), by Stefan Mählqvist and Tord Nygren, Anthony Browne's *Gorilla* (1983), and Ulf Stark and Anna Höglund's *The Jaguar* (1987) supports the objective interpretation that the story is not real, even though the text does not necessarily say explicitly that the protagonist has fallen asleep and is dreaming.[11]

However, this subversive visual element may appear only in the end, as in *Crocodiles,* making it the simplest case; at both the beginning and the end, as in *The Jaguar,* which is slightly more complicated; or all the way through, as in *Gorilla.*

### Visual Subversive Element at the End

In *Come Into My Night, Come Into My Dream* (1978), by Stefan Mählqvist and Tord Nygren, where the title itself encourages a certain type of reading, the text states that the boy wakes up in the middle of the night to experience his nightmarish adventures. The same authors' *I'll Take Care of the Crocodiles* (1977) also starts with bedtime and the child's reluctance to go to sleep. The text says that he "did not want to go to sleep," but we may also read it as "scared to go to sleep." As compared to *Come Into My Night,* which starts with the child's conflict with his parents, the establishing scene of *Crocodiles* may seem idyllic, if we trust the words. The father has read the three-year-old boy a bedtime story, then the mother reads him another bedtime story and sings a song. She leaves a lamp switched on over the bed. The father comes to wipe the boy's nose. The words convey a sense of security. However, the picture that accompanies the words implies something different. It shows the boy alone in his room, crying, with his mouth wide open and his eyes shut.

The nursery in this book is not as frighteningly decorated as in *Come Into My Night,* for it has bright colors and is full of toys. However, there are two adult paintings on the wall, which, exactly as in *Come Into My Night,* provide the sources for the boy's nightmares. One is a full-length portrait of Karl Marx, apparently a scary image for the boy, since Marx will appear recurrently in the dream, and at the end of the story the father will look like him. The other is a picture of Amsterdam, with its typical gables and a vaulted bridge, which provides the landscape that the boy will enter in his dream. While the words insist that the boy is not dreaming—the story is told in the first-person—the second doublespread portrays the famous figure of Scandinavian folklore, best known from Hans Christian Andersen's fairy tale, Willie Winkie with his magical umbrella. In the recto picture, Willie Winkie is sitting on the bedpost, umbrella open, and obviously desperate about ever getting the boy to sleep.

The father offers to lie down by the boy, but in the picture he is still sitting on the edge of the bed, turned from the viewer; he may be looking at the Amsterdam painting, which has very clearly become larger and come closer. In the next spread, the water from the canal starts leaking into the nursery, and all the objects in the room are shaken from their places. The text says: "He surrendered. Tonight it happened quite easily. The adventure started. Anything could happen." These words represent the boy's perspective, which has overcome his father's, for in the picture the father is asleep in the boy's bed,

hugging him. The words "Anything could happen" are expanded in the picture not only by the threatening flood from the canal, but also by the toy airplane transformed into a hybrid created from a plane and a giant fly (in
Swedish, a pun: "flygplan"—"flugplan"), and by the butterfly pattern on the
wallpaper coming alive. Reading the picture objectively, we will state that the
boy has fallen asleep with a sense of security, having his father with him.

Indeed, during the adventure, the father's and the boy's dreams are
blended in a delightful mixture of child and adult allusions. In the next
spread, they have entered the Amsterdam painting (or the painting has completely invaded the bedroom) and are floating on the canal in their bed. Several of the house windows are replaced by famous paintings from the
Amsterdam Art Museum, which will probably be recognized only by the
adult coreader of the book, but which may be familiar for the young protagonist from some art album. The transformation of a paper swallow into a real
bird, depicted in simultaneous succession, evokes the famous picture by
M. C. Escher. The subsequent spreads have more of a child perspective, but
they also present some clear metafictive, frame-breaking features, both in
words and in pictures. For instance, when the boy sees his friend from the day

Dream invading reality in *I'll Take Care of the Crocodiles,* by
Stefan Mählqvist and Tord Nygren.

care and calls her, the father tells him not to shout so loudly because he will wake the whole house.

The encounter with the crocodile follows the same scheme as the battle with the fish in *The Wild Baby:* the child transfers his fears onto someone else, in this case an adult. The picture emphasizes the father's terror: he hides behind a pillow, while the boy displays both courage and wit. It is an obvious irony that the weapon he uses against the monster is a picturebook, also one of the most idyllic books in Swedish literature, *Peter's Adventures in Blueberry Land,* by Elsa Beskow. They are then attacked by an enormous hippopotamus, but are rescued by the birds on the boy's pajamas. The book is quite symmetrical in this episode, but the picture makes the most of the metaphysical transformation, echoing the Escher birds earlier in the book as well as the transformed wallpaper patterns. In the next spread, the birds merge with the stars in the sky, an event not mentioned in words. The father is asleep, turned away from the boy, who is all alone in the big world. The perspective from above stresses that he is small and helpless. The security from the earlier pictures is substantially destroyed.

Two details bring forward the question of modality. The boy says that the adventure must have taken a long time, because his father has grown a beard and reminds him of the portrait of Uncle Karl in his room. Indeed, in the picture, the father bears a close resemblance to Karl Marx. This is part of the dream and therefore not very convincing evidence. But when the adventure is over and the boy is sleeping in his own bed, he wonders whether the birds from his pajamas will be gone when he awakens in the morning. Since the question is not answered, the reader is left in uncertainty (dubitative modality, expressed visually).

### Visual Subversive Element at Both the Beginning and the End

*The Jaguar* (1987), by Ulf Stark and Anna Höglund, is another Swedish bedtime story showing obvious similarities with Sendak's *Where the Wild Things Are,* for it presents a boy conquering his fears and aggressions through play or dream. Among the similarities is the boy's transformation into a carnivorous animal. As in *Wild Things,* this transformation is prompted by an adult: just as Max's mother has apparently endorsed his aggressive games by giving him a wolf suit, Elmer's yellow spotted pajamas stimulate his imagination. However, *The Jaguar* is much more ambivalent both in words and images. In the first doublespread, the full-page verso picture shows Elmer sitting in his pajamas on a rug, in the middle of a rather empty-looking room, reading a book. On the recto black-and-white vignette we instead see a wild animal. Elmer's physical transformation is more complete than that of Max, who is merely disguised as a wolf; Elmer actually becomes a jaguar, at least if we trust the picture. The text says: "When Elmer was going to bed, he became a jaguar [ . . . ] It happens very quickly, in less than a quarter of an hour his body is covered with fur [ . . . ] When he looks at his toes, he sees sharp claws." The transformation is not instant, but takes some time—the time it takes the child to fall asleep on the rug?

The cover illustration may at first sight seem to be merely a close-up of the initial verso. But Elmer on the cover is wearing mittens and soft slippers with claws, while the boy on the verso is barefoot and has normal hands. Furthermore, on the cover he has a long tail, and the shadow on the wall has animal rather than human ears. The cover picture fills the temporal gap between the verso and the vignette of the first spread, showing an intermediate moment in the transformation, but also adding to the ambivalence: is Elmer really turning into a jaguar or is he falling asleep?

Unlike Max, Elmer does not go far away on his journey, but explores the

The cover of *The Jaguar* adds ambiguity to the story.

mysterious night-time Stockholm, so that the blending of fantasy and reality is accentuated. In a child's dream, elements of the everyday and the imaginary are very likely to be intertwined, and this is more probable than the appearance of a magical realm. So, while Max's journey is make-believe, Elmer's is most probably a dream. While the Stockholm of his dreams is like the real city, it also has strong disparities: a jungle invades the streets, buses have elephant trunks and cars rhinoceros horns, neon signs are formed from snakes. This is a typical nightmare where the child is small, scared, and powerless, unlike the empowered Max. But, again unlike Max, Elmer finds a friend in this dream realm in the form of a cat. In the story, Elmer follows the cat home, promising to see her the next morning, and then goes to his own home. In the penultimate spread, the verso picture shows the jaguar lying on the sidewalk between two parking meters, looking longingly up at the brightly lit window. The feeling evoked by this picture is duplicated by words: "He wants to call 'Mama!' but only a growl comes out, because he is a wild animal now. Suddenly he wants to cry and feels cold. For jaguars have no homes." Although we do not directly share the jaguar's literal point of view, the distorted perspective from below stresses his loneliness, helplessness, and his sense of being an outsider.

The recto vignette shows the result of what the next sentence describes: "Elmer is so tired that he merely collapses, and does not notice what happens: his paw becomes a foot with five human toes, and his tail falls off, as well as

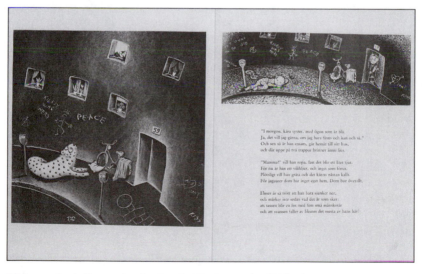

Metamorphosis from animal to boy in *The Jaguar,* by Ulf Stark and Anna Höglund.

most of his fur." In the picture, frontal omniscient perspective is used. The little boy in spotted pajamas is asleep on the sidewalk, just where the jaguar has been lying. Through the doorway, the mother is hurrying. In the next, and last, doublespread, she carries the sleeping boy upstairs. Water is still running down her cheeks, we learn from the text: in the second spread of the book, where the transformed Elmer escapes through the window, the mother is depicted washing her hair. This suggests that Elmer's long adventure has taken just a few minutes of the objective, adult time. One of the possible rational interpretations is that Elmer has been sleepwalking, that he actually goes down the stairs into the street and, exhausted, falls down on the sidewalk, where the worried mother almost immediately discovers him. The transformation and the adventures have then been his dream.

Neither the words nor the pictures support this interpretation directly. Moreover, the penultimate vignette, with the boy sleeping on the sidewalk, also shows his furry tail and ears, which have fallen off and are lying by his side. This pictorial detail subverts the realistic and rational explanation, insisting instead that Elmer has indeed been a jaguar for a while. Unlike *Crocodiles,* where the visual "Mary Poppins evidence" only appears in the end, *The Jaguar* fluctuates between modalities in the pictures, although the words express no doubt about the mimetic nature of the events.

### Visual Subversion throughout the Text

This uncertainty is still more subtle in *Gorilla* (1983), where the child creates an image of a perfect parent when her own father proves insufficient. As in Sendak's book, the imaginary existence, visualized by pictures, seems to be a compensation for lack of parental love rather than a healthy exercise in creativity. The first establishing spreads present a realistic setting, where minute details such as the electric socket amplify the sense of reality. However, already in the third spread we anticipate the power of imagination, when the cone of light from the television, falling on the corner where Hannah sits, transforms the wallpaper, replacing the monsters and ugly plants in its shadowed part with brightly colored sunflowers, mushrooms, and butterflies. This little lighted corner anticipates the imaginary world Hannah will soon enter.

Hannah's disappointment when she gets a toy gorilla for her birthday (cf. the similar motif in *The Wild Baby's Dog*) is magnificently conveyed by the picture composition. The girl is depicted small in her bed, almost obscured by its iron bars—immediately reminiscent of a cage. The picture is contrasted with the next spread, in which the toy gorilla, having come alive, towers over the bed while we share Hannah's point of view, looking right into the creature's eyes. The transformation is only indirectly indicated by words: "In the night something amazing happened." The three small framed pictures on the verso depict the gorilla growing in size; in the third picture, the doll beside the tiny dollhouse is terrified, her hair on end and her mouth wide open. Apparently the doll too comes alive at night. Since the immediately preceding sentence says, "Hannah threw the gorilla into a corner with her other toys and went back to sleep," the verbal text leaves open the possibility that the following events take place in her dream.

The pictures support the optative modality in several ways. First, the gorilla wears the father's clothes—a sheepskin coat and a hat. This may suggest that the image is a combination of Hannah's wish for a caring father and her interest in gorillas, which has been pronounced in the verbal text and amplified by the numerous visual images, including a parody on Mona Lisa on the wall. During the night adventure, several more "postmodern" clues appear in the pictures: a Charlie Chaplin gorilla, a cowboy gorilla, a Superman gorilla, a Che Guevara gorilla, the Statue of Liberty with a gorilla face, and so on. The dream also fulfills many of the girl's wishes: a visit to the zoo, a movie show, a splendid meal in a café, and dancing on a lawn, accompanied by shadowlike greenish gorilla couples. The contrast between the zoo, cinema, and café on one hand and the dance on the other conveys the eclecticism of the dream sequence. The adventure is real and unreal at the same time. Most of its details, as well as the general atmosphere, are only visually expressed; the words are scarce and predominantly in dialogue that is part of the "showing" rather than the "telling" that was the narrative mode of the realistic frame.

At the end of the adventure, the gorilla tells Hannah to go inside and promises to see her in the morning. Waking up and seeing the toy gorilla in the bed beside her, Hannah smiles. Let us remember that last night Hannah has thrown the toy into the corner. The picture of the gorilla by her side suggests two interpretations. If the night adventure has been true, then the magical gorilla has in the daytime become a toy again, having crawled into Hannah's bed just before the transformation (we will not speculate on the incestuous implication of this action). Alternatively, the father has been in her room since she opened the parcel, has seen the toy thrown into the corner, and, full of remorse, has put it beside her.

The sudden change in the father's attitude at the end of the story is not objectively understandable. However, the story is told from Hannah's point of view. The text on the first spread says: "Her father didn't have time to take her to see [a gorilla] at the zoo. He didn't have time for anything." The pictures on this and the subsequent spreads show the father absorbed in his newspaper at the breakfast table, hurrying to work, and at his desk in the evening. The text conveys the iterative frequency by saying: "He went to work *every day* [ . . . ] he *would* say [ . . . ] the next day he was *always* too busy" (emphasis added). The pictures have no direct way of suggesting whether the depicted actions are indeed iterative or singulative, nor can we see directly how much time may have passed between the individual pictures. The sense of a long span of time, intensified by the iterative, may just as well be the longing child's subjective perception. The phrase "They never did anything together" might pertain to a long period of time, but it might also describe just this particular evening. In the birthday picture, Hannah's father is dressed in an unexpectedly youthful manner, in a bright red sweatshirt and jeans instead of the dark suit, shirt, and tie of the first picture. This, too, must be Hannah's subjective vision rather than a real change, as is her linking of her father to the gorilla by the banana tucked into his back pocket. The body contact conveyed by the picture echoes the dream sequence in which the gorilla holds Hannah's hand, holds her by the shoulder, or holds her firmly in his arms.

The last picture repeats the picture in the dream, with the father and Hannah shown from behind, their shadows cast toward the viewer. The only difference is that Hannah is now carrying the toy gorilla in her hand. The image from the dream is in reality divided between the father and the toy. Thus while both the verbal and the visual narrative cooperate on the subjective level, a number of visual details suggest a psychological development and an objective description of the girl's psychological growth as she learns to accept and appreciate her father as he is.

In contrast to the three books discussed in this section, which, similar to *Wild Things,* obviously intend to convey the traumatic experience of a neglected child, another picturebook involving a child-father relationship, Janosch's *Hey Presto! You Are a Bear!* (1977), empowers the child by means of play, reminiscent of *The Wild Baby Goes to Sea.* The power of imagination transforms the boy's nasty classmate into a boar and his little brother into a lion. In the pictures, both transformed characters retain their human clothes as well as the vertical position, therefore the playfulness of the picture is accentuated (similar to the many visual details in *The Wild Baby Goes to Sea*). It takes more effort to transform the father into a bear, but the boy manages this at last, and a wild adventure starts. The realistic setting is contrasted to the absurd, surrealistic plot, and through the preposterous visual and verbal events the imaginative play can be discerned. Interestingly enough, the mother plays the role of the "enemy," interrupting the game and apparently protesting against the destruction it leads to. The picture alone reveals to the reader that the mother is the "enemy."

The book underlines the positive effect of imaginative play rather than its compensatory function. The story's outcome has the child liberating the adult, for the boy encourages his father to be a bear at work the next day and not let his bosses bully him. The boy also makes his father clean his teeth and wash his feet before going to bed, adding that "for once he should feel how it is." The bear-father wears only a shirt, and neither the text nor the pictures question the very fact of transformation (indicative modality). Unlike most of the books discussed earlier, this one has a clear comic tone, which perhaps can best be described in terms of the carnivalesque.

## Two Parallel Modalities

John Burningham's *Come Away from the Water, Shirley* (1977) is a rare example of a picturebook where fantastic and realistic modes are distinctly separated and presented in two parallel narratives, a fact which has been noted by many critics. Consistent with the "home-" and "adventure"-page concept, the verso pictures are static, secure and boring, while the recto pictures are dynamic, full of action, and also more colorful. The fantastic adventure is told only in pictures. The realistic narrative, told by two symmetrical visual-verbal texts, functions as a metafictive comment on the fantastic journey, subverting its credibility and clearly presenting it as Shirley's play. Without the realistic narrative, unsophisticated readers would interpret the journey literally, and the book would lose its ironic tone based on the contrast between the parents' uneventful day on the beach and the child's wild games. The counterpoint leaves no doubt about the adventure being a pretense (impossibility), but this is also the main purpose of the book: the reader is supposed to recognize the adventure as play.[12] In the last realistic picture, where Shirley and her parents are going home, Shirley is stripped of her trophies from the previous fantasy picture—the crown, the necklace, and the sword—so there is no visual evidence of her adventures having actually taken place. The dog, her faithful travel companion, is nowhere to be seen, and he may have been absent from reality as well.

There is no direct correspondence between the visual fantastic narrative and the words of the realistic narrative, but there is some irony in their connection. When the mother says, "Why don't you go and play with those children?" Shirley in her imaginary world is heading toward the pirate ship. The words "Mind you don't get any of that filthy tar on your nice new shoes" match the picture of Shirley approaching the tarred ship. The order "Don't stroke that dog, Shirley, you don't know where he's been" is especially humorous. First, the dog has been around for a while already, and the readers have undoubtedly noticed him while the mother has not. Second, in the fantasy world, the dog "has been" in Shirley's rowboat and is now on the pirate ship with her. Third, right at the moment depicted on the adventurous recto page, the dog is saving Shirley's life by biting the pirate captain's leg. The drink that the mother offers Shirley evokes the barrel on board the ship. Prohibition to throw stones comes when Shirley and the dog throw themselves headfirst from the ship into the waves, and so on. In the penultimate spread, the mother exclaims, "Good heavens! Just look at the time. We are going to be late if we don't hurry," while in Shirley's world it is pitch-black night.

Similarly, in *Time to Get Out of the Bath, Shirley* (1978), while mother is nagging her daughter about having left the soap in the bath, about having a bath more often, and about having thrown her clothes on the floor, Shirley takes the plug out of the tub, is sucked into the plumbing mounted on her rubber duck, and emerges into a landscape that proves to be full of adventure. In this book, it is more difficult to find a coherence between the verbal-visual text of the verso (indicative) and the exclusively visual text of the recto (improbable), except perhaps in the penultimate spread, when Shirley pushes the king from his rubber duck to her mother's comment, "Now there's water everywhere!" This is apparently a reaction to a violent splash in the "real" world that corresponds to Shirley's imaginative contest. On the whole, however, as in the previous book, the uneventful and boring verbal story presents a sharp contrast to the exciting dynamism of Shirley's playful journey. The mother's indifference to her daughter is once again emphasized by her position and actions in the verso pages: the mother is standing on the scales, combing her hair in front of the mirror, cleaning the sink, and so on. Her position of power over Shirley is accentuated by the close-ups, while Shirley's recto pages are consistently portrayed as distant views, except for the picture of the king and queen—possibly Shirley's image of ideal parents.

The books are an excellent illustration of Jacques Lacan's notion of imaginary and symbolic language. The child's imaginative play does not need words for it is preverbal (imaginary in Lacanian terminology). Each picture is so dynamic that the narrative ellipses between pages can easily be filled by the reader's imagination. The adult story is verbal. Throughout the first book, the parents remain in almost the same positions, sitting in their folding chairs, the father reading his newspaper, the mother knitting, apparently oblivious to what is happening around them. Their isolation is further emphasized by the frame and by the negative space or absence of backgrounds. The adult story in the second book is slightly more dynamic as the mother in fact performs some actions. However, the limitation of her narrative is purely spatial: she operates within a few square feet of the bathroom, while her daughter explores a whole world in her imagination. The verbal text in both books consists of banal, prestructured phrases lacking significance and communicating little except for a total absence of interest.

## Unresolved Ambiguous Modality

So far we have been looking at books in which words and images are more or less consonant in their modality, allowing either a mimetic or a symbolic reading, and occasionally enhanced by either verbal or, more often, visual elements. However, a growing number of contemporary picturebooks are totally ambiguous in their modality, just as they are in characterization, perspective, and temporal structures. This ambiguity can be expressed in words, in images, or both; images, being less explicit by nature, allow the picture-book authors to stretch the limits of ambiguity to the utmost. Yet, as in the other areas, words and pictures may collaborate in a number of ways.

### Symmetrical Ambiguity

David McKee's *Not Now, Bernard* (1980) has been analyzed by many scholars as a perfect example of words and pictures telling different stories.[13] We would like to take this discussion a little further. Similar to Sendak's Max, Bernard has no communication with his parents and compensates for his sense of abandonment by getting aggressive. Unlike Sendak's book, the parents are present both in the verbal text—mostly by direct speech, the recurrent phrase "Not now, Bernard"—and in the visual text, busy with all kinds of domestic tasks. The pictures also show that the parents are less than perfect in what they do: the father injures himself with the hammer, the mother spills water when she waters flowers and drops paint when she is painting the walls. Unlike the situation in Sendak's book, the mother does not deny Bernard food, but the food does not signal warmth and community, as it does, for instance, in the *Wild Baby* books. In fact, the mother looks rather irritated as she calls for Bernard to come for dinner; as in everything else, she obviously regards him as a nuisance. In all the pictures the parents' facial expressions convey their own aggressive feelings, which are not manifested in their verbal statements. The story is thus much more fully anchored in the everyday than any of the books discussed above, and there will be no escape into a magical dream realm. Instead, the supernatural will invade this seemingly secure realistic world, whose security is accentuated by the exceedingly bright colors and the details of interior decoration.

On the mimetic level, Bernard is trying to tell his parents that there is a monster in the garden. The pictures do not question his statement: there is indeed a horrible purple creature with horns and sharp teeth (symmetrical indicative modality). The verbal-visual text tells us, matter-of-factly, that the monster eats up Bernard (the act of eating is, however, presented in a visual ellipsis) and goes indoors and tries in vain to attract the parents' attention. Just as they have ignored Bernard, the parents now ignore the monster, to the point where the monster has an identity crisis, no longer quite sure that he is a monster. The psychological implication of the story as we read it on the symbolic level is transparent: the neglected child transforms his aggressions into a monster.[14] However, there is nothing in either text or pictures that directly supports this reading. The monster does not possess any of Bernard's features, he does not disguise himself in Bernard's clothes, and he does not have Bernard's blue eyes, which the illustrations accentuate repeatedly in the beginning of the story. Neither is there any anticipation, verbal or visual, of the transformation, similar to the little drawing of a monster "by Max" in

The monster ate Bernard up, every bit.

Ambivalent message in David McKee's *Not Now, Bernard.*

Sendak's book, or Max's mother's provocative exclamation "Wild thing!" activating Max's fancies. True, the monster eats Bernard's dinner (showing bad table manners), watches the television, reads comics, and breaks a toy, demonstrating human behavior, but he also bites the father's leg, which is an overtly transgressive act. The only detail that may suggest identification of Bernard with the monster is the monster's facial expression showing amazement when he gets no reaction to his behavior. Finally, the penultimate spread, showing the monster going upstairs to bed, presents him as oppressed and defeated, his head drooping, his arms stretched exhaustedly along his body, dragging Bernard's teddy bear after him. The teddy bear, not mentioned in words, is an important key to the monster's/Bernard's emotions, the only source of security and affection. Thus, the pictures do in fact support the objective interpretation, but only for those who are really intent on finding one.

While we can easily see the Wild Things in Sendak's book as visualizations of the boy's aggressive emotions, the situation in *Not Now, Bernard* is more complicated. Bernard disappears from the verbal as well as from the visual text. The monster has replaced the boy; for an unsophisticated reader it has disposed of the hero and usurped his position—a frequent motif in fairy tales. It is also part of the fairy-tale convention that others do not discover the fraud, although it must logically be obvious. However, in fairy tales the false hero is always exposed, and the real hero triumphs. In *Not Now, Bernard,* there is no reverse transformation, or even a hint of it, to suggest that the story has been a play or a compensatory aggressive daydream. There is, equally, no hint on the symbolic level that the boy has mastered his aggressions, "killed the monster," and reconciled with the parents, which we to a certain extent can discern in the closure of *Wild Things.* The story has the nature of indeterminacy typical of postmodern art.

The disturbing ambiguity of *Not Now, Bernard* stands up still more clearly in comparison with McKee's *The Monster and the Teddy Bear* (1989), which can be seen as a companion volume to *Not Now, Bernard,* but which is much more straightforward in its resolution. After a great deal of mischief-making, during which Angela is less and less convinced that she indeed prefers monsters to teddy bears, the teddy bear gets rid of the monster, and the question of consequences arises: "But what will Mummy and Daddy say?" It is natural to interpret the monster and the teddy as the bad and the good side of the child's persona, and it is quite remarkable that, unlike *Not Now, Bernard,* the book allows the good to win without any further complications. To the child's anxious question, the teddy says carelessly, "Let's go back to bed [ . . . ] perhaps they'll never notice." The child protagonist knows that the monster's destructive behavior has been mere play, and that there is not much for the adults to notice. In fact, Angela's baby-sitter obviously notices the noise from the nursery, but does not consider it worth further investigation. Unlike the nice-looking parents, the baby-sitter is depicted as a rather unpleasant lady, fat, her hair in funny curls, with big eyes, a big nose, big teeth, and monstrously big bare feet. She is sitting in front of the television stuffing herself with candy and cookies, dressed in two shades of green that match the monster's color. It is not impossible that her appearance and behavior have prompted Angela's creation of the monster's image, although her initial idea is that "monsters are big and strong and exciting." Thus, in many details the book tends to accentuate the optative modality rather than leave the reader in doubt.

### Contradictory Ambiguity

John Burningham's *Aldo* (1991) is another story full of uncertainties. In the verbal narrative, the nameless female narrator/protagonist knows that Aldo is an imaginary friend, but at the same time the girl firmly believes in his existence and his faithful help. In fact, the story is about the crucial moment in the little girl's life when she is on the verge of abandoning her imaginary helper, and the pictures enhance the depiction of this complicated psychological process. The girl is self-conscious enough to realize that she is lonely, neglected by her mother, and not popular with her classmates. Aldo is a typical compensation for everything she lacks in her real life. Since the story does not mention the girl's father, Aldo is obviously also a father substitute, which is an interesting and important detail, since in most stories imaginary friends are of the same gender (*Gorilla* is another exception).

The words never mention that Aldo is a rabbit, and but for the pictures he could be a human being, some other animal, a monster, a ghost, or indeed anything. It is, however, significant that Aldo is the same size as the girl: he is a friend and not a pet. The picture presenting Aldo shows him as a shy and passive figure, with his arms against his body and his head sunk. Portrayed this way, he is obviously a visualization of the girl's fear and insecurity. The facing page shows Aldo and the girl holding each other by the shoulders, mutually supporting one another. The text says that Aldo appears when something terrible happens, for example when her classmates have been unkind. The next page shows two girls pushing the protagonist and pulling her hair, while in the facing recto Aldo is comforting her, and he has picked up the book and the ruler she has dropped. The text says, "I am sure they fled just because Aldo came." Reading Aldo symbolically, as a purely imaginary creature, we can state that he now plays the role of the girl's self-confidence, and that he helps her to cope with the classmates' bullying.

The narrator further maintains that Aldo takes her to all kinds of wonderful places, and that she is not afraid of anything when she is with him. The pages and doublespreads showing the girl on her imaginary escapades with Aldo are different in graphic design from the rest of the story (much as, we might add, the pictures of Shirley's imaginary journey are different from the pictures of her parents' reality). While most of the pictures are done in so-called negative space, that is, without backgrounds or unnecessary details, the imaginary pages are in full color, which creates depth, and without frames, allowing the viewer to come closer. The difference stresses literally the contrast between flat reality and multidimensional fantasy. With one exception, the fantasy pages are wordless, and there is, as in the Shirley books, no verbal narrative to describe what is happening in these pictures. We may of course see a vague connection between the words "I am not afraid of anything" and the picture in the next spread showing the girl and Aldo balancing on a tightrope high over the roofs of the town; or between "I wish Aldo were with me all the time" and the following spread, in which Aldo rows the girl in a boat over a vast space of water. However, the pictures very obviously expand the words and not merely illustrate them.

The deviating style of the pictures emphasizes that they are the girl's daydreams (desire, optative); however, the verbal text is sufficiently ambiguous on this matter. Following the statement that Aldo is unfortunately only an imaginary friend, we find a doublespread showing the girl on a swing and Aldo pushing the swing for her. The implication is that, although she knows that Aldo is a fancy (impossibility), she still believes in him (possibility), or even that he is as yet real for her (indicative)—a clash between modalities expressed by words and by the picture. In the next spread, the girl wakes up from a nightmare and discovers that Aldo is not there to comfort her, as he apparently has always done before. The text suggests that the protagonist is now losing her faith in Aldo's omnipotence. However, he reappears in the next picture, to reestablish her confidence. The dual narrative is all the time balanced delicately between fantasy and reality, between belief and doubt, and the first-person perspective makes it almost impossible to decide how conscious the protagonist is about her own imagination.

The penultimate spread shows the girl on the swing together with two friends. The text says, "There are of course days when I don't think about him at all, but I know that if the worst thing happens—" The picture is a very clear expression of something that the words only hint at: the girl has outgrown Aldo, she has now established real social contacts. However, the text continues on the next and last page: "—Aldo will always be there." The picture supports the words, showing the girl and Aldo as a much happier couple, dancing and smiling and once again holding each other around the shoulders. They are walking along a path bordered by a row of flowerpots, with a rose arch behind them, all of which creates a sense of unreality (optative). They are also walking in a diagonal from right top to left bottom corner, leading them back into the book, to the time when Aldo always came to the rescue when needed. Both the words and the picture express desire. The word "always," echoing the famous ending of the second Pooh book—"[ . . . ] a little boy and his bear will always be playing"—suggests the iterative frequency, the eternal time of happy childhood.

### Ironic Ambiguity

The recurrent picturebook motif of child-adult conflict is also the focus in Burningham's *John Patrick Norman McHennessy—The Boy Who Was Always Late* (1987). Both the words and the images tell a story we intuitively do not trust: the modality is that of improbability. The story is presented from the boy's point of view and the pictures reflect his inner vision. There is a gap in the text as well as in the pictures about what actually happens to the boy on the way to school. After all, he does come late every day, having lost his gloves, torn his clothes, and got wet. Neither words nor images give us any clue to the real events of the story. However, our skepticism toward the boy's tall tales is shattered when his teacher is kidnapped by a gorilla. Or is this merely another tall tale happening inside his mind? Unlike many other picturebooks, there are no direct tokens of the dubitative and no objective perspective in the text in which, as sophisticated readers, we place ourselves. But the iconotext itself offers no strategy for our interpretation. We know that the boy is telling tales. We can assume the objective position, saying that the boy comes with poor excuses when he is late, and that from his totally oppressed position he takes mental revenge on his teacher by inventing another story. We can equally share the boy's *conceptional* point of view by saying, "Serves the teacher right!" thus empowering the child, which is the way that, for instance, Clare Bradford reads this book.[15] However, to adhere to only one interpretation would be to reduce the impact of the iconotext. The delicate balance between empowering and disempowering is part of the book's complexity. The questions arising are: Do we share the teacher's educational methods? Do we see the author's irony toward him? Do we share the boy's attitude toward school? The only real cue from the author is the recurrent phrase about the boy setting "off along the road to learn," which is overtly ironical, presumably adult, and therefore mocking the child rather than empowering him.

### Embedded Ambiguity

Strange as it may seem, few dream narratives involve girls, that is, the nature of the dream quest is seldom unquestionably female and not possible with a male character (*Through the Red Door,* discussed above, is one of the rare exceptions). *Fanny and the Birds* (1995), by Margareta Strömstedt and Tord Nygren, depicts the character's transformation, but unlike in *The Jaguar* or *Not Now, Bernard,* this transformation is not into a huge and fierce beast, but into a little frail bird (does this reflect the authors' idea of male aggressiveness contra female gentleness?). The wish to be able to fly is a common motif in children's fiction; however, Fanny's metamorphosis is not, as flying is often presented, a matter of carefree adventure (male?), but a result of profound empathy (female?). Fanny wakes up early in the morning to discover that a bird has flown into the glass veranda and been injured. Neither the text nor the illustrations indicate whether this episode is still a dream. The only hint is Fanny's horror-distorted face, which is immediately associated with Edvard Munch's most famous painting, *The Scream.* The nightmarelike figure suggests that perhaps Fanny is still asleep and dreaming. Otherwise, the following events are quite realistic: the father states that the bird is badly injured and that it is a mercy to kill it; Fanny is horrified and bursts into tears. But already in the next spread we must once again decide whether Fanny is dreaming (or pretending), as the injured bird comes to life and flies away. In fact, the flying bird is depicted within a circle with slightly deviating colors, in a manner in which the souls of the dead are sometimes portrayed on medieval paintings. In any case, in the next spread the narrative leaves the realistic level as the bird starts to talk to Fanny, and Fanny talks back. Fanny is in this spread depicted far away in the background, with her back turned to us and to her mother in the foreground. Presumably, she is on the edge between reality and fantasy, or—if the whole story is her dream—going even more deeply into her imagination. The next spread, which shows Fanny growing wings, is the only close-up in the book. She has taken off her red nightgown and is wearing old-fashioned white underpants (the clothes in the book suggests perhaps the 1930s, the author's childhood). Despite this prosaic detail, Fanny is here reminiscent of the Renaissance pictures of Annunciation angels, with a white shimmering light around her emphasizing the connection. When the transformation is complete, Fanny has the body of a bird and a human head and face. A possible association with a harpy is, however, impeded by the absence of

Tord Nygren's allusion to Munch's *The Scream* (1895) in *Fanny and the Birds*.

breasts; further, unlike the vulture-shaped harpies, the bird into which Fanny has turned is a small and vulnerable finch.

The subjective interpretation of the story is supported by the parents' discovering Fanny's absence and searching for her. Fanny reveals herself for her mother saying matter-of-factly, "I am a bird today [ . . . ] but I am coming back to you tonight," to which the mother says, "That's fine," and tells the father and the little sister that Fanny is away visiting an aunt. This verbal statement can naturally be read on different levels again. The mother may be humoring Fanny, who pretends to be a bird. The mother has recognized Fanny's empathy with the dead bird and her need to handle her sorrow through imaginative play. The pictures, conveying Fanny's point of view, contradict this interpretation. In the pictures, as well as in the subjective verbal story, Fanny really is a bird (indicative modality), and she finds security and support in her mother's acknowledgment of her disguise. Further, if the whole story is a dream, there is no need to account for the mother's immediate acceptance of the fact that, if her daughter has decided to be a bird for a day, it is merely part of the dream world. In any case, the mother shows remarkable female solidarity, not only in supporting her daughter's literal flight of imagination, but also in protecting her privacy from the rest of the family.

However, both the visual and the verbal narrative go one modal step further in the next spread, where Fanny returns home in the evening and joins the family at the kitchen table. The still-life of bread, cheese, and cucumber on the table emphasizes the realism of the setting and the whole situation. In the picture, Fanny is still a bird. In the text, the father at first does not recognize his daughter, but when the mother says, "Oh, it's Fanny [ . . . ] She is a bird today," seems to accept this as easily as the mother has done. Once again, the father may, at the mother's prompting, merely be endorsing Fanny's simulation. His understanding is further emphasized by his concerned question "When will you be ordinary Fanny again?" The parents are neither amazed by nor anxious about their daughter's appearance, and Fanny seems to have great confidence in their support. However, Fanny has come home to stay; she is tired and does not want to sleep in the tree with the other birds, but in her own bed.

This may be seen as another gender difference in the structure of the dream story. Boys come home because they are hungry. Fanny returns to the warmth and softness of her bed. However, she is still depicted as a bird, by words as well as by picture: "[ . . . ] mamma [ . . . ] tucks her in carefully not to break her wings." The mother is still supporting the child's play. The picture of Bird-Fanny in her bed is designed as a photograph stuck by the corners into slits in a photo album. This picture within a picture, like the flying bird in a clearly delineated circle, seems to create a borderline between imagination and reality, which so far in the story has been fluctuating. However, the next

Bird or human being? From *Fanny and the Birds,* by Margareta Strömstedt and
Tord Nygren.

spread effaces the border again. "During the night she dreams bird dreams,"
the words say. We see Fanny, in her human shape, asleep in her bed, its con-
tours vague and blurred, while the images of her dream appear in a semicircle
around her: the whole family has turned into birds, and their house a bird nest
up in a tree. The cool blue background is unique in the whole book, which
otherwise uses different shades of warm orange and green. The dream within
the dream both stresses that the previous story was real and further subverts
the reality of the events.

Finally, when Fanny wakes up in the morning, she is her ordinary self.
"But her room is full of small soft, white feathers," the text concludes, in the
"Mary Poppins syndrome," this is evidence, against all odds, that the dream
adventure has been real. The verbal text duplicates the pictures, as if unsure
that the visual ambiguity will be enough. In decoding this book, the reader
must make a series of decisions about modality to apply. Each choice determines the further interpretation and may prove false further on: the modalities
are embedded within each other.

### Alternating Ambiguity

In Anna-Clara and Thomas Tidholm's *Journey to Ugri-La-Brek* (1987), both
the verbal and the visual texts are equally ambivalent, but not symmetrical.

Ulla Rhedin maintains in her analysis of the book that the authors do not merely address children and adults on different levels, but rather address the adult coreader alone, using the child as a pretext.[16] Apart from our reluctance to discuss picturebooks in terms of the young readers' ability to understand them, we also believe that the scope of "understanding" stretches between the objective and subjective interpretation, and in a book like *Journey to Ugri-La-Brek,* the various aspects of the verbal and the visual texts allow a wide variety of different readings. As we read the book, the iconotext repeatedly and consistently subverts modality almost as soon as it has been established, perhaps creating confusion for a less sophisticated reader, but otherwise contributing to the story's exciting complexity.

On the subjective level, the two children set out to seek their grandfather, who has disappeared. Already here the words leave some substantial gaps. For a sophisticated reader, the implication of the disappearance is clear. The verbal text does not say that Grandfather is dead, it says that he "is lost." In the establishing scene, where the two children are introduced, they face the viewer with confused expressions, their arms hanging helplessly by their sides. The verbal text of the second spread states that Grandfather cannot be found in his flat, where his bed and armchair are empty, as are his bathroom, his larder, the hall, and the fridge. "[ . . . ] Grandfather has been kidnapped, he is now in another country / working in the moors / and he has left his glasses behind."[17] The picture expands the words by showing still more signs of desolation: leaves falling from potted plants and lamp plugs removed from their sockets. The somewhat distorted perspective creates a sense of a large, empty space in which the two children look small and desperate.

The verbal text says further: "And Mom doesn't want to say anything / and Dad knows nothing." The parents' inability to cope with death, telling the children that the deceased relative has "gone away," is a recurrent motif in children's literature. In the verbal narrative, the children are focalized, being treated as a collective protagonist (except for one doublespread in which they are focalized separately, the boy on the verso and the girl on the recto). Furthermore, the so-called narrative filter is used in the verbal text, which implies that the reader is supposed to understand more than the protagonists, that is, that Grandfather is dead. The picture of the empty room, especially the empty chair (cf. a similar image in Burningham's *Granpa*), manipulates the reader to make the inference the children are unable to make.

The verbal text of the third spread says that the children must save Grandfather, and on the next spread they pack for the journey. The child perspective is emphasized by the things they take with them: a flashlight, dog food, warm mittens, gingerbread, and lottery tickets (the latter perhaps something that they associate with Grandfather). The two preceding episodes, which seemingly slow down the story, have the purpose of emphasizing the child perspective and the child's apprehension of time. First, the text tells us, the girl must finish her lunch, which she apparently dislikes, and the boy must "wait for 28 years." Then the boy must go to the dentist's, and the girl must "wait for 37 years." This subjective perception of time prepares the reader for a correct interpretation of the children's long journey to Ugri-La-Brek, which lasts "a thousand years" (cf. Max traveling "almost over a year").

In the depiction of the journey, it may seem that the subjective perspective is maintained consistently by the verbal text. The children travel "northward over the football field / because everything that is black and far away is northward / Hundred kilometers, or maybe a thousand / over the desolate plains where nobody wants to live / or as much as ride a bicycle." However, at a closer look, the words are ambivalent in an interesting way. "Everything that is black and far away is northward" is the child's subjective perception of distance. The hundred or thousand kilometers is a typical childish hyperbole, and the mention of the bicycle most probably indicates that the children have never dared to ride their bicycles beyond a certain point. Thus, the child perspective notwithstanding, the words subvert themselves by suggesting that they convey a distorted view of the events. The picture supports the ambiguity. The children are depicted in the middle of the football field, with the dangerous darkness opening beyond the horizon, but the apartment houses are still very close, with their brightly lit windows signaling warmth and security.

In the next spread, the verbal text says that Grandfather has been lost in a dark forest, and the picture shows a tangled pattern of tracks between trees. The text continues to state that the children go past "old abandoned bakeries / and Myran thinks she sees a wolf / and Hinken finds a spear from the Stone age." The picture does not directly contradict the words, but some details suggest that the children most probably play in a backyard or a dump, with carcasses of old cars, stoves, and other junk. In the next spread, they have a picnic by the fire. The text says that it is now "night and dark like when you close your eyes in a cellar." Maybe the cellar is where they are in their game. The text also says, "Far, far away, where you cannot hear it / Mom and Dad call from the balcony / that they must go to bed." The image of the parents on a balcony appears high up in the dark sky as a vague shadow; however, it may signify that the children feel close and secure, even though the parents would not answer their important questions.

The visual images of the next two spreads contradict each other. The first of the two depicts the big World "on the other side of the fence." The many details of the picture are partly duplicated by words, but there are more objects in the picture than enumerated in the verbal description, so that the picture is expanding and encourages close study. The tiny figures of the children, their dog, and their sled are almost lost in the vast space of the spread, which naturally expresses their being small and awed when confronted with the big world. The next spread brings the children to the foreground again, and the setting is much more like a dump, with two dilapidated sheds and lots

Morfar har gått vilse i en svart skog
men Strunt har hittat spåret efter hans tofflor
Han har gått i konstiga krokar för han ser inte så bra
men nu är Hinken och Myran på väg för att rädda honom
och ge honom glasögonen

Här reser dom förbi gamla övergivna bagerier
och Myran tror att hon ser en varg
och Hinken hittar ett spjut från stenåldern
som indianerna hade när dom dödade elefanter
och nu börjar det snöa
för nu har det blivit vinter

Realistic or imaginary landscape? From *Journey to Ugri-La-Brek,* by Thomas and Anna-Clara Tidholm.

of rubbish. The contrasting pictures reflect the duality of the narrative: while the first accentuates the fantastic level, the second takes us back to "reality." The verbal text of the two spreads shows no difference.

In the rest of the story, the verbal and the visual text cooperate to convey the subjective narrative: the children definitely leave their everyday world behind and travel "to the other side of the World," beyond a dark river, where there is "nothing / just nothing and nothing," until they come to Ugri-La-Brek, which, we are informed, means "The-Village-Where-Smoke-Goes-Straight-Up." This imaginative name has a double significance. It is something the children have made up. But the straight smoke symbolizes the lack of movement and change, the realm of eternity, death. The image of the realm on the other side of the world may have been suggested to the children by a painting in Grandfather's flat; however, it is too vague to make a definite connection (the painting is also hanging on the wall in Grandfather's hut in Ugri-La-Brek, so it is significant). The rural landscape and the small wooden huts may just as well be memories from a winter holiday in the country. Thus while the words are mostly indicative, the modality of the pictures fluctuates between doubt and impossibility.

When the children are back in their own world, "someone else's grandfather has moved into their Grandfather's flat." The text suggests that the game has perhaps lasted many days. On the other hand, the parents are still having their afternoon coffee on the balcony, just as they were in the children's shadowy vision several spreads before. The setting includes the football field and a forest just beyond it, which might have been the scenery of the children's imaginary adventures.

There are, as we have shown, at least three different narrative levels in the book, all three intertwining, cooperating, and contradicting each other within the verbal and the pictorial text. To see the different levels more clearly, we may resort to Northrop Frye's "displacement" model, with the five modes: myth, romance, high mimetic, low mimetic, and ironic.[18] On the romance level, two children actually go on a magical journey to find their missing Grandfather. We cannot read the story on a purely mythical level, because the characters are not omnipotent gods but ordinary children. However, like the fairy-tale heroes, they possess supernatural powers that enable them to cross the boundary between the real and the magical realm, to travel for thousands of years without getting older, to survive without food, and the like. The country they enter and from which they successfully return may, if we so wish, be interpreted as the realm of death. The children cross the river to get there—an image that recurs in many myths (e.g. Styx in Greek mythology). They visit their dead Grandfather, assure themselves that he is all right, and return. Like mythical or fairy-tale heroes, they are not surprised by the extraordinary events or by their own abilities. They do not contemplate death, but take their journey for granted. The temporal pattern of the journey is similar to those in traditional fantasy novels: the journey does not take any of the primary time. This level is primarily narrated by words, although several verbal details contradict it. Several of the pictorial settings suggest a magical realm. The modality of this level is indicative.

On the mimetic level (in Frye's terms), the children play a game in the yard. The game is probably initiated by the disappearance of their grandfather. The verbal text often contradicts this reading, since it is narrated from the children's point of view. The pictures mostly contradict it as well, but there are more details in the setting that suggest the children are playing. The overall omniscient visual perspective implies an outside narrator who is very much aware of what is taking place. Thus it is the visual text that takes us down to the ironic level of the story, in which the children are not aware that by playing they investigate their attitude to death, that is, their adventure is also an inner journey, a therapy. This level is metatextual and is only open to a sophisticated reader. The fact that we are dealing with a collective protagonist impedes this reading, since we have to decide whose inner landscape we enter, the boy's or the girl's (note that in all the books discussed above we had an individual protagonist). A way to circumvent the problem is to apply the postmodern notion of intersubjectivity, which again demands a great deal of sophistication.

Only one sentence in the verbal text reveals that the children are indeed very much aware that Grandfather has died. When they talk to him in the village of Ugri-La-Brek, the girl asks, quite unexpectedly, "Is it because we tramped on the stairs?" "No, not at all," Grandfather says, and the conversation continues around other subjects. However, the girl's question reflects her suppressed guilt, which young children, according to psychologists, often feel when a relative or a friend dies. The last sentences of the book repeat the text in the beginning: "Mom doesn't want to say anything / and Dad knows nothing." The text continues: "But Hinken and Myran know / They say nothing." These words indicate reconciliation: the children have come to an understanding of death, whether we interpret the story as true or as play. Further, when the children are visiting the grandfather in his little hut, the text says, "Myran *believes* that she is *maybe* dreaming" (emphasis added). This is the only case of explicit doubt in the verbal text, but it is probably the best guidance to its complex structure.

## Notes

1. Gunther Kress and Theo van Leeuwen, *Reading Images: The Grammar of Visual Design* (London: Routledge, 1996, chapter 5). The use of their definition of "modality" is fruitful for reading visual images and has been used in picturebook analysis, for instance, by John Stephens and Jane Doonan.

2. Cf. David Topper, who argues that "it may be impossible to picture any negation, short of introducing written captions and/or conventional visual adjuncts to the picture, such as an X placed over a burning cigarette." In David Topper, "On Some Burdens Carried by Pictures," *Children's Literature Association Quarterly* 9 (1984) 1: 22. This argument goes radically against Kress and van Leeuwen's approach; see note 1.

3. See further Peter Neumeyer's analysis of dream narratives by Chris Van Allsburg in Peter Neumeyer, "How Picture Books Mean: the Case of Chris Van Allsburg," *Children's Literature Association Quarterly* 15 (1990) 1: 2–8.

4. One of the many theories of the fantastic is to be found in Tzvetan Todorov, *The Fantastic: A Structural Approach to a Literary Genre* (Cleveland: Case Western Reserve University, 1973). Hesitation, Todorov's central notion, is a modality. See also Kathryn Hume, *Fantasy and Mimesis: Responses to Reality in Western Literature* (New York: Methuen, 1984), where fantasy and mimesis are apprehended as two equal constituent elements of a literary work.

5. See, e.g., Kristin Hallberg, "Bilderbokens barn—drömmens och verklighetens resenärer." In *I bilderbokens värld,* ed. Kristin Hallberg and Boel Westin, 11–54 (Stockholm: Liber, 1985). See further Ulla Bergstrand and Maria Nikolajeva, *Läckergommarnas kungarike: Om matens funktion i barnlitteraturen* (Stockholm: Centre for the Study of Childhood Culture, 1999).

6. See Hallberg, op. cit.; Ulla Bergstrand, "Elsa Beskow and Children's Picture Books in Sweden, 1900–1940," *Swedish Book Review* (1990 suppl.): 9–14.

7. J. R. R. Tolkien was one of the first to question the legitimacy of such rational explanations. In his essay "On Fairy Stories," he dismisses *Alice in Wonderland* because in the end the heroine wakes up and her adventures turn out to have been a dream. He would probably dismiss *Paul Alone in the World* on the same grounds. See J. R. R. Tolkien, "On Fairy Stories," in his *Tree and Leaf* (London: Allen & Unwin, 1968): 11–70.

8. Cf. the interpretation of this book in Lena Kåreland and Barbro Werkmäster, *En livsvandring i tre akter* (Uppsala: Hjelm, 1994).

9. As we have clearly shown in our analysis of the translations of the *Baby* books in Chapter 1, the English-language version differs from the original in some essential aspects. Among other things, two key episodes involving the mother are omitted altogether, from the verbal as well as the visual text. We will therefore refer to the Swedish original edition, *Den vilda bebiresan*, quoting from it in our own translation.

10. See, e.g., John Stephens, *Language and Ideology in Children's Fiction* (London: Longman, 1992): 136f; Margery Hourihan, *Deconstructing the Hero: Literary Theory and Children's Literature* (London: Routledge, 1997): 12 and passim; Marina Warner, *No Go the Bogeyman: Scaring, Lulling, and Making Mock* (New York: Farrar, Straus and Giroux, 1998): 147–150.

11. On the psychological aspects of bedtime picturebooks see Mary Galbraight, " 'Goodnight Nobody' Revisited: Using an Attachment Perspective to Study Picture Books about Bedtime," *Children's Literature Association Quarterly* 23 (1998–99) 4: 172–180.

12. Joseph Schwarcz speaks of "the mutual infringement of outer and inner reality" in this book; see Joseph H. Schwarcz, *Ways of the Illustrator: Visual Communication in Children's Literature* (Chicago: American Library Association, 1982): 175.

13. E.g. Peter Hunt, *Criticism, Theory, and Children's Literature* (London: Blackwell, 1991): 128.

14. Cf. Warner, op.cit.: 150f.

15. Clare Bradford, "Along the Road to Learn: Children and Adults in the Picture Books of John Burningham," *Children's Literature in Education* 25 (1994) 4: 207f.

16. Ulla Rhedin, "Resan i barndomen. Om bilderböcker för barn och vuxna," in *Vår moderna bilderbok,* ed. Vivi Edström, 155–188 (Stockholm: Rabén & Sjögren, 1991).

17. In the Swedish text, no punctuation is used, perhaps to present the text as an "inner monologue" and also as a poetic text. We have marked the line breaks with slashes.

18. See Northrop Frye, *Anatomy of Criticism: Four Essays* (Princeton: Princeton University Press, 1957).

From *Come Away from the Water, Shirley,* by John Burningham.

# CHAPTER 7

# Figurative Language, Metafiction, and Intertext

Visual symbolic language as such lies beyond the scope of our present study, if only because it has been investigated thoroughly by many scholars, mainly from the point of view of art criticism. There is a well-developed methodology for the discussion of this aspect. Visual symbols in picturebooks can be very complex and equivocal, contributing to the general complexity of texts, as many studies of, for instance, Maurice Sendak's or Anthony Browne's books clearly show. On the other hand, they can be quite lucid, hardly needing an especially keen eye.

As far as verbal figurative language is concerned, that is, similes, personification, metaphors, and so on, some picturebooks abound in figures of speech, while others do not make use of them at all. Figurative language is based on the shift in the literal meaning of a word and its transferred meaning. The usage of figurative language in the verbal text of picturebooks is not different from novels and does not therefore deserve any special attention.

Instead, in this chapter we will explore some aspects of the text–image counterpoint on the level of language, including the phenomenon we have, for lack of a better term, called intraiconic texts, as well as metafiction and intertextuality.

## Signifier without Signified and Signified without Signifier: Figurative Language in Words and Images

In picturebooks, images can enhance the verbal figurative language. For instance, the simile "fresh as a rose" or the idiom "green with envy" can be treated literally in a picture. Personification especially allows wide possibilities in picturebooks, where the sun and the moon, the four seasons, day and night, the wind, the rain, and so on are ascribed anthropomorphic features. In such cases, words and images cooperate to produce an iconotext.

On the other hand, some picturebook creators make use of stale metaphors to produce unexpected effects, that is, subvert the verbal figures of
speech. "Milky Way" in Sendak's *In the Night Kitchen* (1970) is a literal
interpretation of a verbal set phrase. Normally, when we say "Milky Way"
referring to our galaxy, we do not associate the phrase with milk. In *Michael
Rosen's Book of Nonsense* (1997), illustrated by Clare Mackie, the text states:
"A football should not be round (or oval)—it should look like it sounds—like
a foot," and the picture shows impossible objects in a direct visualization of a
literal interpretation of a compound word. The text goes on to ask whether a
basketball should look like a basket.

Nonsense is a stylistic device often based on the discrepancy between the
literal meaning of the word and its metaphorical meaning, or between its true
meaning and the way the characters interpret it. Visualization of verbal nonsense is a challenge for an illustrator, offering endless possibilities of pictorial
play. Some of the rare examples can be drawn from Ernest Shepard's illustrations to *Winnie-the-Pooh*. Several verbal images, or nonce words, in the book
lack the signified, that is, an object connected with the particular word by
convention. Since the word denotes no object, its illustration is completely
arbitrary. Shepard chooses to illustrate the Heffalump (making him look
rather like an ordinary elephant both in Pooh's and Piglet's visions), but not
woozles and wizzles, nor the Spotted and Herbaceous Backson. In the woozle-
hunt chapter, Pooh is wondering whether he and Piglet are following two
Grandfathers, and what a Grandfather might look like. This is a complete
reversal of notions where the reader is able to create a visual image of a word
that for the character is as nonsensical as "woozle" is for the reader. In the
chapter about the discovery of the North Pole, Shepard makes use of a verbal
pun, illustrating the homonym, in this case the childish objectification of this
abstract term for a geographical location.

In the Disney movie *Winnie-the-Pooh and the Blustery Day,* there is a
dream sequence in which an army of Heffalumps of all kinds, colors, and
shapes attacks Pooh's honey jar. We can evaluate this treatment from two different viewpoints, either saying that the movie interprets the verbal image in a
more imaginative way than the book illustration, or that it denies the viewers
a possibility to create their own images.

A much discussed example of verbal nonsense is the poem "Jabberwocky" from *Through the Looking Glass*.[1] John Tenniel's original illustrations offer readers the visual image of Jabberwocky (a dragonlike monster)
when the poem is first introduced, and of the other creatures, alongside
Humpty-Dumpty's explanations: "[ . . . ] *'toves'* are something like bad-
gers—they're something like lizards—and they're something like cork-
screws." In the Disney movie *Alice in Wonderland,* there is an episode in
which Alice is walking through the woods meeting all kinds of strange creatures who are immediately apprehended as toves, borogoves, and raths, since

the whole scene is accompanied by the "Jabberwocky" poem set to music. Once again, the filmmakers have visualized the verbal images for the reader. Tenniel also chose to illustrate such verbal images as the Mock Turtle, and nonsensical portmanteau constructions such as Rocking-horse-fly and Bread-and-butter-fly.

Both Carroll and Milne approved of the original illustrations to their works, therefore we might assume that the visual images are congenial to their verbal counterparts. Subsequent illustrators have made different decisions about illustrating the nonsensical verbal images of the books. For instance, in a Russian edition illustrated by Boris Diodorov, the Heffalump is not featured in the pictures. Naturally, in foreign editions, many of the images have to be adapted to the verbal solutions presented by the translators.

Our third example comes from the Norwegian novel *The Magic Chalk,* by Zinken Hopp, illustrated by Malvin Neset, in which one of the characters is granted three wishes by a troll and as the first one asks for a "cuprobe." He has earlier boasted about the fine interiors of his ancestral home, including a cuprobe that was "molished and encristed." The troll wonders, of course, what a cuprobe is, to which the boy replies, "I have no idea, but I want one, molished and encristed." Since the troll is a powerful magician, he very soon produces a strange thing that he claims to be a cuprobe. The boy then asks whether the troll has remembered to make it molished and encristed. The troll admits that he has forgotten it, casts some more spells, and the cuprobe becomes molished and encristed. We are not completely helpless when confronted with this scene, because the language used in it has a clear grammatical structure. A cuprobe is apparently a noun, while "molished" and "encristed" are past participles of the verbs "to molish" and "to encrist," which may or may not be associated with existing words. The language follows the same logic as Noam Chomsky's famous example, "Green colorless ideas sleep furiously." However, if we tried to visualize this phrase we would meet with insurmountable problems. The illustrator of *The Magic Chalk* provides a visual image of the molished cuprobe, otherwise the signifier would be left without the signified.

On the other hand, we are constantly dealing with a variety of visual images that lack a signifier. One example is all the creatures and objects in surrealistic painting from Bosch to Dalí and Magritte, which, as already mentioned, have contributed considerably to contemporary picturebooks. In *Shut Up!* (1974), by Patrick Couratin, we meet a chain of visual images that perhaps correspond to portmanteau words: apple-elephant, elephant-hand, hand-rhinoceros, rhinoceros-man, man-duck, duck-hand, and so on. The verbal text offers no names for the depicted objects, but is nonsensical in itself. This book, however, is a mere episodic play with words and images, while in Anthony Browne's *Changes* (1990) a similar visual play is part of a narrative, conveying the young boy's confused mind. The images of the book are also of a portmanteau type: a kettle with cat's ears and tail, a slipper with a wing and a beak, and so on. The images are also dynamic, since the objects constantly shift shape.

A special case is presented in the so-called impossible figures and optical illusions, for instance M. C. Escher's or Oscar Reuterswärd's. These create a pictorial space that has no correspondence to perceptible reality. Gennadi Kalinovsky's illustrations for *Alice in Wonderland* try to convey the absurd world of the novel by depicting impossible space, which is a successful response to the verbal text. The distorted perspective of David McKee's *I Hate My Teddy Bear* (1982) or *Charlotte's Piggy Bank* (1996) is another variation on the theme.

We will now discuss some picturebooks that deliberately make use of the discrepancy between the signifier and the signified, or even the absence of one or the other. The work of Dr Seuss, obviously enough, provides some examples. An author/illustrator combined, Seuss creates a number of nonce words (signifiers that lack the signified) and gives them a visual content, for instance the Grinch in *How the Grinch Stole Christmas* (1957) and especially the many creatures of *Dr. Seuss's ABC* (1963): a duck-dog (not a portmanteau word, but rather a hybrid), a Fiffer-feffer-feff, an Icabod, a quacker-oo, and a Zizzer-Zazzer-Zuzz. Likewise, in *Marvin K. Mooney, Will You Please Go Now* (1972), the nonexisting names of various transportation means are visualized: a Zike-Bike, a Crunk-Car, a Zumble-Zay, and a Bumble-Boat. The strange appearances of these creatures and objects correspond to the funny

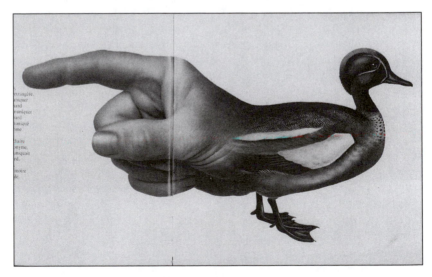

Visual portmanteau in Patrick Couratin's *Chute!*

И она сразу представила себе такую сцену:
«Мисс Алиса! Идите скорей, пора собираться на про-
гулку!»
«Не могу, нянечка! Диночка велели мне посторожить мы-

45

Impossible space: a Gennadi Kalinovsky illustration for *Alice in Wonderland.*

and nonsense-sounding words. *Green Eggs and Ham* (1960) is based on the incongruity between a linguistically correct expression and the absence of its correspondence in the perceptible world. In a picture, the logically impossible green eggs and ham can be easily depicted. Other verbal images that are, although not illogical, highly improbable are magnificently enhanced by pictures, for instance "camel on the ceiling," "Oscar's only ostrich oiled an orange owl," or "policemen in a pail" (from *ABC*). In *The Cat in the Hat* (1957), Seuss does something different again. The naughty cat carries in a big red box, announcing that it contains two things. The word "thing" is in this case a so-called linguistic shifter, that is, an expression the content of which can only be determined by the situation ("a thing" can denote almost anything, although perhaps most often an inanimate object). However, on the

"I didn't know you could sing," said Blue Teddy.

David McKee's impossible spaces in *I Hate My Teddy Bear* and
*Charlotte's Piggy Bank* allude to M. C. Escher.

next page, the word acquires a concrete and tangible signified, as it refers to
two living creatures. The word "thing" ceases to be a shifter and becomes a
regular signifier, while the signified, Thing One and Thing Two, are portrayed
in the picture, thus visualizing the concretized abstraction. Something similar
occurs in *Horton Hears a Who* (1954), where the interrogative pronoun
"who" (a shifter) is turned into a signifier with a signified.

*German Measles* (1988), by P.C. Jersild and Mati Lepp, is a picturebook
wholly based on visualization of nonce words and figurative language. The
Swedish medical term for German measles is "röda hund," which literally
means "red dog." At the end of the story, after the two children have had fun
during their illness, the girl says that she does not want to get well; she wants
to have her "red dog" for ever. One of the helping figures in the story takes the
"red dog", the measles, away from the children, but allows them to keep it in
the form of an image—transforming the stale metaphor into a real little red
puppy.

In the story, the two children are bored during the illness and start to create new words and draw their signifieds—or draw pictures of strange things
and give them names. Mostly, the words and images are of the portmanteau
type: girat (giraffe + rat), storcat (stork + cat), turelk (turtle + elk), and so on.
They even create their own parents: mamoo (mama + kangaroo) and dankey
(daddy + monkey). As the story progresses, the boundary between reality and
imagination is totally obliterated, and all the creatures enter the children's
world. There is no resolution bringing things to order again.

In a verbal narrative, it is possible to make statements like "round
squares" or "bald people with curls" or "green red roses" (the examples are
from a nonsense poem by Lennart Hellsing; cf. Dr. Seuss's "green eggs and
ham"). In a picturebook, an attempt to convey a similar statement visually
would prove difficult if not impossible. However, contemporary picturebooks
often make us aware of the conventionality of language by focusing on the
incompatibility of verbal statements and their visual correspondence. It is
possible to say, "I have seven daddies, but they are rather small." To envision
this statement and to draw the consequences of it is a challenge, successfully

Some visualizations of portmanteau words in *German Measles,* by
P. C. Jersild and Mati Lepp: girat . . .

storcat . . .

turelk . . .

. . . and the parents, mamoo and dankey. Stale metaphor visualized: the red dog.

met in Pija Lindenbaum's *Else-Marie and Her Seven Daddies* (1990). The pictures show the daddies in a variety of situations that are easy to describe by words, but perhaps a venture to visualize, and the humor of the book is derived from the fact that neither Else-Marie nor the surrounding people seem to notice the absurd situation. The book presents a clash of styles: ironic in images, but serious in words.

Pat Hutchins's *Don't Forget the Bacon* (1976) involves another kind of word–image play. The rhymelike order the mother gives her son as she sends him shopping goes: "Six farm eggs, a cake for tea, a pound of pears, and don't forget the bacon." As the boy walks down the street, the visual images he encounters are transformed into words, and the rhyme is successively corrupted. "Six farm eggs" are first changed into "six fat legs" and then into "six clothes pegs." "A cake for tea" becomes, through "a cape for me," "a rake for leaves." "A pound of pears" transforms into "a flight of stairs" and finally into "a pile of chairs." The reverse transformation is equally prompted by the things the boys sees. Since the whole verbal narrative is rendered by the boy's thoughts, in thought balloons, the connection between words and images must be made by the reader, and the comic effect is produced by the discrepancy between the verbal and the visual.

As many linguists have shown, proper names have no direct connection between the signifier and the signified. *The Pirate Book* (1965), by Lennart Hellsing and Poul Ströyer, is based on rhyming the names of the many pirate captains with their actions: "Pirate King / does the fling / pirate Lamotte / does the gavotte / pirate Schmaltz / dances a waltz / pirate Marston / dances the charlestone." From the names alone it is impossible to identify the many characters in this nonsense poem. The reading of the iconotext implies connecting each verbal image with its visual correspondence.

One of the distinctive features of postmodernism is the interrogation of language as an artistic means.[2] Although we have shown that the play with the signifier and the signified occurred already in the works of Lewis Carroll, an increasing number of contemporary picturebooks make use of this device to create an exciting stylistic counterpoint.

## Metafiction

Metafiction is a stylistic device aimed at destroying the illusion of a "reality" behind a text and instead emphasizing its fictionality. Metafictional elements in a text deliberately draw attention to its status as a literary construction and therefore raise questions about the relationship between fiction and reality.[3]

In picturebooks, visual images open wide possibilities for metafictional comments, as several scholars have observed.[4] In fact, mutual visual-verbal comments on modality, discussed in the previous chapter, are highly metafictional.[5] Further, since metafiction is primarily based on the conventionality of language,[6] the examples of the visualized figurative language above can be considered part of metafiction as well.

One of the simplest types of metafiction is direct address to the reader. It is widely used in classical novels for children as well as for adults. In picture-books, it may assume, for instance, the form of an admonition: Do you want to know what happened next?—turn the page. We meet it as a recurrent narrative device in Tove Jansson's *Moomin, Mymble and Little My* (1952), where every page is concluded by the direct question to the reader: "What do YOU think happened then?" The book also carries another interactive element, encouraging the reader to draw a picture of the fillyjonk "when she has calmed herself" in the empty space in a corner of a page.

There is, however, a much more subtle example of metafiction in the same book. The frontispiece of the book carries a picture of a bearded, bespectacled man in a correct suit with a bow tie, holding a pair of oversize scissors. Above him, a round hole is cut in the page, with uneven strips of paper falling down to the bottom of the page, while a clumsy printed inscription announces that "the holes are cut at Gebers." Gebers is the name of Tove Jansson's Swedish publisher (the Finnish translation naturally mentions its publisher, WSOY, and the English translation, Benn's). Since there are no human beings in the Moomin world, the man is not part of the narrative, but he is unmistakably part of the book, that is, the metanarrative that introduces the main narrative and invites the reader to enter it. In doing so, the figure brings forward the clear and yet fluctuating borders between fiction and reality.[7]

In Lingdren and Eriksson's *The Wild Baby's Dog* (1985), there is a short comment that can be apprehended as metafictional. As the baby rips off the dog's blazing tail, the narrator suddenly lifts above the diegetic level: "Such things happen in this world—one day everyone will die! No, not *us,* I mean the dog's tail. We just fly away quickly somewhere else" (author's emphasis). This is the only case where the narrator really exposes itself and refers to itself as "I," also revealing the story as a construction.

Most critics claim that metafictive elements have become prominent in contemporary literature and art since the early 1970s.[8] *Moomin, Mymble and Little My,* published in 1952, shows that this phenomenon is present in a considerably older text. It is true, however, that the number of picturebooks wholly based on metafictional play is rapidly increasing. One author who has made it his trademark is Jon Scieszka, who has collaborated with a number of different illustrators on his metafictional picturebooks. The simplest is perhaps *The True Story of the Three Little Pigs, by A. Wolf* (1989), illustrated by Lane Smith, in which the traditional story is told in the first person by the wolf himself. On the verbal side, the book is a witty and humorous reversal of the well-known plot, with many contemporary allusions, such as: "It's not my fault wolves eat cute little animals like bunnies and sheep and pigs [ . . . ] If cheeseburgers were cute, folks would probably think you were Big and Bad,

A metafictive figure in Tove Jansson's *Moomin, Mymble and
Little My.*

too." Statements like this one are illustrated by funny and thought-provoking
pictures, which, however, are not metafictional as such. The only genuinely
metafictional visual element is the cover, representing a page of a newspaper
titled "Daily Wolf," with a large heading "The True Story of the 3 little pigs."
In the right bottom corner of the cover we see a pig's foot holding the newspaper. The story's existence as an artifact is subtly emphasized.

*The Stinky Cheese Man and Other Fairly Stupid Tales* (1992), perhaps
Scieszka's best-known book, illustrated by Lane Smith, has a metanarrative
with a narrator portrayed in the pictures as well as one of the characters constantly commenting on the story. The narrator frequently addresses the

reader—or perhaps the character, the Little Red Hen. The narrator is, incidentally, Jack Up the Hill, who tells his own story, so the widespread metafictive play with narrator/character reversal is applied too. The narrator even pretends that he does not know the outcome of the story. Although the main focus of the book is the many fractured tales it contains, its metafictional nature contributes to the whole impression.

The most overtly metafictional of Scieszka's creations is *The Book That Jack Wrote* (1994), illustrated by Daniel Adel. The first spread shows a painting in a heavy wooden frame of a very thick volume, with the same cover as the book itself. The volume is lying on a black-and-white checkered surface. In front of it we see a pair of round spectacles, and from under the book, a pair of red shoes are showing (perhaps reminiscent of the Wicked Witch of the East killed by Dorothy's house in *The Wizard of Oz* movie). The text states simply: "This is the Book that Jack Wrote." In the next spread, the book is opened and we see an idyllic rural landscape, framed in a similar heavy wooden frame. The double frame removes the readers from the story, "alienates" them. Next, a rat "falls" into the picture. The rat is outside the inner frame, but entering the landscape, transgressing the borders between two framed pictorial spaces. In this third spread, the picture of the book inside the outer frame has moved closer to us, so that the checkered background is no longer seen, the spectacles have disappeared beyond the frame, and the shoes are barely visible. The next spread, portraying "the cat, that ate the Rat," has only one frame, and the picture of the open book is gone. It is impossible to decide whether we have now entered the outer frame or whether the inner narrative has invaded the outer frame. The rest of the story (the Dog that chased the Cat, the Cow that spooked the Dog, the Baby humming the tune, the Pie flying through the air, and so on) takes place within this undeterminable frame; however, the frame itself changes from rectangular to a variety of shapes and forms evoking paintings in a museum. Every now and then a little detail sticks out of the frame as if trying to force the border. Some of the characters allude to Lewis Carroll's figures (Humpty-Dumpty, the Hatter) as well as Tenniel's illustrations of them. On the Hatter spread, we see a framed picture on the wall replicating the cover and the first spread (the so-called mis-en-abyme, see below). We also see the black-and-white checkered floor: the story is literally rounding up. "The bug, that frayed the rug, that tripped the Hatter . . ." in the next spread is wearing red buckled shoes, and in its half-blurred face human traits begin to be discernible, with a reddish pointed nose and round spectacles. It is easy to anticipate the metamorphosis in the next spread, where we see "the Man in the tattered coat," whom we immediately recognize from the cover and the first spread. Behind him, slightly obstructed by the outer frame, we see the replica of the picture with the open book. However, the next episode is perhaps less predictable, as the heavy volume comes tumbling from above, transgressing the frame and, in the final spread, squashing the man. We are thus brought to realize that the spectacles and the red shoes from the earlier spread are what is left of the squashed man. However, this last spread also breaks the border between the reader and the narrative, since the wooded frame of the painting is splintered too. As readers, were are now inside the narrative, and the fictionality of our own reality is suggested, just as it happens in *Through the Looking-Glass* as Alice contemplates the question "Which dreamed it?"

## Framing

The notion of framing, so apparent in *The Book That Jack Wrote,* is central in the theory of metafiction.[9] Scieszka and Adel's book is an extreme, but not the only picturebook using the device. *The Tangled Tale* (1994), by the Estonian mother-daughter team Aino Pervik and Piret Raud, presents a challenge for the most sophisticated reader. The verbal text contradicts itself on every level of the story. The character presentation on the first spread goes: "Once upon a time there was a little hare," and continues, in another frame: "Or, if you prefer birds, there was a big owl." The setting is described partly as: "It was a warm summer," partly as: "On the other hand, if you love snow, it was a cold winter, and snow covered everything." This first spread contains four frames within each other, and it is only the reader's competence that prompts

Frames are metafictive devices in *The Tangled Tale,* by Aino Pervik and Piret Raud.

the correct reading strategy. The words "Once upon a time" suggest that this is the beginning of the narrative, and we are compelled to start reading from the inner frame, which, visually, contains the presentation of the character, a little hare, in his natural setting, a green meadow. Turning outward into the next frame, we find the other character, the owl, and the contradictory setting, a winter night landscape. The third frame confirms the first setting, and the final, outer frame repeats the winter setting. However, while the linearity of the verbal text compels us to seek a reasonable order of reading, the visual images of the four frames can be perceived in any order or all at once. The doublespread sets the main pattern of the story on the verbal as well as the visual level: polarity and self-contradiction.

In the next spread, we find three frames, but since the inner one is shifted to the right, our left-to-right reading habit makes us start reading the verbal text in the upper left-hand corner, which happens to be in the middle frame. This frame depicts the little hare eating clover in the summer meadow. We are then guided to proceed into the outer frame, reading the verbal text in the lower left-hand corner, which states that in winter there was no clover to be found. The frame depicts a winter night landscape. Finally, we get into the inner frame, with a close-up of the owl against a snowy background, the text saying, "In any case, if it was an owl, she did not like clover. Instead she had a taste for small hares." The owl's beak is sticking out from the frame, as if she

were trying to break through the border dividing the two space-times and get the little hare in the middle frame.

In the next spread, the division between frames is definitely broken. There are only two frames, both have a winter landscape, and the owl has managed to penetrate the inner frame and is tugging at one of the two little hares. However, this hare in itself presents a frame-breaking, or rather a visual portmanteau, since it has a hare's head that extends into a heap of clover. The verbal text does not help the confused reader, since it first states, in the outer frame, that the owl had hard times finding dry clover under snow, while the inner frame claims that it was not the owl, but the hare who found the clover.

The fourth spread contains three frames with fluctuating borders. The inner frame contains the owl pecking "fresh juicy clover in the summer meadow all day," the middle frame hurries to say that it wasn't the owl, but the hare, who did not peck, but chew, and not all day, but all night. The last statement does not, however, make sense, since the night is associated with the owl. The outer frame, with a winter landscape, points this out: ". . . wait a minute, that means it was the owl after all." The "wait a minute," and the narrator's attempt to clarify the story, is just another metafictive trait, amplified in the next spread by the so-called comment on discourse: "This story is getting mixed-up." Although the spread contains two frames, they do not separate two space-times, but are part of the same picture, at least as far as the setting is concerned. The two characters on the other hand are presented in a typical impossible-figure manner, stretching through the inner frame as if it were empty. And while the little hare looks normal, the owl has metamorphosed into a visual portmanteau with one half, in the outer frame, a hare and the other, in the inner frame, an owl. The verbal text, too, jumps between frames within one sentence, starting with "Let's choose the little hare" in the upper left-hand corner, continuing as "and not the big old owl," in the inner frame, and concluding with: "who let the little hare go, and they both went to the meadow to eat clover." While we have in previous discussions seen either words or pictures performing impossible acrobatics, in this book they both do it in perfect interaction, the language used to enhance the unlimited possibilities of visual play.

A special type of framing, widely discussed in contemporary art criticism and adopted by literary critics as well, is "mis-en-abyme." It can be defined as a text—visual or verbal—embedded within another text as its miniature replica. For instance, the little picture within the larger identical picture on the cover of *The Book That Jack Wrote* is an excellent example of visual mis-en-abyme. Tord Nygren's *The Red Thread* (1987) contains several cases of mis-en-abyme. In Sven Nordqvist's *Fox Hunt* (1986), there is a picture in a heavy gilded frame among the many objects in Festus's toolshed. The picture portrays Festus and Mercury preparing explosives, that is, exactly

Pettson gick tillbaka in i snickarboden och började leta i alla gamla
färgburkar som stod på kaminen.
— Var är smällarna, om jag får fråga? sa han och såg grymt på Findus.
Här var fullt med smällare i förrgår och nu är de slut. Findus???
— Såvitt jag vet brukar de alltid ligga i hattasken bredvid dörren,
sa Findus tålmodigt.
— Ja, det kan hända. Det stämmer det, mumlade Pettson och plockade fickorna
fulla med smällare och stubintråd och bengaliska eldar ur hattasken.

Mis-en-abyme in Sven Nordqvist's *Fox Hunt.*

what they are doing in the main text and picture. The little picture does not
directly duplicate the large one, but nevertheless mirrors it. The function of
the little picture is a metafictional comment on the story.

## Intertextuality

Some scholars include intertextuality among metafictional elements. Intertextuality naturally brings to our attention the existence of other "realities"
outside the given text, as seen from the discussion of *The Stinky Cheese Man*
and *The Book That Jack Wrote*. However, it also has other functions.

The notion of intertextuality refers to all kinds of links between two or more texts: irony, parody, literary and extraliterary allusions, direct quotations or indirect references to previous texts, fracturing of well-known patterns, and so on. In picturebooks, intertextuality, as everything else, works on two levels, the verbal and the visual. As all other aspects of the iconotext, intertextuality can be symmetrical and counterpointing. The latter implies that the intertextual link can be only present in the verbal or in the visual text, and it is naturally the visual intertextual ("intervisual") elements that are of special interest for us.

Let us, however, start with some obvious and elementary examples of intertextuality in picturebooks. Ever-increasing numbers of picturebooks are based on fractured fairy tales. Most of them use as their main artistic devices a change of setting (*Snow White in New York,* by Fiona French, 1987), reversed gender roles (*Prince Cinders* by Babette Cole, 1987), and reversed power positions (*The Three Little Wolves and the Big Bad Pig,* by Eugene Trivizas and Helen Oxenbury, 1993). In all these cases, intertextuality works symmetrically on the verbal and the visual levels. However, many contemporary illustrators create a counterpoint, for instance by making pictures deliberately anachronistic. Anthony Browne's version of *Hansel and Gretel* (1995) includes a television set as part of the interior.[10]

Intertextuality presupposes the reader's active participation in the decoding process; in other words, it is the reader who makes the intertextual connection. It means that the allusion only makes sense if the reader is familiar with the hypotext (the text alluded to). It is therefore not surprising that most fractured-tale picturebooks are based on well-known plots, as the few examples above clearly demonstrate. In Scieczka's *The Stinky Cheese Man* and *The Frog Prince Continued* (1991), several tales are blended. These two books illustrate two diverse types of intertextuality, anagram and contamination. The various topsy-turvy tales in *The Stinky Cheese Man* can be easily recognized and the original tales reconstructed from them, just as we can decode the original message from an anagram (a coded message in which the order of letters is deliberately mixed up). In *The Frog Prince Continued,* the story contains elements from many other famous tales; it is "contaminated" by other texts without naming them overtly: "Sleeping Beauty," "Snow White," "Hansel and Gretel," and "Cinderella." In both books, the reader must know the original stories to appreciate the parody; the worldwide knowledge of the parodied texts makes the book equally appreciated by any reader.

In other cases, intertextuality may be culturally dependent. *The Tale of the Little, Little Cat* (1997), by Thomas Halling and Gunna Grähs, is a parodic sequel to the classic Swedish picturebook *The Tale of the Little, Little Old Woman* (1897) by Elsa Beskow, which ends by the woman chasing her cat away from her house. The modern picturebook, written to celebrate the centenary of Beskow's beloved classic, continues from this episode and, moreover, is told, verbally as well as visually, from the cat's point of view. Once again, the conventional power position is interrogated, and the weak and oppressed figure is empowered. The pictorial style of the book is deliberately caricature-like, contrasting sharply with the pastoral style of the original. The hundred years separating the two books are clearly visible in the parody.

*Look Max's Grave* (1991), by Barbro Lindgren and Eva Erkisson, is a self-parody on the innumerable Max (Sam in the English translation) books: *Max's Ball, Max's Teddy Bear, Max's Wagon,* to name a few. The book may be an ironic response to the publisher demanding more Max books; it may also address parents who are sick and tired of reading Max books to their children, as well as young parents who listened to Max books as children. The verbal style of the book does not differ from the parodied originals: it is written in baby talk, with grammatically incorrect sentences of no more than three or four words (the specific device of Max books that caused much discussion when they first appeared). Unlike the original Max books, the text is handwritten. The pictures are stylistically different from the originals in layout and color scheme, but similar in their reduced settings and simple props. The plot takes Max, the one-year-old protagonist of the original books, through his whole life with school, job, marriage, children, divorce, and senility to the last spread in which a group of mourning relatives visits Max's grave. The text–image interaction is full of humor and irony. For instance, the

"Max looks papers," from *Look Max's Grave,* by Barbro Lindgren and Eva Eriksson.

text "Max looks papers" is accompanied by Max at his desk looking with great interest into his blond secretary's low-cut dress. The text "Max wants chewing tobacco" is illustrated by an angry old man in a wheelchair, with a frustrated nurse in the background. There are also allusions to popular TV shows evidently meant to be recognized. While the book can perhaps be enjoyed in its own right, much of its delight is lost if the reader is not familiar with (and probably fed up with) the hypotext.

All the discussed examples, although they make extensive use of visual artistic devices, are basically symmetrical in their text–image relationship. It is perhaps a greater challenge to discover more subtle intertextual links based on visual images. Several scholars have observed the pictorial allusion to John Bauer's fairy tale about princess Tussock-grass in Tove Jansson's *The Dangerous Journey* (1977).[11] A less-noticed allusion is to be found in Lena Anderson's *Maja's Alphabet* (1984), where the letter Ö is illustrated by wintergreen ("ögonljus" in Swedish). Whether this picture also alludes to Tove Jansson's is dubious. Rather both Jansson and Anderson respond to one of the most famous pictures in Swedish art (it has even been featured on a postal

Intervisuality: John Bauer's *Princess Tussock-grass* (above), Lena Anderson's *Maja's Alphabet* (top right), and Tove Jansson's *The Dangerous Journey* (bottom right).

ÖGONLJUS

stamp) in quite different ways. Jansson's picture is a representation of fear, in a clear contrast to Bauer's fairy-tale idyll. Susanna's reflection in the pond is a monster—a projection of the dark side of her Self. Anderson's picture is as peaceful and pensive as Bauer's, although it lacks the fairy-tale atmosphere. Maja is not pretty like princess Tussock-grass, and her stripy hair, big round eyeglasses, and modern clothes signal a different kind of character. Since *Maja's Alphabet* also has a dialogic relationship to Bauer's contemporary, Ottilia Adelborg, this link must be more intentional than a possible side wink to Jansson.

More obvious pictorial allusions, which address a less sophisticated audience, are produced by famous books featured in the pictures, for instance Beskow's *Peter's Adventures in Blueberry Land* (1901) used as a weapon in *I'll Take Care of the Crocodiles* (1977). For a Swedish adult reader, this episode may remind of Selma Lagerlöf's *The Saga of Gösta Berling,* where a volume of Corinna is thrown into the gaping mouth of an attacking wolf. However, this allusion is not visual and may even be totally unintentional. Beskow's book, a companion of every Swedish child, will be easily recognized, and the way it is utilized creates a humorous effect. In Pija Lindenbaum's *Else-Marie and Her Seven Daddies,* we can discern the cover and title of the book the daddies are reading in bed for Else-Marie: *The Little Prince.* Such direct allusions are common in picturebooks as well as novels, and they are used to create a sense of continuity.[12]

There is another type of intertextuality in *Else-Marie,* sometimes referred to as intratextuality: the authors' allusions to their own texts. On her way to school, Else-Marie thinks with horror about the neighbor's fierce dog. The dog, reappearing in a later spread when Else-Marie is going home with her daddies, is a self-quotation from *Boodil My Dog* (1991). It is featured in

Self-quotations: the author's favorite dog in *Boodil My Dog* (above), *Britten and Prince Benny* (top right), and *Else-Marie and Her Seven Daddies* (bottom right), by Pija Lindenbaum.

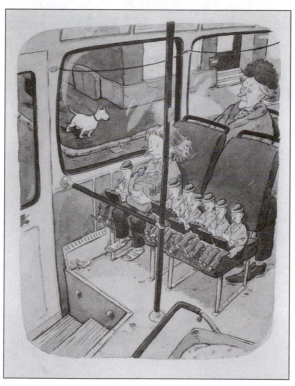

still another picturebook by the same author, *Britten and Prince Benny* (1996), without ever being mentioned by words. A reader not familiar with Boodil will probably not even notice this little detail, but for an initiated reader it is highly enjoyable. Many picturebook creators seem to amuse themselves, perhaps also addressing their audience, by scattering such minor details from their own texts in the books. In *Come Into My Night, Come Into My Dream* (1978), we can see the previous book by the same authors, *I'll Take Care of the Crocodiles,* lying on the floor in the nursery. As many scholars have observed, Anthony Browne's books abound in pictorial self-quotations, especially the images of gorillas and pigs. Another feature that appears in many of his books—*Look What I've Got* (1980), *Gorilla* (1983), *The Tunnel* (1989), *Changes* (1990), *Zoo* (1992), and others—is the brick wall as a background, which has different functions in the books, but is a detail meant

Inger and Lasse Sandberg "quote" their own characters in *ABCD*.

to be recognized. Less subtle use of intratextuality appears in Inger and Lasse Sandberg's *ABCD* (1986), where most of the characters from their previous books are portrayed, representing the letters of the alphabet. All these elements also have metafictive functions, since they draw our attention to the essence of the text as an artistic construction.

Still another widely used intertextual element in contemporary picturebooks is allusion to famous works of art.[13] Sendak's allusion to Rodin's sculpture *The Thinker* in *Where the Wild Things Are* has been noticed by all critics discussing the book. *La Gioconda* is a favorite object for pictorial parody in picturebooks, perhaps because it is assumed to be widely known even by less sophisticated readers. In *The Cat's Terror* (1992), by Fam Ekman, a whole museum hall is filled with distorted masterpieces with feline associations.[14] In Browne's *The Tunnel,* we can see the famous illustration by Walter Crane to "Little Red Riding Hood" on a wall in the girl's room, which will be echoed by the girl's red hooded coat. A less prominent intertextual link has been suggested in a Swedish art anthology for children, where the bathing scene from *The Wild Baby* is juxtaposed with Anders Zorn's famous painting.[15]

It is, however, essential not to go too far in search of visual intertexts. The image of the forest in *The Tunnel* is a locus communus (common place) rather than a specific allusion to any of the forests in world painting or in picturebooks. Stylization is not the same as intertextuality either, for instance the deliberate Pre-Rafaelite style in Susan Hill and Angela Barrett's *Beware, Beware* (1993).

## Intraiconic Texts

In earlier chapters we have examined the nature of intraiconic texts, particularly from the dual audience perspective and in the nature of the decoding process. We want to address it again in order to understand the stylistic and metafictive aspects of this technique, where the accepted division between verbal and iconic texts is violated and an ongoing dialogue between the two takes precedence.

A brief study of Maurice Sendak's work provides some insight into the flowering of this technique. Both *Where the Wild Things Are* (1963) and *Outside Over There* (1981) make a very clear distinction between the verbal narrative and the illustration. In *Outside Over There,* the text and illustrations are emphatically separated, either by placing the words in a framed and bordered label on the picture, on a separate page, or on the white margin at the bottom of the illustrated page. Only the frontispiece, title page, and final page do not draw a distinct line or frame separating the wording and the picture. This follows the pattern established in *Wild Things,* where a few words appear either on the page facing the illustration or clearly demarcated below it. In some

A picturebook illustration alluding to a painting: *The Wild Baby* and Anders Zorn's *The First Bath* (1888).

cases there are as few as two words stimulating illustration, and in the six pages of wild rumpus no words at all appear.

Other works of Sendak's reveal a different pattern. In *The Sign on Rosie's Door* (1960), the pictures of Rosie and her friends are sometimes on separate pages, sometimes given borders to separate them from the text, but most often appear in various places on the page, above, below, or within the text. However, they remain clearly separate in function, the words telling the story, the pictures illustrating it. In *Wild Things*, the only word appearing in illustrations is "Max" as the name of the boat, and "by Max" on the picture hanging on the wall in the second illustration. The merging of text and illustration begins in a variety of ways in *In the Night Kitchen* (1970). Words in the text are absorbed into the illustrations, predominantly in cartoonlike balloons identifying spoken language. In addition, all kinds of contrapuntal noises and signs being to appear: thumps and bumps, oohs and aahs, the aptly named "Mickey Oven," labels on flour, salt, and jam.

The sounds providing the "racket in the night" that pulls Mickey out of his bed, out of his clothes, and into the Night Kitchen might be interpreted as the knocking of his subconscious mind, his dream life pulling him into its sphere, just as the music in *Outside Over There* opened the way for the goblins representing Ida's inner feelings. But where Max and Ida move into a wordless visionary state, a clear otherworld of experience very different from their usual existence, Mickey's journey takes him into a world of sensations in which language is all around. Just as he is submerged in the cake batter, so is he in words.

At this stage in Sendak's development, the words are very much in harmony with both the picture and the text. "Thump, dump, clump, lump, bump" go the noises. "Quiet down there!" cries Mickey, standing on his bed. The words could be taken from a reading primer, and Mickey's words and actions are simple and straightforward. As he falls through the dark, he arrives smiling and with a soft landing in the bowl of batter, and the words that follow are plain and uncomplicated, easily recognizable to a child. Generally the words in the illustrations reflect their referent well: the jar labeled "jam" has a picture of strawberries, "flour" is printed on an appropriately shaped bag, "salt" on a round box, and "cream" on a carton. But some of the representations include ironic little jokes—"phoenix baking soda," shortening that characterizes itself as "fabulous, good and great" all at once, and cream that "may be sold only at midnight." In these cases the words are establishing a new relationship with their signified, creating a verbal dialogue that plays with the nature of meaning in its relationship between object and word, and between words and other words. Also easily recognizable is the transformation of kitchen containers into the box, carton, and bottle-shaped buildings of the cityscape, complete with rows of lighted windows and decorated with magnified kitchen implements: beaters, whisks, spoons, graters, which we noted earlier. Here it is the nature of images in dialogue with other images that

parallels the interactive play of words. These container-buildings offer infor-
mative and promotional labels that are the most distracting of all the words in
the illustrations: "TA-KA-KAKE"; "CHASE-O washes and blues at one
time"; "ROLLED WHITE OATS, first cheapest best." These messages and
jokes on the buildings are not part of the story line, but vie with it for the
reader's attention, in essence diverting it from action to sensation. Nonetheless, while the words that have crossed the border into the illustrations create
a dialogue with those in the text, this dialogue is harmonious and complementary, and reflects the relationship between the character's ordinary life
and his night or dream vision, each adding richness to the other.

In *We Are All in the Dumps with Jack and Guy* (1993), the invasion of the
graphic borders involves a process of multiple dialogue that reaches a
crescendo of extraordinary pitch and complexity whose allusions have risen
well beyond the child's frame of reference. Sendak's choice of the nursery
rhyme as his formal verbal narrative is a brilliant entrée into a book that presents such a speaking picture of the world's ills in social, political, and economic terms. Unlike his earlier illustrations of others' works, for example
those inspired by Grimm's "Dear Mili" (1980), the official verbal text of the
first half of *Dumps,* featuring the first of the two nursery rhymes Sendak has
selected and combined, is almost buried in words of his own. For this section
Sendak thus assumes the role of writer as well as that of illustrator, and here
the city is both the everyday and the otherworld merged into one. The text has
completely invaded the illustrations, and its coherence, hard to understand
even on its own, is in continual conflict with the words that appear in all parts
of the illustrations: as dialogue in balloons, as signposts, as lettering on dis-
carded cartons, but most of all as newspaper headlines, articles, and advertisements that make sad, ironic, and bitingly satiric comments on the plight of
the children, on the state of the community at large, and on the rapaciousness
of some and poverty of others in an economically turbulent world. Interspersed among these complex and sophisticated messages are personal messages and autobiographical notes from Sendak's own life.

The initial nursery rhyme provides the context for the title and cover
illustration, the first half of the book, and its finale. As the book proceeds, the
layering of text, illustration, other dialogue, word messages, and references
contrives a collage of meaning that reflects and comments upon itself in a
truly postmodern, metafictive manner. The rats' bridge game takes place in
the shadow of a real bridge; the children cry "Trumped" beneath the Trump
Tower; a child wears a T-shirt with a Wild Thing on it; references to Sendak's
doctor are hidden in the illustration. In counterpoint with the text of the continuing nursery rhyme, Sendak continues his own rhythmic chorus until the
children's last cries of "Lost! Tricked Trumped Dumped!" At this point the
newspaper text emerges to continue the verbal commentary. Presented initially on the front cover by the headlines "Leaner Times, Meaner Times,"

"Homeless Shelters," and the more fanciful "Children Triumph," "Kid Elected President," the newspapers' print becomes increasingly legible as the children's voices fail, giving the effect of a rising volume of social commentary to replace their cries.

From an initial mention of AIDS and ozone, in pages alternating with nursery rhyme text, the newspapers erupt into pointed comments focusing on real estate advertisements for smart housing with no kids allowed, and investment property and mortgages, including one headline suggesting that we "profit from our losses." The poignancy of their message is accentuated by the fact that the papers are serving as clothing for the homeless children. This subversive text continues in headlines identifying a homeless shelter system, bank gains, crime, and economic downturn, while the children watch the rat making off with the baby. As the first nursery rhyme ends, the papers make their final comments about layoffs, chaos in shelters, famine, and babies starving, and then fall silent, their print moving back into illegibility, and ultimately the newspapers disappear.

Colin Thompson, like Sendak, packs his illustrations with words, but these tend to be more tangential to the narrative development than do Sendak's commentaries and are predominantly playful, with the words taking on an independence and arbitrariness regardless of their context. The majority of the references in *Looking for Atlantis* (1993) do embellish the theme of water, though sometimes in a byzantine convolution. But many others are just amusing in their own right and set up dialogue of their own. "Spring water, dilute to taste" exemplifies the joke with a water referent, but "silicon chips" on a package of potato chips has gone off on a journey of its own. Other spin-offs might be illustrated by the three boxes in the boy's room labeled "nurse costume," "junior feminist outfit," and "chartered accountant outfit." These have nothing to do with the Atlantis theme, though one could agree they provoke imagination. The nurse outfit is easily predicted, and the red crosses on the box support this, but its very predictability jars with the others, which may similarly refer to stereotyped roles, but whose form is not apparent.

Ultimately these techniques draw attention to the presence of the picture-book creator and serve as an alternative text, which can easily derail the narrative flow.

# Notes

1. See, e.g., Jean-Jacques Lecercle, *Philosophy of Nonsense: The Intuitions of Victorian Nonsense Literature* (London: Routledge, 1994).

2. See, e.g., Linda Hutcheon, *A Poetics of Postmodernism: History, Theory, Fiction* (New York: Routledge, 1988), especially chapter 5.

3. See Patricia Waugh, *Metafiction: The Theory and Practice of Self-Conscious Fiction* (London: Methuen, 1984): 2. For a more detailed discussion of metafiction in

children's literature, see Maria Nikolajeva, *Children's Literature Comes of Age: Toward a New Aesthetic* (New York: Garland, 1996): 189ff.

4. See David Lewis, "The Constructedness of Texts: Picture Books and the Metafictive," *Signal* 62 (1990): 131–146; Margaret Mackey, "Metafiction for Beginners: Allan Ahlberg's Ten in a Bed," *Children's Literature in Education* 21 (1990) 3: 179–187; John Stephens, " 'Didn't I Tell You about the Time I Pushed the Brothers Grimm off Humpty Dumpty's Wall?' Metafictional Strategies for Constituting the Audience as Agent on the Narratives of Janet and Allan Ahlberg," in *Children's Literature and Contemporary Theory,* ed. Michael Stone, 63–75 (Wollongong, University of Wollongong, 1991). Also, scholars such as Clare Bradford and Jane Doonan observe metafictive elements in their studies of picturebooks.

5. Patricia Waugh includes fantastic worlds in her very broad definition of metafiction. See Waugh, op. cit.: 108ff.

6. Waugh, op. cit.: 3.

7. In their analysis of the book, Lena Kåreland and Barbro Werkmäster observe the figure and interpret him as an old-fashioned theater manager opening the curtains to present the performance. They do not make use of the notion of metafiction. See Lena Kåreland and Barbro Werkmäster, *En livsvandring i tre akter* (Uppsala: Hjelm, 1994): 41.

8. E.g. Waugh, op. cit.: 21ff. She does, however, admit the presence of metafictive traits in *Don Quixote* and *Tristram Shandy*.

9. See Waugh, op. cit.: 28–34.

10. See further Jane Doonan, "Talking Pictures: A New Look at Hansel and Gretel," *Signal* 42 (1983): 123–131.

11. See, e.g., Boel Westin, "Resan till mumindalen. Om Tove Janssons bilderboksestetik," in *I bilderbokens värld,* ed. Kristin Hallberg and Boel Westin (Stockholm: Liber, 1985): 241; Ulla Rhedin, *Bilderboken: På väg mot en teori* (Stockholm: Alfabeta, 1993): 137.

12. The title of Isabelle Nières's essay "Writers Writing a Short History of Children's Literature Within Their Texts" pinpoints this aspect. See Isabelle Nières, "Writers Writing a Short History of Children's Literature within Their Texts," in *Aspects and Issues in the History of Children's Literature,* ed. Maria Nikolajeva, 49–56 (Westport: Greenwood, 1995).

13. Jane Doonan discusses this phenomenon in Anthony Browne's picturebooks. See Jane Doonan, "Drawing Out Ideas: A Second Decade of the Work of Anthony Browne," *The Lion and the Unicorn* 23 (1998) 1: 30–56.

14. Sandra Beckett discussed this book and several others in her paper "Parodic Play with Painting in Picture Books," presented at the 20th conference of the Childrens' Literature Association, Paris, July 1998.

15. See *Min nya skattkammare: Bildriket,* ed. Harriet Alfons (Stockholm: Natur och kultur, 1984): 22–23.

# CHAPTER 8

# Picturebook Paratexts

Almost nothing has been written about the paratexts of picturebooks such as titles, covers, or endpapers.[1] These elements are, however, still more important in picturebooks than in novels. If the cover of a children's novel serves as a decoration and at best can contribute to the general first impact, the cover of a picturebook is often an integral part of the narrative, especially when the cover picture does not repeat any of the pictures inside the book. The narrative can indeed start on the cover, and it can go beyond the last page onto the back cover. Endpapers can convey essential information, and pictures on title pages can both complement and contradict the narrative. Since the amount of verbal text in picturebooks is limited, the title itself can sometimes constitute a considerable percentage of the book's verbal message.

In this chapter we will consider some paratextual elements of picturebooks, especially those that contribute to a word–image tension.[2]

## Format

The format of the book belongs to the category described by Genette as the publisher's peritexts.[3] Format is an extremely important feature of a picturebook, and there is a considerably greater variation in formats of picturebooks as compared to novels. While the discussion of the format as such lies beyond the scope of our interest, being part of book design, we can still raise some questions that concern the aesthetic aspects of the actual size of a picturebook. How does the format of a picturebook affect our appreciation of it? Can we imagine a Beatrix Potter book in a Babar format? And what happens with Potter's delicate watercolors when they are blown up to a full A4 page? On the other hand, what happens to the tiny details of a Sven Nordqvist double-spread if it is reduced to a three-by-five-inch miniature? The format is thus not accidental, but part of the book's aesthetic whole.

Why do artists sometimes use standing (vertical) and sometimes lying (horizontal) formats? The lying formats are more or less unique to picturebooks, for we seldom if ever meet them in novels. Obviously, lying formats allow a horizontal composition, which is especially useful in depicting space and movement. The lying format is similar both to a theater stage and to a movie screen. There are also square picturebooks.[4]

It is evident that some picturebook creators prefer particular formats that suit their personal style. There are at least two contrasting concepts about what format is "best" for young readers: small books are better for small hands, or large books are more attractive and easier for small hands, to hold and handle. Both arguments sound reasonable. Picturebook creators who work in different formats, for instance Inger and Lasse Sandberg, apparently have some ideas about choosing a format to suit their purpose.

There are many examples of picturebooks produced in different formats. Eric Carle's *The Very Hungry Caterpillar* (1969) is available both in a large and a small format, which hardly affects our appreciation of the pictures. Paperback and other serial editions are usually in a smaller format, which occasionally may make the pictures less distinct and even disturb the balance between pictures and words.[5]

## Titles

First some general remarks on book titles.[6] Book titles are important parts of the text as an entity, and many empirical studies show that young readers often choose (or reject) books because of titles. In their general function, picturebook titles do not differ radically from novel titles. The most traditional titles of children's books are so-called nominal, comprising the main character's name: *Aunt Green, Aunt Brown and Aunt Lavender* (1918), by Elsa Beskow, *Eloise* (1955), by Kay Thompson and Hilary Knight, *Princess Smartypants* (1986), by Babette Cole (cf. *Robinson Crusoe, Winnie-the-Pooh,* or *Mary Poppins*). Another common pattern for the traditional title is a combination of a name and an epithet or appellation: H. A. Rey's *Curious George* (1941), Dr. Seuss's *The Cat in the Hat* (1957), Inger and Lasse Sandberg's *Little Ghost Godfrey* (1965), Ulf Nilsson and Eva Eriksson's *Little Sister Rabbit* (1983), Eric Carle's *The Very Hungry Caterpillar*. The adjective "little" is used to emphasize the character's closeness to the supposed audience. The epithets "curious" or "hungry" immediately indicate the central conflict of the story. However, in *Curious George,* the adjective contains an evaluation of the character, which definitely comes from an adult, didactic narrator. The nominal title of John Burningham's *John Patrick Norman McHennessy—The Boy Who Was Always Late* (1987) is of course highly ironic.

Collective characters are often featured in the title, for example Elsa

Beskow's *Children of the Forest* (1910). The character's name can also be combined with a place: *Ida-Maria from Arfliden* (1977), by Ann-Madeleine Gelotte (cf. *Anne of Green Gables*). An extremely popular combination is also *The Tale of . . . (Peter Rabbit)* or *The Story of . . . (Babar, the Little Elephant)*. The practice of having the protagonist's name in the title is, at least in children's literature, a didactic narrative device, giving the young reader some direct and honest information about the content of the book, its genre (animal story), and its audience: a girl's name will probably be associated with a book for girls, a boy's name with a book for boys.

Instead of the protagonist's name a nominal title can also contain the central object of the story: Lindgren and Eriksson's *Sam's Teddy Bear* (1981), David McKee's *Charlotte's Piggy Bank* (1996), Lennart Hellsing and Svend Otto S.'s *The Wonderful Pumpkin* (1975), Sven Nordqvist's *Pancake Pie* (1985). Virginia Lee Burton's title *The Little House* (1942) is different, since the inanimate object, the house, is the protagonist of the story, not the character's attribute or possession (cf. *The Little House on the Prairie*). Likewise, in Lennart Hellsing and Fibben Hald's *The Egg* (1978), the title object is the protagonist.

Another traditional type of title may be called narrative, that is, a title that in some way sums up the essence of the story. Such titles can either be formed with a verb—*Thomas Goes Out* (1969), by Gunilla Wolde, *The Wild Baby Goes to Sea* (1982), by Lindgren and Eriksson, *Lily Takes a Walk* (1987), by Satoshi Kitamura—or as a nominative phrase, *Peter's Voyage* (1921), by Elsa Beskow, *Bedtime for Frances* (1960), by Russell Hoban and Garth Williams, *Rosie's Walk* (1968), by Pat Hutchins, or *The Hat Hunt* (1987), by Sven Nordqvist. The word *journey* seems to be popular, and it is often ambiguous, since it allows the "objective" as well as the "subjective" interpretation: Ivar Arosenius's *Journey with a Cat* (1908), Tove Jansson's *The Dangerous Journey* (1977), Anna-Clara and Thomas Tidholm's *Journey to Ugri-La-Brek* (1987). The journey of the title is often supposed to be apprehended as an inner journey. However, Mitsumasa Anno's *Journey* (1977) is much more literal.

In picturebooks, titles may both clarify and contradict the double narrative. It is obvious that Tord Nygren's title *The Red Thread* (1987), which is the only verbal text of this wordless story, makes the reader aware of the visual image of the thread and manipulates the reading. The title is metafictive, since it gives the reader an interpretive strategy: follow the red thread. The titles *Sunshine* (1981) and *Moonlight* (1982), by Jan Ormerod, are a more poetical way of saying "Morning" and "Evening," or "Getting Up" and "Going to Bed," giving a fairly honest description of what the books are about.

The nominal title *Aldo* (1991), by John Burningham, is mystifying: the title figure is not the protagonist of the book, and it is from the pictures alone that we learn that Aldo, the girl's imaginary friend, is a rabbit. The nominal title *Granpa* (1984), by Burningham, is somewhat misleading: the intersubjective nature of both the visual and the verbal narrative makes the title highly ambiguous. The title *Spotty* (1945), by Margret and H. A. Rey, is nominal, but at the same time it suggests the main conflict of the story, supported by the cover picture: the little spotted rabbit is not like other rabbits.

The "topographical" titles of Maurice Sendak's picturebooks signify places that are either imaginary—*Where the Wild Things Are* (1963), *Outside Over There* (1981)—or transformed by magic—*In the Night Kitchen* (1970). None of the titles reveal the plot or the conflict of the narrative. They are thus rather symbolic and mystifying.

Titles like *I Don't Want to Go to Bed* (1947), by Astrid Lindgren and Birgitta Nordenskjöld, or *I Can Drive All Cars* (1965), by Karin Nyman and Ylva Källström, present a problem both with the pictures and the rest of the verbal text, since the first-person perspective of the title does not correspond to the omniscient perspective of the narrative. On the other hand, the title *Else-Marie and Her Seven Daddies* (1990), by Pija Lindenbaum, uses the third-person perspective, while the story is told in the first person. By comparison, the titles *I'll Take Care of the Crocodiles* (1977) and *Come Into My Night, Come Into My Dream* (1978), by Stefan Mählqvist and Tord Nygren, reflect the "subjective" nature of the story, conveying the first-person narrator's perspective. *Come Into My Night . . .* is a very ambiguous title, since its narratee is unclear. Who is the narrator inviting into his dream? The reader? The absent parents? Since in the previous book the father participated in the dream journey, it is possible that the title is an appeal to the father to join in the magical adventure once again. On the other hand, titles like *Come Away From the Water, Shirley* (1977) and *Time to Get Out of the Bath, Shirley* (1978), by John Burningham, convey the adult perspective, while the narrative is based on the contrast between the adult and the child perspective. Depending on our position as readers, the title either amplifies the adult perspective or creates an additional ironic counterpoint.

The title *Röda Hund* (1988), by P. C. Jersild and Mati Lepp, is a pun in Swedish: as previously mentioned it denotes the name of an illness, German measles, suffered by the children in the story, but it means literally "red dog," and this metaphorical red dog appears as a character in the story. The verbal expression, which has lost its literal meaning, is visualized in the narrative.

Thus the titles of picturebooks are a very important part of the text–image interplay and contribute to all the types of interaction we have observed inside the books themselves.

We can also take a brief look at what happens to titles in translation. The Swedish title *Mamman och den vilda bebin* ("Mama and the wild baby") emphasizes the warm relationship between the mother and her child; the fact that the mother stands first in the title gives her a special importance. The

English title *The Wild Baby* focuses solely on the baby. The British title of the sequel, *The Wild Baby's Dog,* is nominative, making the dog the central character of the story, which contradicts the story itself, especially in the British translation, where the dog's personality, vague in the original, is further muted. The American title, *The Wild Baby Gets a Puppy,* is closer to the original and accentuates the central event of the story, with its action verb at the center of the title.

## Titles and Covers

The titles of picturebooks naturally appear on covers, and picturebook covers always, without exception, display a picture. It can be a picture that is repeated inside the book, or it can be unique. A cover picture that is repeated, even with a slight variation, inside the book anticipates the plot and together with the title, especially a clear-cut title like "The Tale of . . ." or "The Journey to . . . ," provides some information about the book's story, genre, and addressee.

However, the cover may contradict the story itself (as we have shown, for instance, in *Peter's Voyage*), or the title may mystify rather than clarify the cover. The title *Rosie's Walk,* in combination with the cover picture, is ambiguous. We do not know whether Rosie is the name of the hen or the fox or neither. It is not until the first doublespread that we learn the title character is the hen. The title *Not Now, Bernard* (1980), by David McKee, is still more confusing. We do not know whether Bernard is the name of the boy or the monster, and the utterance "Not now, Bernard" comes from neither of them.

Sam books have identical covers with a picture of the boy and the object featured in the title: *Sam's Ball, Sam's Teddy Bear,* and so on. But the cover also advertises the other titles in the series, portraying the teddy bear, the lamp, the cake, the bowl, and the ball, as well as the boy's two "enemies," the cat and the dog.

In the layout of the cover, the artist may use different fonts, sizes, and configurations for the title, which occasionally can affect our understanding of the book. For instance, the arch-formed title of Anthony Browne's *The Tunnel* (1989) evokes the central image of the book.[7] In the title of *The Jaguar* (1987), by Ulf Stark and Anna Höglund, the letters are yellow and furry, with black spots. The word "alphabet" in Lena Anderson's *Maja's Alphabet* (1984) is composed of letters made of twigs. The title *The Dangerous Journey* (on the title page, not on the cover) is dissolving in water, anticipating the perilous balloon flight over the stormy ocean.[8]

Normally, we do not pay much attention to the layout of the title. However, the examples above show how this device helps to enhance the message of the book. We see this clearly when we compare original publications with foreign translations, which quite often use a different font for the title. Also,

The cover of each Sam book features objects from the other books.

paperback editions sometimes destroy the effect. In fact, the arch-formed title of *The Tunnel* is, in the Walker Book edition, replaced by a straight one.

The choice of the cover picture reflects the authors' (or in some cases perhaps the publishers') idea of the most dramatic or enticing episode in the story. It would be reasonable to expect that the plot and the conflict of the book should not be revealed in the cover. Yet, amazingly, many picturebooks destroy the suspense created by an enticing title by featuring the setting or the antagonist on the cover, for instance in *Where the Wild Things Are*. It may feel wrong to have seen the Wild Things before they appear in the story. Likewise, the mysterious green elf in *Come Into My Night, Come Into My Dream* is presented on the cover, and the surprise caused by his appearance inside the book is diminished. By comparison, since crocodiles are mentioned in the title of *I'll Take Care of the Crocodiles,* the cover picture does not reveal too much of the plot. Moreover, it is rather contradictory to the title, because the boy on the cover is scared and confused, even though he is hugging two crocodiles and stepping carelessly on a third.

The title *The Wild Baby Gets a Puppy* is revealing enough, but the cover picture, with the baby and his toys dancing merrily on a rock under a starry sky, anticipates too early the happy outcome of the conflict. On the contrary, the cover picture of *The Wild Baby Goes to Sea,* portraying the baby sailing in the wooden crate, does not reveal more than the title does. The cover of the first book, *The Wild Baby,* shows Mama hugging the baby, which emphasizes her love and the great security it provides for the little child. This central picture, which can be seen as both the starting and the ending point of the whole book, is surrounded by nine images of the baby in different postures, in a dynamic circular movement anticipating the recto of the first spread.

Quite often, the cover picture, whether it is unique or repeats a picture from inside the book, is placed within a frame. Framing creates a sense of detachment, and together with the title and the author's name on the cover, it emphasizes the existence of the book as an artifact.[9]

## Endpapers

In the vast majority of picturebooks, endpapers are white or neutral. Unlike novels, picturebooks may also lack endpapers altogether, instead having the title page and copyright page/frontispiece directly inside the cover. However, a growing number of picturebook creators have discovered the possibilities of endpapers as additional paratexts that can contribute to the story in various ways.[10]

A common device is to depict the main character several times on endpapers, performing various actions, most often not mentioned inside the book. For instance, in Barbro Lindgren and Cecilia Torudd's *A Worm's Tale* (1985), the twenty-five images of the little worm fill the gaps in the visual–verbal story between the episodes described, suggesting that there are many more adventures to be told about this funny creature. Original editions of H. A. Rey's *Curious George* have multiple figures of the little monkey on endpapers, and many editions of *Babar* have fascinating rows of elephants. Endpapers of Margareta Strömstedt and Tord Nygren's *Fanny and the Birds* (1995) repeat the pattern of wallpaper in Fanny's room. The front endpaper of *German Measles* is decorated with red spots. *Where the Wild Things Are* has some exotic-looking flowers. *Else-Marie and Her Seven Daddies* shows diagonal rows of tiny felt hats alternating with lollipops, which the daddies bring to Else-Marie. In Astrid Lindgren and Ilon Wikland's *Look, Mardy, It's Snowing* (1983), endpapers show a panoramic view of the little town—a view that does not appear inside the book. The function of the endpaper is that of an establishing scene. Endpapers of Kay Thompson and Hilary Knight's *Eloise* (1955) show the naughty little heroine rushing off the right edge, while a little turtle crawls after her in the left-hand corner—an obvious allusion to Achilles and the turtle.

The endpapers of John Burningham's *Come Away from the Water, Shirley*

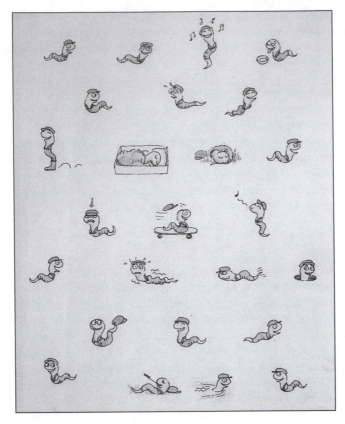

Endpaper from Barbro Lindgren and Cecilia Torudd's
*A Worm's Tale.*

(1977) carry a map of Shirley's imaginary journey. Maps as endpapers are
widely used in children's novels, for instance *The Wind in the Willows* or *Winnie-the-Pooh,* so picturebooks are not unique in this respect. *Island Boy*
(1988), a historical picturebook by Barbara Cooney, shows the map of the
described area on endpapers. Endpapers are not merely a decoration, but convey important additional information. In *Shirley,* for instance, we may
assume that the map is something Shirley has seen in a book or in a museum;
it is conceivable that she has this map in her room or in the family's living
room, and that it has stimulated her imagination. But it may equally be a
"mind map" that instead stimulates the reader's imagination. In *Island Boy,*
the map has an educational function.

The endpapers in Sendak's *We're All in the Dumps with Jack and Guy*

(1993) are made of brown kraft paper, coarse and crinkly-textured, in contrast to the rest of the book's more standard medium. This paper prepares us for the book's unusual socially provocative theme, suggesting the rawness of a life devoid of the usual "civilized" resources, and the need to use and reuse the detritus of a richer life, like the cardboard boxes the children sleep in. It also presents the "third world" theme immediately picked up on the half-title page where the baby, a child of color dressed only in a tattered loincloth, howls. The color of the endpaper matches the color of the baby's skin, and the rough texture suggests the discomfort of life on the edges of civilization.

We have mentioned in earlier chapters how endpapers can add to the narrative itself and even influence our interpretation. In Astrid Lindgren and Ilon Wikland's *I Don't Want to Go to Bed* (1988), the endpapers showing the boy playing with his stuffed animals manipulate us to apprehend the story as play. The endpapers of *Come Into My Night, Come Into My Dream* show the boy's head in profile, merging with some images from his nightmares: the green elf, green-brown leaves, the owl, the frog, the moon; the images themselves are blurred and fluctuating, for instance the beads in the elf's chain transform into dewdrops. The endpaper illustration emphasizes the interpretation of the story as the boy's dream, something that takes place inside his mind.

The endpapers of John Burningam's *John Patrick Norman McHennessy—the Boy Who was Always Late* show uneven handwritten lines of the boy's assignment: "I must not tell lies about crocodiles and I must not lose my gloves." On closer examination we notice that the right-page lines instead say: "I must not tell *lise* about crocodiles . . ." (emphasis added). The endpapers add a highly ironic comment to the story. In the Swedish translation of the book, the misspelled word has been omitted, and at least part of the irony lost.

Occasionally, the picturebook narrative can start on the front endpaper, for instance in Tord Nygren's *The Red Thread* (1987), where the double-spread of the carousel precedes the title page. The back endpaper brings together a number of characters and themes from throughout the book, again reinforcing the notion of linearity, but again undermining this expectation by giving a false sense of an ending. There is no real integration of characters or themes, and the movement of the children and of the pointing hand simply signals us on, following the thread, which takes us to the beginning again.

In most picturebooks, front and back endpapers are identical. However, they can be used to emphasize the changes that have taken place within the book. The endpapers of *The Tunnel* have the "female" space (the flowery wallpaper) on the verso and the "male" space (brick wall) on the recto. On the front endpaper, there is a book—the girl's attribute—lying in front of the flowery wall. On the back endpaper, the book has been moved over to the boy's space and is accompanied by a soccer ball, the boy's attribute. The union of the book and the ball reflect the reconciliation of the brother and sister in the book.

## Title Page

The title page normally contains the title, the name of the author and illustrator, and, optionally, the name of the publisher. Occasionally picturebooks have a half-title page (a page with the title only, immediately preceding the title page) or a dedication page. It is quite common to have a small picture on the title page and half-title page, which most often is a detail of some picture inside the book, probably with the background cut off. The function of such a picture is purely decorative, anticipating the plot. It is not unusual to have a picture of the main character, which then serves as an introduction, instead of the verbal "Here is . . ." or "Meet . . .". If we had doubts about the protagonist from the cover of *Not Now, Bernard,* the picture of the boy on the title page suggests that Bernard is indeed the name of the boy, which is immediately confirmed in the first spread.

The picture on the title page of Sven Nordqvist's *Willie in the Big World* (1985) shows a forget-me-not, which will be featured in the story. The title page of *Rosie's Walk* is an establishing picture, giving a whole panoramic view of the setting, the details of which will appear on the subsequent spreads.

However, the title-page picture may, just as the cover picture, suggest and amplify a certain interpretation. On the title page of *Journey to Ugri-La-Brek,* we see an empty blue rocking chair which will appear toward the end of the story when the children finally find their lost grandfather. This rocking chair is not featured in the "real" world, so the children must either have made it up or perhaps seen it somewhere during their imaginary quest. The empty chair suggests that the journey takes place in the children's minds.

Occasionally, the narrative can start on the title page. In *I'll Take Care of the Crocodiles,* we see the boy sitting with his back to us but turning his head and saying, in a speech balloon, "When you are almost just three years old and as big as myself and don't want to go to sleep . . ." (see page 252). We are thus introduced to the narrator/protagonist, and the verbal story continues on the first spread.

Stephen Roxburgh's interpretation of *Outside Over There* presupposes that the narrative starts on the half-title page, where Ida is holding her baby sister by the hands teaching her to walk. A squatting goblin is lurking by the fence. On the title page, which actually is a doublespread, Ida has taken up the baby, appears afraid, and looks suspiciously right at the reader. The goblin is getting up, and three more are hurrying from the other side, so Ida is now surrounded by enemies (whether they are real or imaginary is another ques-

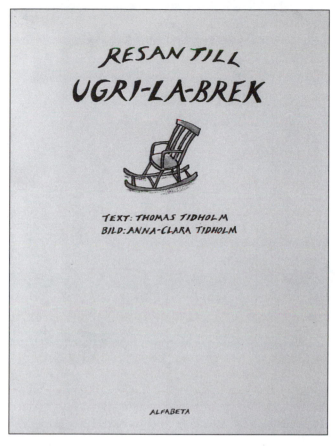

RESAN TILL

UGRI-LA-BREK

TEXT: THOMAS TIDHOLM
BILD: ANNA-CLARA TIDHOLM

ALFABETA

Title-page picture of *Journey to Ugri-La-Brek* adds to the book's uncertainty.

tion). On the next page, which carries the dedication—another paratext—Ida is hurrying away from the reader and into the picture, pursued by a goblin. None of the three paratextual pictures have any backgrounds. When the story as such starts, the spreads have fully depicted settings, occasionally framed. The story may thus be interpreted as Ida's fancies or a fairy tale which she is telling her sister. On the last page, Ida and her sister are back by the fence, and Roxburgh suggests that the journey has taken place between the two steps taken by the baby.[11] With this interpretation, the visual paratexts constitute the primary narrative, while the journey is a fantastic paralepsis.

We have already mentioned the dedication page of *Outside Over There,* which besides the verbal dedication carries important visual information.

The narrative in *I'll Take Care of the Crocodiles* starts on the
title page.

Dedications, mottoes, and the like are rare in children's fiction and still more
rare in picturebooks. However, they do exist. For instance, in Sendak's *In the
Night Kitchen,* the dedication is accompanied by the picture of Mickey in his
airplane, with a speech balloon saying "MAMA PAPA."

In film, it is quite common that the narrative starts before the title and the
credits. For practical reasons, it is not possible to start the narrative on the
cover of a book and wait until the title page to give the title and the name of
the authors. By starting the story on the front endpaper, the half-title page, the
frontispiece, or the title page, picturebook creators provide a variety of pictorial solutions corresponding to the above-mentioned device from film. Unfortunately, these elements very often disappear or are corrupted in translations,
reprints, and paperback editions.

## Back Cover

In many picturebooks, the back cover continues the front cover, so that, if folded out, the cover constitutes a whole picture. However, there are seldom any essential details on the back cover that complement or contradict the story. Presumably, this is based on our reading conventions: when we have finished reading the verbal text of the book, we assume that the story is over and do not pay much attention to the back cover.

A number of contemporary picturebook authors deliberately challenge this convention by letting a decisive clue of the story appear on the back cover. One frequently discussed example is Jörg Steiner and Jörg Müller's *The Bear Who Wanted to be a Bear* (1976), where the final picture inside the book has a pessimistic tone, depicting a winter landscape, which suggests the protagonist's defeat and possibly death. The back cover, however, shows a picture of spring, evoking hope and, in contrast to death, resurrection and new life.[12]

The cover of *We're All in the Dumps* reverses our expectation by putting the large-captioned title of the book on the back cover. The front cover offers an upbeat, if perhaps fanciful note to the homeless children's situation by positing "Kid elected President" as a newspaper headline, and showing the baby emerging from the mouth (which we later learn to identify as the moon) holding a sprig of grain, a clear "rebirth" suggestion. One is tempted to consider these as they would ordinarily appear, with the picture providing a positive ending on the back cover.

In *The Red Thread,* the thread continues on the back cover, leading the reader back to the front and into the book once again, in a neverending, circular story.

However, back covers seldom carry any verbal text that is part of the narrative. On the contrary, back covers are frequently used for paratexts such as a brief plot summary, a presentation of author and illustrator (sometimes with a photo), a recommendation on the reader's age, excerpts from reviews, information on other books by the same authors, and the like. As any educational texts, these are often strongly didactic, presenting the book as "funny," "magnificently told," and so on. Often they impose on the reader just one of the many interpretative strategies, for instance maintaining that the character makes an exciting journey in his imagination.

Such educational instructive paratexts can also be placed elsewhere in the book. Colin Thompson's *Looking for Atlantis* (1993) is a very interesting example of a pedagogical context grafted on to the original format. Unlike the British edition, the later American Dragonfly edition uses the endpapers to offer instructions on how to turn the book into a practical training exercise. At the beginning, readers are encouraged to hunt through the book to count among other things the number of fish, doors, mice, stairs, and/or ladders to be found. They are given exercises in observation in real life: "Look at the next person who enters the room. Then close your eyes and see how much you remember" about such details as the person's eye and hair color, shoes and shirt. And they are asked to draw pictures of what might be found behind a closed closet door. The back endpaper introduces "fun facts" about surrealism and Atlantis, and suggests both imaginary and observational exercises. The back cover has some final advice for parents: "Read to a Child! The most important 20 minutes of your day," thus specifying even the appropriate amount of time to devote to this activity. A statement on the back cover notes that this book is "in the field of social studies"; whether or not we agree with this categorization, it is sure that the addition of this pedagogical context significantly alters the nature of the reading experience.

## Postmodern Play with Paratexts

A contemporary "postmodern" picturebook may deliberately question the paratextual conventions, which is probably best illustrated by Jon Scieszka and Lane Smith's *The Stinky Cheese Man* (1992). The story—or rather its metafictive frame—begins on the frontispiece. The title page carries the inscription "Title Page." The dedication, "to our close, personal, special friend: (your name here)," is supplied with the comment: "Who ever looks at that dedication stuff anyhow?" There is an introduction by the narrator, Jack Up the Hill, and a stamp imitating the well-known warning from cigarette packs. The table of contents comes after the first tale. The back endpaper comes before the last tale. Finally, the back cover says, "What is this doing here? This is ugly! Who is this ISBN guy?" Perhaps only a very keen eye will notice some small-type additions on the copyright page, such as "The illustrations are rendered in oil and vinegar" and—after the usual "This book is sold under condition," and so forth—"Anyone caught telling these fairly stupid tales will be visited, in person, by the Stinky Cheese Man."

Like all postmodern games, the book presupposes that the reader is familiar with the way paratexts normally function in a book. The titles of the tales, as the tales themselves, are all parodic: "The Princess and the Bowling Ball," "Little Red Running Shorts," "Cinderumpelstiltskin," "The Tortoise and the Hair," and so on.

## Picturebook Sequels and Series

Just like novels for children, successful picturebooks are often followed by successors involving the same characters and sometimes the same settings. Sequels and series are still more common in picturebooks than in novels. While we most often associate series of seven or more novels with popular fiction, it is quite normal to have over twenty picturebooks involving the same character. Since the plot and the time span of picturebooks are limited, often focused upon one episode, picturebooks allow an endless string of such episodes. We have therefore five books about Frances, six books about Curious George, seven original books about Babar, twenty-two books about Alfie Atkins, eight Festus and Mercury books, and so on (to these must be added the various spin-off products such as coloring books, ABC and counting books, calendars, exhibit books, and more).[13] When evaluating this phenomenon, we must take into account both commercial (extraliterary) and aesthetic aspects. The commercial demands publishers put on writers mean that a successful book is supposed to be followed by a sequel. Titles often contribute to this, featuring the name of the popular character. The aesthetic aspect, as stated above, means that since a book only depicts a short time span, there is always room for further development. However, most picturebook follow-ups are series rather than sequels.

Series differ from sequels in that the individual books stand on their own without any organizational relationship to the others, so that they can be read in any order. The series characters do not change and do not get older. It is perhaps essential to read the first Curious George book or the first Babar book to understand the character's background (George comes over from Africa, Babar meets the old lady; notably, both characters are introduced into Western civilization), but it is not of overall importance. The later books can be enjoyed on their own, and the first books, if read afterward, can function as flashbacks. It is even possible to omit them altogether and still appreciate the rest of the series. Details in the Curious George sequels refer to events from previous books; for instance, in *Curious George Goes to the Hospital* (1966), the man in the yellow suit reminds George of a hospital episode in *Curious George Takes a Job* (1947). However, this is not essential to understanding the plot.

On the other hand, the Wild Baby books have an inner structure and sequence, although vague. For instance, the cock the baby finds on the voyage in *The Wild Baby Goes to Sea* is later featured, in the visual text only, in *The Wild Baby Gets a Puppy*. Since the puppy is not featured in the two other books, we assume that they take place before the appearance of the puppy. However, these details are fairly insignificant for the general appreciation of the Wild Baby books. One of the Alfie Atkins books describes Alfie's first day in school, which marks the flow of time. Actually, in some books Alfie is stated to be four years old, and in some others he is five or six or seven, but it does not affect the plots or the psychological development of the character. In the Festus and Mercury series, some books take place in summer, others in autumn or winter, but these seasonal changes do not bring about any growth or maturation of the character. Thus, since many picturebooks are simply episodic in nature, we do not wholly share Joseph Schwarcz's opinion that serialization allows full character development.[14] Some picturebooks have been treated by critics as trilogies: Sendak's *Where the Wild Things Are, In the Night Kitchen,* and *Outside Over There,*[15] or Stefan Mählqvist and Tord Nygren's *I'll Take Care of the Crocodiles, Come Into My Night,* and *The Dragon Mountain* (1981). While the idea is enticing, this kind of labeling is arbitrary. The books may belong together thematically (for instance, being representations of the protagonists' dreams), but in our opinion this is not sufficient to call them sequels. Both Sendak and Nygren, as well as a number of other contemporary picturebook illustrators, such as Anthony Browne, work extensively with self-quotations, but this gives even less reason to identify books as being directly connected together.

Some of the most exciting and challenging picturebooks have a nonepisodic, progressive plot, and a definite closure in the end. The plot and the character's development in these books reach a stage where any further development is superfluous.

The contribution of paratexts to the picturebook is clearly highly significant, especially since they frequently carry a substantial percentage of the book's verbal and visual information. We find it interesting that this aspect has generally been neglected by critics.

## Notes

1. The only scholar who devotes considerable attention to format, covers, and endpapers as narrative elements is Ulla Rhedin, *Bilderboken: På väg mot en teori* (Stockholm: Alfabeta, 1993): 141–160.

2. For a general introduction to paratexts, see Gérard Genette, *Paratexts: Thresholds of Interpretation* (Cambridge: Cambridge University Press, 1997).

3. Genette, op. cit.: 17–22.

4. We are not discussing here the vast variety of so-called toy books: movable, shaped, pop-up, concertina, panoramic, etc. See Göte Klingberg, *Denna lilla gris går till torget* (Stockholm: Rabén & Sjögren, 1987).

5. See further on format: Perry Nodelman, *Words About Pictures. The Narrative Art of Children's Picture Books* (Athens: University of Georgia Press, 1988): 44ff.

6. See further Maria Nikolajeva, "Reflections of Change in Children's Books Titles," in *Reflections of Change: Children's Literature Since 1945,* ed. Sandra L. Beckett 85–90 (Westport, CT: Greenwood, 1997).

7. We are indebted for this particular observation to Clare Bradford, who brought this to our attention during her CD-ROM demonstration in Stockholm October 15, 1998.

8. Cf. Rhedin op. cit.: 155.

9. Cf. Nodelman op. cit.: 50ff.

10. Cf. Peter Neumeyer's remarks on the significance of endpapers; Peter Neumeyer, *The Annotated Charlotte's Web* (New York: HarperCollins, 1994): xxxiii.

11. Stephen Roxburgh, "A Picture Equals How Many Words? Narrative Theory and Picture Books for Children," *The Lion and the Unicorn* 7–8 (1983): 20–33.

12. Cf. Rhedin op. cit.: 152f.

13. Margaret Mackey's *The Case of Peter Rabbit* (New York: Garland, 1998) makes a thorough study of the range and impact of commercial spin-offs.

14. Joseph H. Schwarcz and Chava Schwarcz, *The Picture Book Comes of Age* (Chicago: American Library Association, 1991): 39; Alfie Atkins books are among Schwarcz's examples of "successful cases.")

15. Schwarcz, op. cit.: 194–205. In his analysis, Schwarcz first questions Sendak's own statement about his books comprising a trilogy, and then demonstrates by elegant argument why this is true.

Endpapers (front and back) from *The Tunnel*, by Anthony Browne.

From *Gorilla*, by Anthony Browne.

# Conclusion

Throughout this study we have deliberately focused on picturebooks where words and images work actively together to create the book's impact. The most effective examples create some tension between the information included in the words and in the pictures, so that they collaborate rather than simply repeat redundantly what is communicated in the other mode of expression. Even a very brief glance at our bibliography reveals that most of the texts we find interesting to discuss from this angle have their origins in the 1980s and 1990s.

At the beginning of the 20th century, the dynamic relationship between word and image involves a variety of techniques: the enrichment of understanding through detail; the creation of affective impact both through the use of words and through the use of pictorial design including style and color; the presentation of different perspectives and points of view in text and illustration; and the use of ironic interplay between the two. In many cases specific visual clues open up the text, and words choices sharpen the reader's scrutiny and analysis of the picture. In these early 20th-century works, notably Beatrix Potter's or Elsa Beskow's picturebooks, the intention is to expand and enrich the readers' understanding and involve them in the situations depicted.

As the century progresses, the author/illustrators' intention and impact change. Rather than the text–illustration relationship clarifying and making more apparent the detail, perspective, and events of the twofold narrative, the works increasingly challenge the reader, introducing ambiguity that is sometimes so intense that the more often the text is read, the more closely the illustrations are examined, the more uncertain the communication appears. The result of this is that readers are required to bring their own answers, their own resolutions to the works, and to join forces with the author/illustrators in creating the scenario, the story, and the interpretation.

*259*

In some cases this methodology leads to a fuller and more intense involvement in decoding, with just a few questions remaining about the meaning or the import. But in other cases, even an intense decoding effort leaves the reader with such basic questions about what is being communicated that the sense of ambiguity is all-encompassing. We have demonstrated this in the works of such authors as Anthony Browne, John Burningham, Inger Edelfeldt, David McKee, Sven Nordqvist, Maurice Sendak, and Colin Thompson, as well as author-illustrator teams such as Barbro Lindgren and Eva Eriksson, Stefan Mählqvist and Tord Nygren, and Ulf Stark and Anna Höglund.

All these uncertain iconotexts, where the readers are drawn into decoding aspects of the picturebooks that frequently remain ambiguous despite their attention, reflect in their methodologies the way life has changed in the last century. We have shifted from absolutes to relativities, from understood rules of behavior to personal preference, from shared values to situational ethics, from community to anomie. Like the reader who must work to find meaning, or even to create it, contemporary picturebooks represent the fin-de-siècle dilemmas that challenge us as the new century begins.

One may argue that there is nothing unique about picturebooks in the general tendency of contemporary children's fiction toward complexity and ambivalence. In fact we have repeatedly pointed out this growing complexity in other contexts.[1] When confronted with works by certain contemporary children's writers, we must either admit that they do not write for children— as some of them have declared they do not, although their books are marketed as books for children—or radically redefine our notion of what constitutes children's literature. Increasingly, a large part of what is today written and published as children's literature, including picturebooks, is transgressing its own boundaries and coming closer to mainstream literature. This phenomenon has repeatedly brought the critics' attention to the question of the audience for whom these books are created.

While in our study of picturebooks we have to a great extent avoided the problem of audience, the question certainly remains and demands attention. Should we exclude from our concept of children's literature most of the wide scope of texts that we have discussed? We have demonstrated that they diverge from the traditional concept of children's books as "simple," if by simple we mean such aspects as clear-cut narrative structures, a chronological order of events, an unambiguous, preferably didactic narrative voice, and, not least, clearly delineated and fixed borders between "fantasy" and "reality," between the objective truth and subjective perception. In most of the picturebooks we have discussed, we can observe a shift in artistic representation from the mimetic toward the symbolic. This shift in approach may be correlated with the postmodern interrogation of the arts' ability to reflect reality by means of language, or indeed by visual means. Although a number of critics have pointed out that contemporary children's literature adopts many traits of postmodernism, we must agree that the distinctive features of postmodern literature—such as eclecticism, heteroglossia, heterotopia, intersubjectivity, or metafiction—are not the features we normally associate with children's literature. However, the recent concept of crosswriting has given us a new instrument to evaluate children's texts that do not lend themselves to such labels as "simple, action-oriented, didactic and optimistic," to refer to Perry Nodelman's definition of children's fiction.[2]

While many of the works that have drawn the attention of critics fascinated by the dual-audience or cross-audienced phenomenon offer opportunities for intricate analysis of narrative technique, perspective, symbolism, and characterization, we believe that picturebooks provide a special occasion for a collaborative relationship between children and adults, for picturebooks empower children and adults much more equally. While illustrated books certainly encourage the less experienced child reader, picturebooks are specifically designed to communicate by word, by image, and by a combination of both. This form has redrawn boundaries, and in so doing has challenged accepted forms and learned expectations. Those less bound to the accepted conventions of decoding text are freer to respond to less traditional work, so children's very naivete serves them well in this arena, making them truer partners in the reading experience. As in the "find Waldo" books, children's ability to perceive and sift visual detail often outdistances that of the adult.

Looking at this dilemma from a psychological point of view, we may resort to some arguments based on the ideas of Jacques Lacan,[3] as we have indeed done throughout the study. In Lacan's theory, a significant distinction is made between the imaginary and the symbolic. If we relate these categories to the notions that we started with in our Introduction, the iconic and the conventional, we can easily see how the interrelation between word and image in picturebooks can be described in Lacan's terms. The imaginary in Lacan's theory comes from "image" = picture, iconic sign. "Imaginary stage" in Lacanian psychology implies communication by preverbal signs, before the child has mastered the language, or, in adult life, deliberately rejecting verbal language as a means of communication. Imaginary communication is nonlinear and nonstructured.

The symbolic refers to the semiotic concept of "symbol" (not the ordinary meaning), which is the same as a conventional sign. The symbolic stage, according to Lacan, is verbal, because language is based on conventional signs. The symbolic stage, in Lacan's theory, is linear, ordered—male (or, if we adapt it to children's literature, adult).

The third, "real" stage is an attempt—according to Lacan, often failed—to reconcile the two previous ones. Since Lacan connects the imaginary stage with the mother, the child must inevitably reject the mother in order to transfer into the symbolic stage (Father's Law, as Lacan calls it). Julia Kristeva has further developed Lacan's ideas to show how female creativity is based on the restoration of the imaginary. We can apply this idea to demonstrate how picturebooks bridge the gap between the verbal and nonverbal, creating an artistic form equally appealing to sophisticated and to less sophisticated readers.

The common prejudice that picturebooks are literature for very young children is apparently based on Lacan's notion of the preverbal, imaginary language, which is, if not dominant, then conspicuous in picturebooks as compared to novels. As it appears, picturebooks, successfully combining the imaginary and the symbolic, the iconic and the conventional, have achieved something that no other literary form has mastered.

In our study we have attempted to present some useful tools for exploring the word–picture dynamic, which we find so rich and so promising in its ability to penetrate and unlock the intricacies of picturebook communication. While our book uses this methodology to explore many aspects of picturebooks, it also opens up many new opportunities for further work.

## Notes

1. See, e. g., Maria Nikolajeva, *Children's Literature Comes of Age: Toward a New Aesthetic* (New York: Garland, 1996); Maria Nikolajeva, "Exit Children's Literature?" *The Lion and the Unicorn* 22 (1998) 2: 221–236; Carole Scott, "Dual Audience in Picture Books," in *Transcending Boundaries: Writing for Dual Audience of Children and Adults,* ed. Sandra Beckett 99–110. (New York: Garland, 1999).

2. Perry Nodelman, *The Pleasures of Children's Literature* (New York: Longman, 1992): 190.

3. Jacques Lacan, *Écrits: A Selection* (New York: Norton, 1977).

# Bibliography

## Primary Sources

The picturebooks are arranged by the author of the text, followed by the illustrator if different. For books that are discussed in the Swedish original, both the original and the English translations are included. English titles of books not translated into English are given in parenthesis and quotation marks.

Adams, Jeanie. *Pigs and Honey.* Norwood, South Australia: Omnibus Books, 1989.

Adelborg, Ottilia. *Prinsarnes blomsteralfabet* (1892). Stockholm: Bonnier, 1968 ("The Princes' Flower Alphabet").

Andersen, H. C., and Arlene Graston. *Thumbelina.* Retold by Jennifer Greenway. New York: Delacorte, 1996.

Andersen, H. C., and Susan Jeffers. *Thumbelina.* Retold by Amy Ehrlich. New York: Dial Books, 1976.

Andersen, H. C., and Robyn Officer. *Thumbelina.* Retold by Jennifer Greenway. Kansas City: Andrews and McMeel, 1991.

Andersen, H. C., and Svend Otto S. "Thumbelina." In *Hans Andersen's Fairy Tales.* Copenhagen: Carlsen, 1990.

Andersen, H. C., and Lisbeth Zwerger. *Thumbelina.* New York: Simon & Schuster, 1985.

Andersen, H. C. and Kaj Beckman. *Tummelisa.* Stockholm: Tiden, 1967 ("Thumbelina").

Andersen, H. C., and Elsa Beskow. *Tummelisa* (1907). Stockholm: BonnierCarlsen, 1994.

Andersen, H. C., and Linda Lysell. *Tummelisa.* Stockholm: Barnboksförlaget, 1982.

Andersen, H. C., and Einar Nerman. *Tummelisa.* Stockholm: Corona, 1974.

Andersen, H. C., and Elisabeth Nyman. *Tummelisa.* Stockholm: Natur och kultur, 1991.

Andersen, H. C., and Charlotta Rege. *Tummelisa.* Höganäs: Wiken, 1982.

Anderson, Lena. *Majas alfabet.* Stockholm: Rabén & Sjögren, 1984 ("Maja's Alphabet").

Anno, Mitsumasa. *Anno's Journey*. London: Bodley Head, 1977.

Arosenius, Ivar. *Kattresan*. Stockholm: Bonnier, 1908 ("Journey with a Cat").

Barker, C. M. *Flower Fairies*. London: Blackie and Son, 1923.

Bergström, Gunilla. *Is There a Monster Alfie Atkins*. New York: Farrar/R & S, 1988 (*Alfons och odjuret*, 1979).

Bergström, Gunilla. *Who is Scaring Alfie Atkins?* New York: Farrar/R & S, 1987 (*Vem spökar Alfons Åberg*, 1983).

Bergström, Gunilla. *You are a Sly One Alfie Atkins*. New York: Farrar/R & S, 1988 (*Aja baja Alfons Åberg*, 1973).

Bergström, Gunilla. *You Have a Girlfriend, Alfie Atkins*. New York: Farrar/R & S, 1988 (*Alfons och Milla*, 1985).

Beskow, Elsa. *Aunt Green, Aunt Brown and Aunt Lavender*. London: Harper, 1938 (*Tant Grön, tant Brun och tant Gredelin*, 1918).

Beskow, Elsa. *Children of the Forest*. New York: Delacorte, 1969 (*Tomtebobarnen*, 1910).

Beskow, Elsa. *Peter's Voyage*. New York: Knopf, 1931 (*Lillebrors segelfärd*, 1921).

Beskow, Elsa. *Peter's Adventures in Blueberry Land*. New York, Delacorte, 1975 (*Puttes äventyr i blåbärsskogen*, 1901).

Beskow, Elsa. *The Tale of the Little, Little Old Woman*. Edinburgh: Floris Books, 1988 (*Sagan om den lilla, lilla gumman*, 1897).

Blake, Quentin. *Clown*. London: Jonathan Cape, 1995.

Boulton, Jane, and Barbara Cooney. *Only Opal: The Diary of a Young Girl*. New York: Philomel, 1994.

Browne, Anthony. *Changes*. London: Julia MacRae Books, 1990.

Browne, Anthony. *Gorilla*. London: Julia MacRae Books, 1983.

Browne, Anthony. *Look What I've Got!* London: Julia MacRae Books, 1980.

Browne, Anthony. *Piggybook*. London: Julia MacRae Books, 1986.

Browne, Anthony. *The Tunnel*. London: Julia MacRae Books, 1989.

Browne, Anthony. *Zoo*. London: Julia MacRae Books, 1992.

de Brunhoff, Jean. *Babar the King*. New York: Random House, 1935 (*Babar le roi*, 1933).

de Brunhoff, Jean. *The Story of Babar, the Little Elephant*. New York: Random House, 1933 (*Babar*, 1931).

Burningham, John. *Aldo*. London: Jonathan Cape, 1991.

Burningham, John. *Come Away from the Water, Shirley*. London: Jonathan Cape, 1977.

Burningham, John. *Granpa*. London: Jonathan Cape, 1984.

Burningham, John. *John Patrick Norman McHennessy—The Boy Who Was Always Late*. London: Jonathan Cape, 1987.

Burningham, John. *Time to Get Out of the Bath, Shirley*. London: Jonathan Cape, 1978.

Burton, Virginia Lee. *The Little House*. Boston: Houghton Mifflin, 1942.

Carle, Eric. *Do You Want to Be My Friend?* New York: Crowell, 1971.

Carle, Eric. *The Very Hungry Caterpillar*. New York: World Publishing, 1969.

Cederqvist, Simone. *Jag ser inte vad du ser*. Stockholm: Tiden, 1976 ("I Don't See What You See").

Cole, Babette. *Prince Cinders*. London: Hamish Hamilton, 1987.

Cole, Babette. *Princess Smartypants*. London: Hamish Hamilton, 1986.

Cole, Babette. *Tarzanna*. London: Hamish Hamilton, 1991.

Cole, Babette. *The Trouble With Gran*. London: Heinemann, 1987.

Cole, Babette. *The Trouble With Grandad*. London: Heinemann, 1988.

Cole, Babette. *The Trouble With Mum*. London: Kaye and Ward, 1983.

Cooney, Barbara. *Island Boy*. New York: Viking, 1988.

Couratin, Patrick. *Chut!* Paris: Harlin Quist, 1974 ("Shut Up!").

Edelfeldt, Inger. *Genom den röda dörren*. Stockholm: BonniersJunior, 1992 ("Through the Red Door").

Edelfeldt, Inger. *Nattbarn*. Stockholm: Alfabeta, 1994 ("Nightchild").

Edelfeldt, Inger. *Stackars lilla Bubben*. Stockholm: Alfabeta, 1996 ("Poor Little Bubble").

Ekman, Fam. *Kattens skrekk*. Oslo: Cappelen, 1992 ("The Cat's Terror").

Ekman, Fam. *Rødhatten og ulven*. Oslo: Cappelen, 1985 ("Red Cap and the Wolf").

Freeman, Don. *Corduroy*. New York: Viking, 1968.

French, Fiona. *Snow White in New York*. New York: Oxford University Press, 1987.

Gág, Wanda. *Millions of Cats*. New York: Coward, 1928.

Gelotte, Ann-Madeleine. *Ida-Maria från Arfliden*. Stockholm: Tiden, 1977 ("Ida-Maria from Arfliden").

Gelotte, Ann-Madeleine. *Tyra i 10:an Odengatan*. Stockholm: Tiden, 1981 ("Tyra in Odengatan no. 10").

Gelotte, Ann-Madeleine. *Vi bodde i Helenelund*. Stockholm: Tiden, 1983 ("We Lived in Helenelund").

Greene, Grahame, and Edward Ardizzone. *The Little Train*. London: The Bodley Head, 1973.

Grimm, Wilhelm and Jacob, and Binette Schoeder. *Froschkönig*. Moenchalt, Nord-Süd Verlag, 1989 ("The Frog King").

Grimm, Wilhelm and Jacob, and Anthony Browne. *Hansel and Gretel*. London: Julia MacRae, 1982.

Grimm, Wilhelm and Jacob, and Jane Ray. *Hansel and Gretel*. New York: Candlewick Press, 1997.

Grimm, Wilhelm and Jacob, and Svend Otto S. *Hansel and Gretel*. New York: Larousse, 1983.

Grimm, Wilhelm and Jacob, and Paul O. Zelinsky. *Hansel and Gretel*. New York: Penguin, 1984.

Grimm, Wilhelm and Jacob. *The Juniper Tree and Other Tales from Grimm*. Selected by Lore Segal and Maurice Sendak. Pictures by Maurice Sendak. New York: Farrar, Straus and Giroux, 1973.

Halling, Thomas, and Gunna Grähs. *Sagan om den lilla, lilla katten*. Stockholm: Natur och kultur, 1997 ("The Tale of a Tiny, Tiny Cat").

Hellsing, Lennart, and Fibben Hald. *Ägget*. Stockholm: Rabén & Sjögren, 1978 ("The Egg").

Hellsing, Lennart, and Poul Ströyer. *The Pirate Book*. New York: Delacorte, 1972 (*Sjörövarbok*, 1965).

Hellsing, Lennart, and Svend Otto S. *The Wonderful Pumpkin*. New York: Atheneum, 1976 (Den underbara pumpan, 1975).

Hill, Eric. *Where's Spot?* New York: Putnam, 1980.

Hill, Susan, and Angela Barrett. *Beware, Beware*. London: Walker Books, 1993.

Hoban, Russell, and Lillian Hoban. *A Baby Sister for Frances*. New York: Harper, 1964.

Hoban, Russell, and Lillian Hoban. *A Bargain for Frances*. New York: Harper, 1970.

Hoban, Russell, and Lillian Hoban. *A Birthday for Frances*. New York: Harper, 1968.

Hoban, Russell, and Lillian Hoban. *Bread and Jam for Frances*. New York: Harper, 1964.

Hoban, Russell, and Garth Williams. *Bedtime for Frances*. New York: Harper, 1960.

Hoban, Russell, and Emily Arnold McCully. *The Twenty-Elephant Restaurant*. New York: Atheneum, 1978.

Höglund, Anna. *Mina och Kåge*. Stockholm: Alfabeta, 1995 ("Mina and Kåge").

Hutchins, Pat. *Don't Forget the Bacon*. London: The Bodley Head, 1976.

Hutchins, Pat. *Rosie's Walk*. London: The Bodely Head, 1968.

Jackson, Ellen, and Kevin O'Malley. *Cinder Edna*. New York: Lothrop, 1994.

Janosch. *Hey Presto! You're a Bear!* Boston: Little, Brown, 1980 (*Ich sag, du bist ein Bär,* 1977).

Janosch. *I'll Make You Well, Tiger, Said the Bear*. New York: Adama Books, 1985 (*Ich mach dich gesund, sagte der Bär*).

Janosch. *A Trip to Panama*. Boston: Little, Brown, 1981 (*Oh, wie schön ist Panama,* 1978).

Jansson, Tove. *The Dangerous Journey*. London: Benn, 1978 (*Den farliga resan,* 1977).

Jansson, Tove. *Moomin, Mymble and Little My*. Seattle: Blue Lantern, 1996 (*Hur gick det sen? Boken om Mymlan, Mumintrollet och lilla My,* 1952).

Jansson, Tove. *Who Will Comfort Toffle?* New York: Walck, 1969 (*Vem ska trösta knyttet?,* 1960).

Janus Hertz, Grete, and Bengt Janus. *Strit*. Copenhagen: Hirschsprung, 1943.

Jersild, P. C., and Matti Lepp. *Röda hund*. Stockholm: Carlsen/if, 1988 ("German Measles").

Kharms, Daniil et al., and Nikolai Radlov. *Picture Stories*. Moscow: Raduga, 1987 (*Rasskazy v kartinkakh,* 1958).

Kitamura, Satoshi. *Lily Takes a Walk*. New York: Dutton, 1987.

Kreidolf, Ernst. *Dream Garden*. La Jolla, CA: Green Tiger Press, 1979 (*Der Traumgarten*).

Kreidolf, Ernst. *Flower Fairy Tales*. La Jolla, CA: Green Tiger Press, 1979 (*Blumen-Märchen*).

Lindenbaum, Pija. *Boken om Bodil*. Stockholm: Bonnier, 1991.

Lindenbaum, Pija. *Boodil My Dog*. New York: Holt, 1992 (*Boken om Bodil,* 1991).

Lindenbaum, Pija. *Britten och prins Benny*. Stockholm: Alfabeta, 1996 ("Britten and Prince Benny").

Lindenbaum, Pija. *Else-Marie and Her Seven Daddies*. New York: Holt, 1991 (*Else-Marie och småpapporna,* 1990).

Lindgren, Astrid, and Ilon Wikland. *Christmas in Noisy Village*. New York: Viking, 1964 (*Jul i Bullerbyn,* 1963).

Lindgren, Astrid, and Ilon Wikland. *I Don't Want to Go to Bed*. New York: Farrar/R & S, 1988 (*Jag vill inte gå och lägga mig,* 1988).

Lindgren, Astrid, and Ilon Wikland. *I Want a Brother or Sister.* New York: Farrar/R & S, 1988 (*Jag vill också ha ett syskon,* 1978).

Lindgren, Astrid, and Ilon Wikland. *I Want to Go to School Too.* New York: Farrar/R & S, 1987 (*Jag vill också gå i skolan,* 1979).

Lindgren, Astrid, and Birgitta Nordenskjöld. *Jag vill inte gå och lägga mig.* Stockholm: Rabén & Sjögren, 1947 ("I Don't Want to Go to Bed").

Lindgren, Astrid, and Birgitta Nordenskjöld. *Jag vill också gå i skolan.* Stockholm: Rabén & Sjögren, 1951 ("I Want to Go to School Too").

Lindgren, Astrid, and Birgitta Nordenskjöld. *Jag vill också ha ett syskon.* Stockholm: Rabén & Sjögren, 1954 ("I Want a Brother or Sister").

Lindgren, Astrid, and Ilon Wikland. *Springtime in Noisy Village.* New York: Viking, 1966 (*Vår i Bullerbyn,* 1965).

Lindgren, Astrid, and Ilon Wikland. *Titta, Madicken, det snöar.* Stockholm: Rabén & Sjögren, 1983 ("Look, Mardy, It's Snowing")

Lindgren, Barbro, and Eva Eriksson. *Mamman och den vilda bebin.* Stockholm: Rabén & Sjögren, 1980.

Lindgren, Barbro, and Eva Eriksson. *Sam's Ball.* New York: Morrow, 1983 (*Max boll,* 1982).

Lindgren, Barbro, and Eva Eriksson. *Sam's Bath.* New York: Morrow, 1983 (*Max balja,* 1982).

Lindgren, Barbro, and Eva Eriksson. *Sam's Car.* New York: Morrow, 1988 (*Max bil,* 1981).

Lindgren, Barbro, and Eva Eriksson. *Sam's Cookie.* New York: Morrow, 1988 (*Max kaka,* 1981).

Lindgren, Barbro, and Eva Eriksson. *Sam's Lamp.* New York: Morrow, 1982 (*Max lampa,* 1982).

Lindgren, Barbro, and Eva Eriksson. *Sam's Potty.* New York: Morrow, 1986 (*Max potta,* 1986).

Lindgren, Barbro, and Eva Eriksson. *Sam's Teddy Bear.* New York: Morrow, 1982 (*Max nalle,* 1981).

Lindgren, Barbro, and Eva Eriksson. *Sam's Wagon.* New York: Morrow, 1986 (*Max dockvagn,* 1986).

Lindgren, Barbro, and Eva Eriksson. *Titta Max grav.* Stockholm: Eriksson & Lindgren, 1991 ("Look Max's Grave").

Lindgren, Barbro, and Eva Eriksson. *Den vilda bebiresan.* Stockholm: Rabén & Sjögren, 1982.

Lindgren, Barbro, and Eva Eriksson. *Vilda bebin får en hund.* Stockholm: Rabén & Sjögren, 1985.

Lindgren, Barbro, and Eva Eriksson. *The Wild Baby.* Translated by Jack Prelutsky. New York: Greenwillow, 1981.

Lindgren, Barbro, and Eva Eriksson. *The Wild Baby.* Translated by Alison Winn. London: Hodder & Stoughton, 1981.

Lindgren, Barbro, and Eva Eriksson. *The Wild Baby Gets a Puppy.* Translated by Jack Prelutsky. New York: Greenwillow, 1988.

Lindgren, Barbro, and Eva Eriksson. *The Wild Baby Goes to Sea.* Translated by Jack Prelutsky. New York: Greenwillow, 1983.

Lindgren, Barbro, and Eva Eriksson. *The Wild Baby's Dog*. Translated by Alison Winn. London: Hodder & Stoughton, 1986.

Lindgren, Barbro, and Cecilia Torudd. *A Worm's Tale*. New York: Farrar/R & S, 1988 (*Sagan om Karlknut,* 1985).

Lionni, Leo. *Little Blue and Little Yellow*. New York: McDowell, 1959.

Lobel, Arnold. *Frog and Toad Are Friends*. New York: Harper & Row, 1970.

Lobel, Arnold. *Days with Frog and Toad*. New York: Harper & Row, 1979.

Löfgren, Åke, and Egon Möller-Nielsen. *Historien om någon*. Stockholm: Rabén & Sjögren, 1951 ("The Story About Somebody").

Lööf, Jan. *Pelles ficklampa*. Stockholm: Carlsen/if, 1978 ("Peter's Flashlight").

Lööf, Jan. *Sagan om det röda äpplet*. Stockholm: Carlsen/if, 1974 ("The Story of the Red Apple").

Mählqvist, Stefan, and Tord Nygren. *Come Into My Night, Come Into My Dream*. London: Pepper Press, 1981 (*Kom in i min natt, kom in i min dröm,* 1978).

Mählqvist, Stefan, and Tord Nygren. *Drakberget*. Stockholm: Rabén & Sjögren, 1981 ("The Dragon Mountain").

Mählqvist, Stefan, and Tord Nygren. *I'll Take Care of the Crocodiles*. New York: Atheneum, 1978 (*Inte farligt pappa, krokodilerna klarar jag,* 1977).

Mayer, Mercer. *There's a Nightmare in My Closet*. New York: Dial Books, 1968.

McKee, David. *Charlotte's Piggy Bank*. London: Andersen Press, 1996.

McKee, David. *I Hate My Teddy Bear*. London: Andersen Press, 1982.

McKee, David. *The Monster and the Teddy Bear*. London: Andersen Press, 1989.

McKee, David. *Not Now, Bernard*. London: Andersen Press, 1980.

Munsch, Robert N., and Michael Martchenko. *The Paper Bag Princess*. Toronto: Annick Press, 1980.

Nilsson, Ulf, and Eva Eriksson. *Little Sister Rabbit*. Boston: The Atlantic Monthly Press, 1984 (*Lilla syster kanin,* 1983).

Nordqvist, Sven. *Festus and Mercury Go Camping*. Minneapolis: Carolrhoda, 1993 (*Pettson tältar,* 1992).

Nordqvist, Sven. *Festus and Mercury: Ruckus in the Garden*. Minneapolis: Carolrhoda, 1991 (*Kackel i trädgårdslandet,* 1990).

Nordqvist, Sven. *Festus and Mercury: Wishing to Go Fishing*. Minneapolis: Carolrhoda, 1991 (*Stackars Pettson,* 1987).

Nordqvist, Sven. *The Fox Hunt*. New York: Morrow, 1988 (*Rävjakten,* 1986).

Nordqvist, Sven. *The Hat Hunt*. New York: R & S Books, 1988 (*Hattjakten,* 1987).

Nordqvist, Sven. *Merry Christmas, Festus and Mercury*. Minneapolis: Carolrhoda, 1989 (*Pettson får julbesök,* 1988).

Nordqvist, Sven. *Pancake Pie*. New York: Morrow, 1985 (*Pannkakstårtan,* 1985).

Nordqvist, Sven. *Willie in the Big World*. New York: Morrow, 1986 (*Minus och den stora världen,* 1985).

Nygren, Tord. *The Red Thread*. Stockholm: R & S Books, 1988 (*Den röda tråden,* 1987).

Nyman, Karin, and Ylva Källström. *Jag kan köra alla bilar*. Stockholm: Rabén & Sjögren, 1965 ("I Can Drive All Cars").

Nyman, Karin, and Tord Nygren. *Jag kan köra alla bilar*. Stockholm: Rabén & Sjögren, 1997 ("I Can Drive All Cars").

Ormerod, Jan. *Moonlight.* London: Lothrop, 1982.

Ormerod, Jan. *Sunshine.* London: Lothrop, 1981.

Pastuchiv, Olga. *Minas and the Fish.* Boston: Houghton Mifflin, 1997.

Pervik, Aino, and Piret Raud. *Keeruline lugu.* Tallinn: Tiritamm, 1994 ("The Tangled Tale").

Potter, Beatrix. *Ginger and Pickles.* London: Warne, 1909.

Potter, Beatrix. *The Pie and the Patty-Pan.* London: Warne, 1905.

Potter, Beatrix. *The Tailor of Gloucester.* London: Warne, 1903.

Potter, Beatrix. *The Tale of Jemima Puddleduck.* London: Warne, 1908.

Potter, Beatrix. *The Tale of Johnny Town-Mouse.* London: Warne, 1918.

Potter, Beatrix. *The Tale of Mrs. Tiggy-Winkle.* London: Warne, 1905.

Potter, Beatrix. *The Tale of Peter Rabbit.* London: Warne, 1902.

Potter, Beatrix. *The Tale of Pigling Bland.* London: Warne, 1913.

Potter, Beatrix. *The Tale of Tom Kitten.* London: Warne, 1907.

Pyle, Howard, and Trina Schart Hyman. *King Stork.* Boston: Little, Brown, 1973.

Rey, H. A. *Curious George.* Boston: Houghton Mifflin, 1941.

Rey, H. A. *Curious George.* Boston: Houghton Mifflin, 1969.

Rey, H. A. *Curious George Flies a Kite.* Boston: Houghton Mifflin, 1958.

Rey, H. A. *Curious George Gets a Medal.* Boston: Houghton Mifflin, 1957.

Rey, H. A. *Curious George Goes to the Hospital.* Boston: Houghton Mifflin, 1966.

Rey, H. A. *Curious George Learns the Alphabet.* Boston: Houghton Mifflin, 1963.

Rey, H. A. *Curious George Rides a Bike.* Boston: Houghton Mifflin, 1952.

Rey, H. A. *Curious George Takes a Job.* Boston: Houghton Mifflin, 1947.

Rey, H. A. *Nicke Nyfiken.* Stockholm: Rabén & Sjögren, 1967 (*Curious George,* 1941).

Rey, Margret, and H. A. Rey. *Spotty.* New York: Harper, 1945.

Rosen, Michael, and Clare Mackie. *Michael Rosen's Book of Nonsense.* Hove, U.K.: Wayland, 1997.

Sandberg, Inger, and Lasse Sandberg. *ABCD.* Stockholm: Rabén & Sjögren, 1986.

Sandberg, Inger, and Lasse Sandberg. *Daniel and the Coconut Cakes.* London: Black, 1973 (*Mathias bakar kakor,* 1968).

Sandberg, Inger, and Lasse Sandberg. *Dusty Wants to Borrow Everything.* New York: Putnam & Grosset/R & S, 1988. (*Låna den, sa Pulvret,* 1984).

Sandberg, Inger, and Lasse Sandberg. *Dusty Wants to Help.* New York: Farrar/R & S, 1987. (*Hjälpa till, sa Pulvret,* 1983).

Sandberg, Inger, and Lasse Sandberg. *Jaa, det får du, sa Pulvret.* Stockholm: Rabén & Sjögren, 1993 ("Yes, You May, Dusty Said").

Sandberg, Inger, and Lasse Sandberg. *Little Anna and the Magic Hat.* New York: Lothrope, Lee & Shepard, 1965 (*Lilla Anna och trollerihatten,* 1965).

Sandberg, Inger, and Lasse Sandberg. *Little Ghost Godfrey.* New York: Delacorte, 1968 (*Lilla spöket Laban,* 1965).

Sandberg, Inger, and Lasse Sandberg. *Nicholas' Red Day.* New York: Delacorte, 1967 (*Niklas röda dag,* 1964).

Sandberg, Inger, and Lasse Sandberg. *Titta där, sa Pulvret.* Stockholm: Rabén & Sjögren, 1983 ("Look There, Dusty Said").

Sandberg, Inger, and Lasse Sandberg. *Vit och svart och alla de andra.* Stockholm: Rabén & Sjögren, 1986 ("White and Black and All the Others").

Sandberg, Inger, and Lasse Sandberg. *What Anne Saw*. New York: Lothrope, Lee & Shepard, 1964 (*Vad Anna fick se,* 1964).

Scieszka, Jon, and Daniel Adel. *The Book That Jack Wrote*. New York: Viking, 1994.

Scieszka, Jon, and Steve Johnson. *The Frog Prince Continued*. New York: Viking, 1991.

Scieszka, Jon, and Lane Smith. *The Stinky Cheese Man and Other Fairly Stupid Tales*. New York: Viking, 1992.

Scieszka, Jon and Lane Smith. *The True Story of the 3 Little Pigs, by A. Wolf*. New York: Viking, 1989.

Sendak, Maurice. *Dear Mili*. New York: Farrar, Straus, Giroux, 1980.

Sendak, Maurice. *In the Night Kitchen*. New York: Harper, 1970.

Sendak, Maurice. *Outside Over There*. New York: Harper & Row, 1981.

Sendak, Maurice. *The Sign on Rosie's Door*. New York: Harper, 1960.

Sendak, Maurice. *We Are All in the Dumps with Jack and Guy*. New York: Harper-Collins, 1993.

Sendak, Maurice. *Where the Wild Things Are*. New York: Harper, 1963.

Seuss, Dr. *ABC*. New York: Random House, 1963.

Seuss, Dr. *The Cat in the Hat*. New York: Random House, 1957.

Seuss, Dr. *Green Eggs and Ham*. New York: Random House, 1960.

Seuss, Dr. *Horton Hears a Who*. New York: Random House, 1954.

Seuss, Dr. *How the Grinch Stole Christmas*. New York: Random House, 1957.

Seuss, Dr. *Marvin K. Mooney, Will You Please Go Now?* New York: Random House, 1972.

Sigsgaard, Jens, and Arne Ungermann. *Paul Alone in the World*. St Louis: McGraw-Hill, 1964 (*Palle alene i verden,* 1942).

Stark, Ulf, and Eva Eriksson. *När pappa visade mej världsalltet*. Stockholm: Bonnier-Carlsen, 1998 ("When Daddy Showed Me the Universe").

Stark, Ulf, and Anna Höglund. *Jaguaren*. Stockholm: BonniersJunior, 1987 ("The Jaguar").

Stark, Ulf, and Anna Höglund. *Min syster är en ängel*. Stockholm: Alfabeta, 1996 ("My Sister Is an Angel").

Stark, Ulf, and Matti Lepp. *Storebrorsan*. Stockholm: BonnierCarlsen, 1995 ("The Big Brother").

Steele, Mary Q., and Lena Anderson. *Anna's Summer Songs*. New York: Greenwillow, 1988.

Steig, William. *Sylvester and the Magic Pebble*. New York: Windmill Books, 1969.

Steiner, Jörg, and Jörg Müller. *The Bear Who Wanted to Be a Bear*. New York: Atheneum, 1977 (*Der Bär der ein Bär bleiben wollte,* 1976).

Strömstedt, Margareta, and Tord Nygren. *Fanny och fåglarna*. Stockholm: Eriksson & Lindgren, 1995 ("Fanny and the Birds").

Thompson, Colin. *How to Live Forever*. London: Julia MacRae, 1995.

Thompson, Colin. *Looking for Atlantis*. London: Julia MacRae, 1993.

Thompson, Colin. *Looking for Atlantis*. New York. Dragonfly, 1997.

Thompson, Kay, and Hilary Knight. *Eloise*. New York: Simon & Schuster, 1955.

Tidholm, Anna-Clara, and Thomas Tidholm. *Resan till Ugri-La-Brek*. Stockholm: Alfabeta, 1987 ("The Journey to Ugri-La-Brek").

Trivizas, Eugene, and Helen Oxenbury. *The Three Little Wolves and the Big Bad Pig.* New York: Margaret McElderly, 1993.

Ungerer, Tomi. *Crictor.* New York: Harper, 1958.

Wheatley, Nadya, and Donna Rawlins. *My Place.* North Blackburn, Australia: CollinsDove, 1988.

Wieslander, Jujja and Thomas, and Sven Nordqvist. *Mamma Mu åker bobb.* Stockholm: Natur och kultur, 1994 ("Mamma Moo Rides the Bob").

Wieslander, Jujja and Thomas, and Sven Nordqvist. *Mamma Mu bygger koja.* Stockholm: Natur och kultur 1995 ("Mamma Moo Builds a Hut").

Wieslander, Jujja and Thomas and Sven Nordqvist. *Mamma Mu gungar.* Stockholm: Natur och kultur, 1993 ("Mamma Moo on the Swing").

Wieslander, Jujja and Thomas, and Sven Nordqvist. *Mamma Mu städar.* Stockholm: Natur och kultur, 1997 ("Mamma Moo Cleans Up").

Wikland, Ilon. *Var är Sammeli?* Stockholm: Rabén & Sjögren, 1995 ("Where Is My Puppy?" Original illustrations for a Japanese edition).

Wolde, Gunilla. *Betsy's First Day at Nursery School.* New York: Random House, 1976 (*Emmas första dag på dagis,* 1976).

Wolde, Gunilla. *Thomas Goes Out.* New York: Random House, 1971 (*Totte går ut,* 1969).

Zolotow, Charlotte, and Maurice Sendak. *Mr. Rabbit and the Lovely Present.* New York: Harper & Row, 1962.

# References

Alderson, Brian. *Looking at Picture Books.* London: National Book League, 1973.

Alfons, Harriet, ed. *Min nya skattkammare: Bildriket.* Stockholm: Natur och kultur, 1984.

Ardizzone, Edward. "Creation of a Picture Book." In *Only Connect: Readings on Children's Literature,* ed. Sheila Egoff et al., 289–298. Toronto: Oxford University Press, 1980.

Arnheim, Rudolf. *Art and Visual Perception.* Berkeley: University of California Press, 1974.

Bader, Barbara. *American Picturebooks: From Noah's Ark to the Beast Within.* New York: Macmillan, 1976.

Bakhtin, Mikhail. "The Forms of Time and Chronotope in the Novel." In his *The Dialogic Imagination,* 84–258. Austin: University of Texas Press, 1981.

Bal, Mieke. *Narratology: Introduction to the Theory of Narrative.* 2nd ed. Toronto: University of Toronto Press, 1997.

Bang, Molly. *Picture This: Perception and Composition.* Boston: Little, Brown, 1991.

Barr, John. *Illustrated Children's Books.* London: The British Library, 1986.

Baumgärtner, Alfred Clemens, ed. *Aspekte der gemalten Welt. 12 Kapitel über das Bilderbuch von heute.* Weinheim: Verlag Julius Beltz, 1968.

Baumgärtner, Alfred Clemens. "Erzählung und Abbild. Zur bildnerischen Umsetzung literarischer Vorlagen." In *Aspekte der gemalten Welt: 12 Kapitel über das Bilderbuch von heute,* ed. Alfred Clemens Baumgärtner, 65–81. Weinheim: Verlag Julius Beltz, 1968.

Baumgärtner, Alfred Clemens. "Das Bilderbuch. Geschichte - Formen - Rezeption." In *Bilderbücher im Blickpunkt verschiedener Wissenschaften und Fächer,* ed. Bettina Paetzold and Luis Erler, 4–22. Bamberg: Nostheide, 1990.

Bergstrand, Ulla. "Det var en gång—om mötet mellan sagan och bilderboken." In *I bilderbokens värld,* edited by Kristin Hallberg and Boel Westin, 143–163. Stockholm: Liber, 1985.

Bergstrand, Ulla. "Elsa Beskow and Children's Picture Books in Sweden, 1900–1940." *Swedish Book Review* (1990 supplement): 9–14.

Bergstrand, Ulla. *En bilderbokshistoria: Svenska bilderböcker 1900–1930.* Stockholm: BonniersJunior, 1993 (Studies Published by the Swedish Institute for Children's Books, no. 44). With a summary in English: The History of Swedish Picture-books 1900–1930.

Bergstrand, Ulla. *Bilderbokslandet Längesen.* Uppsala, Sweden: Hjelm, 1996 (Studies Published by the Swedish Institute for Children's Books, no. 59).

Bergstrand, Ulla, and Maria Nikolajeva. *Läckergommarnas kungarike. Om matens funktion i barnlitteraturen.* Stockholm: Centre for the Study of Childhood Culture, 1999.

Blount, Margaret J. *Animal Land. The Creatures of Children's Fiction.* New York: Morrow, 1974.

Booth, Wayne C. *The Rhetoric of Fiction.* Chicago: University of Chicago Press, 1961.

Bradford, Clare. "The Picture Book: Some Postmodern Tensions." *Papers: Explorations in Children's Literature* 4 (1993) 3: 10–14.

Bradford, Clare. "Along the Road to Learn: Children and Adults in the Picture Books of John Burningham." *Children's Literature in Education* 25 (1994) 4: 203–211.

Bradford, Clare. "Playing With Father: Anthony Browne's Picture Books and the Masculine." *Children's Literature in Education* 29 (1998) 2:79–96.

Carr, David. *Time, Narrative and History.* Bloomington: Indiana University Press: 1986.

Cavallius, Gustaf. "Bilderbok och bildanalys." In *Bilden i barnboken,* edited by Lena Fridell, 31–60. Gothenburg, Sweden: Stegeland, 1977.

Caws, Mary Ann. *The Eye in the Text. Essays on Perception, Mannerist to Modern.* Princeton, NJ: Princeton University Press, 1981.

Chatman, Seymor. *Story and Discourse. Narrative Structure in Fiction and Film.* Ithaca, NY: Cornell University Press, 1978.

Chatman, Seymor. *Coming to Terms.* Ithaca, NY: Cornell University Press, 1990.

Chukovsky, Kornei. *From Two to Five.* Berkeley: University of California Press, 1963.

Cianciolo, Patricia. *Illustrations in Children's Books.* Dubuque, IA: Wm. C. Browne, 1970.

Culler, Jonathan. *Structuralist Poetics. Structuralism, Linguistics and the Study of Literature.* London: Routledge, 1975.

Daniels, Morna. *Victorian Book Illustration.* London: The British Library, 1988.

Darling, Harold, and Peter Neumeyer, eds. *Image & Maker: An Annual Dedicated to the Consideration of Book Illustration.* La Jolla, CA: Green Tiger Press, 1984.

*De ritar och berättar.* Lund, Sweden: Bibliotekstjänst, 1987.

DeLuca, Geraldine. "Rudolf Arnheim's Art, Illusion and Children's Picture Books." *Children's Literature Association Quarterly* 9 (1984) 1: 21–23.

Docherty, Thomas. *Reading (Absent) Character: Toward a Theory of Characterization in Fiction*. Oxford: Clarendon Press, 1983.

Doonan, Jane. "Talking Pictures: A New Look at Hansel and Gretel." *Signal* 42 (1983): 123–131.

Doonan, Jane. "Outside Over There: A Journey in Style." *Signal* 50 (1986): 92–103, and 51 (1986): 172–187.

Doonan, Jane. "The Object Lesson: Picture Books of Anthony Browne." *Word and Image* 2 (1986): 159–172.

Doonan, Jane. "Satoshi Kitamura: Aesthetic Dimensions." *Children's Literature* 19 (1991): 107–137.

Doonan, Jane. *Looking at Pictures in Picture Books*. Stroud: Thimble Press, 1993.

Doonan, Jane. "Into the Dangerous World: We Are All in the Dumps with Jack and Guy." *Signal* 75 (1994): 155–171.

Doonan, Jane. "The Modern Picture Book." In *International Companion Encyclopedia of Children's Literature*, edited by Peter Hunt, 231–241. London: Routledge, 1996.

Doonan, Jane. "Drawing Out Ideas: A Second Decade of the Work of Anthony Browne." *The Lion and the Unicorn* 23 (1998) 1: 30–56.

Edström, Vivi, ed. *Vår moderna bilderbok*. Stockholm: Rabén & Sjögren, 1991 (Studies Published by the Swedish Institute for Children's Books, no. 40). With a summary in English: The Modern Swedish Picture-Book.

Feaver, William. *When We Were Young: Two Centuries of Children's Book Illustrations*. London: Thames and Hudson, 1977.

Fridell, Lena. "Text och bild. Några exempel." In *Bilden i barnboken,* edited by Lena Fridell, 61–83. Gothenburg, Sweden: Stegeland, 1977.

Fridell, Lena, ed. *Bilden i barnboken*. Gothenburg, Sweden: Stegeland, 1977 (Studies Published by the Swedish Institute for Children's Books, no. 7). With a summary in English: On Pictures in Children's Books.

Frye, Northrop. *Anatomy of Criticism. Four Essays*. Princeton, NJ: Princeton University Press, 1957.

Galbraight, Mary. " 'Goodnight Nobody' Revisited: Using an Attachment Perspective to Study Picture Books about Bedtime." *Children's Literature Association Quarterly* 23 (1998–99) 4: 172–180.

Gannon, Susan. "Rudolf Arnheim's 'Psychology of the Creative Eye' and the Criticism of Illustrated Books for Children." *Children's Literature Association Quarterly* 9 (1984) 1: 15–18.

Genette, Gérard. *Narrative Discourse. An Essay in Method*. Translated by Jane E. Lewin. Oxford: Oxford University Press, 1982.

Genette, Gérard. *Paratexts: Thresholds of Interpretation*. Cambridge: Cambridge University Press, 1997.

Golden, Joanne M. *The Narrative Symbol in Childhood Literature: Exploration in the Construction of Text*. Berlin: Mouton, 1990.

Gregersen, Torben. "Småbørnsbogen." In *Børne- og ungdomsbøger: Problemer og analyser,* edited by Sven Møller Kristensen and Preben Ramløv, 243–271. Copenhagen: Gyldendal, 1974.

Grünewald, Dietrich. "Kongruenz von Wort und Bild: Rafik Schami und Peter Knorr: Der Wunderkasten." In *Neue Erzählformen im Bilderbuch,* edited by Jens Thiele, 17–49. Oldenburg, Germany: Isensee, 1991.

Hagemann, Sonja. *De tegnet for barna: Norske kunstneres illustrasjoner i bøker for barn.* Oslo: Tiden, 1986.

Hallberg, Kristin. "Litteraturvetenskapen och bilderboksforskningen." *Tidskrift för litteraturvetenskap* 3–4 (1982): 163–168.

Hallberg, Kristin, and Boel Westin, eds. *I bilderbokens värld.* Stockholm: Liber, 1985.

Hallberg, Kristin. "Bilderbokens barn—drömmens och verklighetens resenärer." In *I bilderbokens värld,* edited by Kristin Hallberg and Boel Westin, 11–54. Stockholm: Liber, 1985.

Hallberg, Kristin. "Swedish Illustrated Children's Books." *Swedish Book Review* (1990 supplement): 15–21.

Hallberg, Kristin. "Det moderna rummet. Inger och Lasse Sandbergs bilderböcker." In *Vår moderna bilderbok,* edited by Vivi Edström, 71–103. Stockholm: Rabén & Sjögren, 1991.

Holländer, Tove. *Från idyll till avidyll. Tove Janssons illustrationer till muminböckerna.* Tampere: Finlands barnboksinstitut, 1983 (Studies published by Finland's Institute for Children's Books; 4). English summary.

Hourihan, Margery. *Deconstructing the Hero. Literary Theory and Children's Literature.* London: Routledge, 1997.

Hume, Kathryn. *Fantasy and Mimesis. Responses to Reality in Western Literature.* New York: Methuen, 1984.

Hunt, Peter. *Criticism, Theory, and Children's Literature.* London: Blackwell, 1991.

Hürlimann, Bettina. *Picture-Book World.* Translated and edited by Brian W. Alderson. London: Oxford University Press, 1968.

Hutcheon, Linda. *A Poetics of Postmodernism: History, Theory, Fiction.* New York: Routledge, 1988.

Iser, Wolfgang. *The Implied Reader.* Baltimore: The Johns Hopkins University Press, 1974.

Iser, Wolfgang. *The Act of Reading: A Theory of Aesthetic Response.* London: Routledge & Kegan Paul, 1978.

Jones, Glyn W. *Tove Jansson.* Boston: Twayne, 1984.

Kåreland, Lena, and Barbro Werkmäster. *En livsvandring i tre akter.* Uppsala, Sweden: Hjelm, 1994 (Studies Published by the Swedish Institute for Children's Books, no. 54). With a summary in English: Life's Journey in Three Acts: An Analysis of Tove Jansson's Picture-books "The Book about Moomin, Mymble and Little My," "Who Will Comfort Toffle?" and "The Dangerous Journey."

Klemin, Diana. *The Art of Art for Children's Books.* New York: Clarkson N. Potter, 1966.

Klingberg, Göte. *Denna lilla gris går till torget och andra brittiska toy books i Sverige 1869–79.* Stockholm: Rabén & Sjögren, 1987 (Studies published by the Swedish Institute for Children's Books, no. 26). With a summary in English: British Toy Books in Sweden 1869–79.

Kress, Gunther, and Theo van Leuwen. *Reading Images. The Grammar of Visual Design.* London: Routledge, 1996.

Kuznets, Lois. *When Toys Come Alive. Narratives of Animation, Metamorphosis and Development.* New Haven: Yale University Press, 1994.

Lacy, Lyn Ellen. *Art and Design in Children's Picture Books: An Analysis of Caldecott Award–Winning Illustrations.* Chicago: American Library Association, 1986.

Lagerroth, Ulla-Britta, et al., eds. *Interart Poetics: Essays on the Interrelations of the Arts and Media.* Amsterdam: Rodopi, 1997.

Lanes, Selma. *The Art of Maurice Sendak.* New York: Abrams, 1980.

Lecercle, Jean-Jacques. *Philosophy of Nonsense. The Intuitions of Victorian Nonsense Literature.* London: Routledge, 1994.

Lent, Blair. "There's Much More to the Picture than Meets the Eye." In *Signposts to Criticism of Children's Literature,* edited by Robert Bator, 156–161. Chicago: American Library Association, 1988.

Lewis, David. "The Constructedness of Texts: Picture Books and the Metafictive." *Signal* 62 (1990): 131–146.

Lotman, Yuri. *Semiotics of Cinema.* Ann Arbor: University of Michigan Press, 1976.

Lowe, Virginia. "Snufkin, Sniff and Little My: The 'Reality' of Fictional Characters for the Young Child." *Papers* 2 (1991) 2: 87–96.

Lukens, Rebecca. *A Critical Handbook of Children's Literature.* 4th ed. New York: HarperCollins: 1990.

Mackey, Margaret. *The Case of Peter Rabbit: Changing Conditions of Literature for Children.* New York, Garland, 1998.

Mackey, Margaret. "Metafiction for Beginners. Allan Ahlberg's Ten in a Bed." *Children's Literature in Education* 21 (1990) 3:179-187.

McCann, Hugo, and Claire Hiller. "Narrative and Editing Choices in the Picture Book: A Comparison of Two Versions of Roberto Innocenti's Rose Blanche." *Papers* 5 (1994) 2-3: 53–57.

McCloud, Scott. *Understanding Comics.* Northampton, MA: Tundra, 1993.

MacMath, Russ. "Recasting Cinderella: How Pictures Tell the Tale." *Bookbird* 32 (1994) 4: 29–34.

Marantz, Kenneth. "The Picture Book as Art Object: A Call for Balanced Reviewing." In *Signposts to Criticism of Children's Literature,* edited by Robert Bator, 152–156. Chicago: American Library Association, 1988.

Marantz, Sylvia and Kenneth Marantz. *Artists of the Page: Interviews with Children's Book Illustrators.* Jefferson, NC: McFarland, 1992.

Matthias, Margaret, and Graciela Italiano. "Louder than a Thousand Words." In *Signposts to Criticism of Children's Literature,* edited by Robert Bator, 161–165. Chicago: American Library Association, 1988.

Mellon, Constance. "Folk Tales as Picture Books: Visual Literacy or Oral Tradition?" *School Library Journal* 33 (1987) 10: 46–47.

Mitchell, W. J. T. *Picture Theory: Essays on Verbal and Visual Representation.* Chicago: University of Chicago Press, 1994.

Moebius, William. "Introduction to Picturebook Codes." *Word and Image* 2 (1986) 2: 141–158. Also in *Children's Literature: The Development of Criticism,* edited by Peter Hunt, 131–147. London: Routledge, 1990.

Moebius, William. "Room with a View: Bedroom Scenes in Picture Books." *Children's Literature* 19 (1991): 53–74.

Neumeyer, Peter. "How Picture Books Mean: The Case of Chris Van Allsburg," *Children's Literature Association Quarterly* 15 (1990) 1: 2–8.

Neumeyer, Peter. *The Annotated Charlotte's Web.* New York: HarperCollins, 1994.

Nières, Isabelle. "Des illustrations exemplaires: "Max et les Maximonstres" de Maurice Sendak." *Le francais aujourd'hui* 50 (1980): 17–29.

Nières, Isabelle. "Et l'image me fait signe que le livre est fini." In *Culture, texte et jeune lecteur,* edited by Jean Perrot, 209–217. Nancy, France: Presses universitaires de Nancy, 1993.

Nières, Isabelle. "Writers Writing a Short History of Children's Literature Within Their Texts." In *Aspects and Issues in the History of Children's Literature,* edited by Maria Nikolajeva, 49–56. Westport, CT: Greenwood, 1995.

Nikolajeva, Maria. "Bilderboken som försvann. Några tendenser i den sovjetiska bilderbokskonsten." In *I bilderbokens värld,* edited by Kristin Hallberg and Boel Westin, 127–142. Stockholm: Liber, 1985.

Nikolajeva, Maria. *The Magic Code: The Use of Magical Patterns in Fantasy for Children.* Stockholm: Almqvist & Wiksell International, 1988 (Studies Published by the Swedish Institute for Children's Books, no. 31).

Nikolajeva, Maria. *Children's Literature Comes of Age: Toward a New Aesthetic.* New York: Garland, 1996.

Nikolajeva, Maria. "Literature for Children and Young People." In *A History of Swedish Literature,* edited by Lars Warme, 495–512. Lincoln: University of Nebraska Press, 1996.

Nikolajeva, Maria. *Introduction to the Theory of Children's Literature.* 2nd ed. Tallinn, Estonia: Tallinn University Press, 1997.

Nikolajeva, Maria. "Reflections of Change in Children's Books Titles." In *Reflections of Change. Children's Literature Since 1945,* edited by Sandra L. Beckett, 85–90. Westport, CT: Greenwood, 1997.

Nikolajeva, Maria. *Barnbokens byggklossar.* Lund, Sweden: Studentlitteratur, 1998.

Nodelman, Perry. "Of Nakedness and Children's Books," *Children's Literature Association Quarterly* 9 (1984) 1: 25–30.

Nodelman, Perry. "How Picture Books Work." In *Image & Maker: An Annual Dedicated to the Consideration of Book Illustration,* edited by Harold Darling & Peter Neumeyer, 1–12. La Jolla, CA: Green Tiger Press, 1984.

Nodelman, Perry. *Words About Pictures: The Narrative Art of Children's Picture Books.* Athens: The Univerity of Georgia Press, 1988.

Nodelman, Perry, ed. *Touchstones: Reflections on the Best in Children's Literature.* Vol. 3: Picture Books. West Lafayette, IN: ChLA, 1989.

Nodelman, Perry. "The Eye and the I: Identification and First-Person Narratives in Picture Books." *Children's Literature* 19 (1991): 1–30.

Nodelman, Perry. *The Pleasures of Children's Literature.* New York: Longman, 1992. 2nd ed. 1996.

Ovenden, Graham. *Nymphets and Fairies: Three Victorian Children's Illustrators.* London: Academy Editions, 1976.

Paetzold, Bettina, and Luis Erler, eds. *Bilderbücher im Blickpunkt verschiedener Wissenschaften und Fächer.* Bamberg, Germany: Nostheide, 1990.

Peltsch, Steffen, ed. *Auch Bilder erzählen Geschichten.* Special issue of *Beiträge Jugendliteratur und Medien* 8 (1997).

Peterson, Lars. "Om upprorets lust och en frigörande bananrevy: Sex bilderboksanalyser." In *I bilderbokens värld,* edited by Kristin Hallberg and Boel Westin, 164–189. Stockholm: Liber, 1985.

Prince, Gerald. *A Dictionary of Narratology.* Lincoln: University of Nebraska Press, 1987.

Rayner, Mary. "Some Thoughts on Animals in Children's Books." *Signal* 28 (1979): 81–87.

Rhedin, Ulla. "Resan i barndomen. Om bilderböcker för barn och vuxna." In *Vår moderna bilderbok,* edited by Vivi Edström, 155–188. Stockholm: Rabén & Sjögren, 1991.

Rhedin, Ulla. *Bilderboken: På väg mot en teori.* Stockholm: Alfabeta, 1993 (Studies Published by the Swedish Institute for Children's Books, no. 45). With a summary in English: The Picture Book—Towards a Theory.

Rimmon-Kenan, Shlomith. *Narrative Fiction: Contemporary Poetics.* London: Methuen, 1983.

Romberg, Bertil. *Studies in the Narrative Technique of the First-Person Novel.* Stockholm: Almqvist & Wiksell, 1962.

Roxburgh, Stephen. "A Picture Equals How Many Words? Narrative Theory and Picture Books for Children." *The Lion and the Unicorn* 7–8 (1983): 20–33.

Schaffer, Barbro. "Solen som lingonbröd. Bilden i den moderna bilderboken." In *Vår moderna bilderbok,* edited by Vivi Edström, 104–154. Stockholm: Rabén & Sjögren, 1991.

Schapiro, Meyer. *Words and Pictures. On the Literal and the Symbolic in the Illustration of a Text.* The Hague: Mouton, 1973 (Approaches to Semiotics no. 11).

Scholes, Robert. *Semiotics and Interpretation.* New Haven: Yale University Press, 1982.

Schwarcz, Joseph H. *Ways of the Illustrator: Visual Communication in Children's Literature.* Chicago: American Library Association, 1982.

Schwarcz, Joseph H. and Chava Schwarcz. *The Picture Book Comes of Age.* Chicago: American Library Association, 1991.

Scott, Carole. "Between Me and the World: Clothes as Mediator Between Self and Society in the Works of Beatrix Potter." *The Lion and the Unicorn* 16 (1992) 2: 192–198.

Scott, Carole. "Clothed in Nature or Nature Clothed: Dress as Metaphor in the Illustrations of Beatrix Potter and C. M. Barker." *Children's Literature* 22 (1994): 70–89.

Scott, Carole. "The Subversion of Childhood: Maurice Sendak and the American Tradition." In *Gunpowder and Sealing-wax: Nationhood in Children's Literature,* edited by Ann Lawson Lucas, 39–47. Hull, England: Troubador, 1997.

Scott, Carole. "Dual Audience in Picture Books." In *Transcending Boundaries: Writing for Dual Audience of Children and Adults,* edited by Sandra Beckett 99–110. New York: Garland, 1999.

Shulevitz, Uri. *Writing with Pictures: How to Write and Illustrate Children's Books.* New York: Waton-Guptill Publications, 1985.

*Siest du das? Die Wahrnehmung von Bildern in Kinderbücher—Visual Literacy.* Zurich: Chronos, 1997.

Sipe, Lawrence R. "The Private and Public Worlds of *We Are All in the Dumps with Jack and Guy.*" *Children's Literature in Education* 27 (1996) 2 87–107.

Sipe, Lawrence R. "How Picture Books Work: A Semiotically Framed Theory of Text–Picture Relationships." *Children's Literature in Education* 29 (1998) 2: 97–108.

Skalin, Lars-Åke. *Karaktär och perspektiv. Att tolka litterära gestalter i det mimetiska språkspelet.* Uppsala, Sweden: Uppsala University press, 1991. With a summary in English: Character and Perspective: Reading Fictional Figures in the Mimetic Language Game.

Spitz, Ellen Handler. *Inside Picture Books*. New Haven: Yale University Press, 1999.

Stanton, Joseph. "The Dreaming Picture Books of Chris Van Allsburg." *Children's Literature* 24 (1996): 161–179.

Stephens, John. "Language, Discourse and Picture Books." *Children's Literature Association Quarterly* 14 (1989) 3: 106–110.

Stephens, John. " 'Didn't I Tell You about the Time I Pushed the Brothers Grimm off Humpty Dumpty's Wall?' Metafictional Strategies for Constituting the Audience as Agent on the Narratives of Janet and Allan Ahlberg." In *Children's Literature and Contemporary Theory,* edited by Michael Stone, 63–75. Wollongong, Australia: University of Wollongong, 1991.

Stephens, John. *Reading the Signs: Sense and Significance in Written Texts*. Kenthurst, Australia: Kangaroo, 1992.

Stephens, John. *Language and Ideology in Children's Fiction*. London: Longman, 1992.

Stephens, John. "Representation of Place in Australian Children's Picture Books." In *Voices From Far Away: Current Trends in International Children's Literature Research,* edited by Maria Nikolajeva, 97–118. Stockholm: Centre for the Study of Childhood Culture, 1995.

Stephens, John. "Gender, Genre and Children's Literature." *Signal* 79 (1996): 17–30.

Stewig, John Warren. *Looking at Picture Books*. Fort Atkinson, WI: Highsmith Press, 1995.

Stybe, Vibeke. *Fra billedark til billedbog: Den illustrerede boernebog i Danmark indtil 1950*. Copenhagen: Nyt nordisk forlag, 1983.

Sunesson, Göran. *Pictorial Concepts: Inquiries into the Semiotic Heritage and Its Relevance for the Analysis of the Visual World*. Lund, Sweden: Lund University Press, 1989.

Svensson, Sonja. "Barnböcker utan barn." In *Barnkultur—igår, idag, imorgon,* edited by Ann Banér, 73–102. Stockholm: Centre for the Study of Childhood Culture, 1999.

Tabbert, Reinbert. "The Impact of Children's Books—Cases and Concepts." In *Responses to Children's Literature,* edited by Geoff Fox and Graham Hammond, 34–58. München, Germany: Saur, 1980.

Tabbert, Reinbert, ed. *Maurice Sendak: Bilderbuchskünstler*. Bonn: Bouvier Verlag Herbert Grundmann, 1987.

Tabbert, Reinbert. "National Myth in Three Classical Picture Books." In *Aspects and Issues in the History of Children's Literature,* edited by Maria Nikolajeva, 151–163. Westport, CT: Greenwood, 1995.

Thiele, Jens, ed. *Neue Erzählformen im Bilderbuch*. Oldenburg, Germany: Isensee, 1991.

Todorov, Tzvetan. *The Fantastic: A Structural Approach to a Literary Genre*. Cleveland: Case Western Reserve University, 1973.

Tolkien, J. R. R. "On Fairy Stories." In his *Tree and Leaf*. London: Allen & Unwin, 1968: 11–70.

Topper, David. "On Some Burdens Carried by Pictures." *Children's Literature Association Quarterly* 9 (1984) 1: 23–25.

Trites, Roberta Selinger. *Waking Sleeping Beauty: Feminist Voices in Children's Novels.* Iowa City: University of Iowa Press, 1997.

Wagner, Peter, ed. *Icons—Texts—Iconotexts. Essays on Ekphrasis and Intermediality.* Berlin: de Gruyter, 1996 (European Cultures: Studies in Literature and the Arts; 6).

Wall, Barbara. *The Narrator's Voice: The Dilemma of Children's Fiction.* London: Macmillan, 1991.

Ward, John L., and Marian Nitti Fox. "A Look at Some Outstanding Illustrated Books for Children." *Children's Literature Association Quarterly* 9 (1984) 1: 19–21.

Warner, Marina. *No Go the Bogeyman: Scaring, Lulling, and Making Mock.* New York: Farrar, Straus and Giroux, 1998.

Waugh, Patricia. *Metafiction: The Theory and Practice of Self-Conscious Fiction.* London: Methuen, 1984.

Westin, Boel. "Det flerdimensionella samspelet. En modell för interaktionsanalys av muminböckernas text och bild." *Tidskrift för litteraturvetenskap* 3–4 (1982):148–162.

Westin, Boel. "Bilderbokens estetik. Tove Jansson som bilderbokskonstnär." *Svensk lärareföreningens årssskrift* (1983): 60—79.

Westin, Boel. "Konsten som äventyr. Tove Jansson och bilderboken." In *Vår moderna bilderbok,* edited by Vivi Edström, 51–70. Stockholm: Rabén & Sjögren 1991.

Westin, Boel. "Resan till mumindalen. Om Tove Janssons bilderboksestetik." In *I bilderbokens värld,.* edited by Kristin Hallberg and Boel Westin, 235–253. Stockholm: Liber, 1985.

Westin, Boel. "Superbarn, vardagsbarn och vilda bebisar: Svenska bilderböcker 1945–1980." In *I bilderbokens värld* edited by Kristin Hallberg and Boel Westin, 55–98. Stockholm: Liber, 1985.

Whalley, Joyce Irene, and Tessa Rose Chester. *A History of Children's Book Illustration.* London: John Murray, 1988.

Whalley, Joyce Irene. "The Development of Illustrated Texts and Picture Books." In *International Companion Encyclopedia of Children's Literature,* edited by Peter Hunt, 220–230. London: Routledge, 1996.

# Index of Names

# Index of Titles

# Subject Index

Page numbers after concepts used throughout the study (e.g., doublespread, iconotext) refer to the first occurrence, where the concept is introduced and explained.